High Definition and 24P Cinematography

Dedication

To

William and Annabel

who are the future

High Definition and 24P Cinematography

Paul Wheeler BSC FBKS

AMSTERDAM • BOSTON • HEIDELBERG • LONDON • NEW YORK • OXFORD
PARIS • SAN DIEGO • SAN FRANCISCO • SINGAPORE • SYDNEY • TOKYO
Focal Press is an imprint of Elsevier

Focal Press
An imprint of Elsevier
Linacre House, Jordan Hill, Oxford OX2 8DP
30 Corporate Drive, Burlington, MA 01803

First published 2003
Reprinted 2004. 2005 (twice)

British Library Cataloguing in Publication Data
Wheeler, Paul, 1945–
  High definition and 24P cinematography
  1. Cinematography
  Title
  778.5′3

Library of Congress Cataloguing in Publication Data
A catalogue record for this book is available from the Library of Congress

ISBN 0 240 51676 1

For information on all Focal Press publications
visit our website at www.focalpress.com

Working together to grow
libraries in developing countries

www.elsevier.com | www.bookaid.org | www.sabre.org

ELSEVIER   BOOK AID
            International   Sabre Foundation

Typeset by Keyword Typesetting Services Ltd
Printed and bound in Great Britain by MPG Books Ltd, Bodmin, Cornwall

Contents

Preface

I joined the BBC film department in 1963 just as they were opening their second channel and moving over from 35 mm black and white to 16 mm colour. I left to go freelance 25 years later, by which time I had become one of the six Senior Film Cameramen. At the time I resigned the BBC was just introducing portable video kits for film cinematographers; these consisted of an analogue camera with a separate U-Matic recorder. I have to confess that the introduction of this kit was a contributing factor to my decision to resign – compared with the 16 mm film cameras we were using at that time they were heavier, brought back the umbilical cord between the camera and the recorder, and to my eyes there was a huge drop in picture quality.

I never did take to the analogue cameras but, in the years since then, I have come to appreciate Digi Beta, a much more stable format. Until recently, however, I still preferred to shoot on film, particularly 35 mm. That is now changing, and it is the Common Image Format (CIF) and the HDCAM system that is very much behind that change.

In December 2000, Panavision Europe asked me to become an Associate of the company to help introduce their version of the Sony HDW F900 high definition camera. Panavision's philosophy was that, as I was well versed in both film and in digital cinematography, I ought to be the right person to introduce the new technology to all branches of the profession. I still spend at least half of every year as very much a working DoP shooting on any format I believe suits the script. Far from having reservations about HD shooting at 24P, I immediately fell in love with the system. It gives me the convenience of Digi Beta, saves the producer money, even when compared with 16 mm film, and has an image quality comparable with 35 mm film. What more could I ask?

This book has been harder to write than my previous two, *Practical Cinematography* and *Digital Cinematography*, for it has been a race to learn enough before writing any given chapter. Indeed, several chapters were updated in the last week before handing over the manuscript to my publisher. I do believe, though, that the book was finished at a turning point in the introduction of HD, when more and more people are wanting to learn about it because they have seen pictures that they have genuinely admired, and this is intriguing them. Undoubtedly HD will be a considerable part of the future of recording and displaying the moving image.

About the Author

Paul Wheeler has a wealth of practical experience both as a Film and Digital Cinematographer, combined with wide experience as a highly respected trainer. He is the author of *Practical Cinematography*, which covers much the same areas in this book but for Film Cinematographers, and *Digital Cinematography*, which primarily concentrates on the Digi Beta arena. After 25 years with the BBC, by the end of which he was one of only six Senior Film Cameramen out of a total of 63 DoPs employed there at that time, he left to go freelance.

Since leaving the BBC, Paul has had a flourishing career which has bought him many awards, including two Independent Producers Association (INDIE) awards for Digital Cinematography, two BAFTA nominations and a nomination from the Society of Lighting Directors. In between shoots he has stood in as Head of Cinematography at the National Film and Television School several times and also as Head of Cinematography at the Royal College of Art. He is a regular visiting tutor at the London International Film School. He has designed and run the highly respected Digital Cinematography course at the National Short Course Training Programme, part of the National Film School.

In December 2000, Paul was invited to join Panavision Europe as an associate of the company in order to help introduce the Panavision HD cameras to the European film and television community. He had the luck to join Panavision Europe just 3 days before they got their first HD camera so was in, by a whisker, just before the start! Paul now spends about half his working life with Panavision – shooting schedules permitting.

Paul is a member of the British Society of Cinematographers (BSC) and a Fellow of the British Kinematograph, Sound and Television Society (FBKS).

Acknowledgements

My thanks to:

Alan Piper, European Technical Director, Panavision Europe, for inviting me to become an associate of Panavision Europe a couple of days before they received their first HD camera – an invitation which subsequently led to this book.

Peter Swarbrick, Head of Digital Imaging, Panavision Europe, for being wonderfully supportive and a great friend and colleague.

Alex Golding for his considerable help in taking the photographs in this book.

And most importantly, my wife Anne for her encouragement, support and her patience with reading my drafts.

All the illustrations in this book are the copyright of the author with the exception of:

The front cover – copyright Panavision.
Figures 3.1 and 3.2 – copyright Barco plc
Figures 23.2 and 23.4 – copyright Screen 2 Screen

My thanks to Alan Piper, Mike Coleman and Chris Atkins for their permission to use the illustrations listed above.

Introduction

HD and 24P cinematography is a new acquisition format which, I believe, is set to revolutionize much of the theatrical film world and, perhaps, even more of television. Film, with its utterly superb image capture capabilities, is nonetheless an anachronism in a television environment, and with more and more digital effects appearing in feature films it is inevitable that, on occasion, there will be advantages in originating in the same image format as that which is to be used for the post-production.

HD picture quality is arguably every bit as good as 35 mm film, yet the pre-cutting room costs are going to be less than shooting 16 mm film. Make no mistake about it, the drive to HD is fiscal, so let we cinematographers be thankful that the picture quality, the range of cameras and lenses, and their ease of use is nearly always to our advantage. It's not just the saving in film stock and processing that is driving this engine. There is a huge value, especially to the distributors of feature films, to deliver the product to the screen without the cost of making and shipping release prints. Fortunately for cinematographers there has been a contemporaneous advance in digital projection equipment and it is now possible to be very proud indeed of one's work, even if it has never left the digital domain.

In my previous books, *Practical Cinematography* and *Digital Cinematography*, I have kept close to the cinematographer's craft; in this book I have covered most of that ground but included a considerable amount of information for both directors and producers, for it is these crafts, as much if not more so than the cinematographer, who will influence the decision to shoot on HD.

I am a great believer that people from a visual world gain as much information from pictures as they might from words, therefore I often produce the illustrations first and then write the text to them; in this book there are 144 illustrations.

A top of the range HD camera with the finest lenses and recording in the HDCAM format is now my camera of choice – always – not bad for a man whose grandfather joined the British film industry only 2 years after the Lumière brothers showed the first on-film moving picture in Regents Street, London. Grandfather was late by the way, his brother had joined 6 months earlier!

Part 1

Why Choose HDCAM?

1
What is 24P and HDCAM?

The enthusiasm for tape shot at a frame rate of 24 fps (frames per second) using a progressive scanning technique together with the HDCAM recording format has come about because, for the first time, with a tape-based recording system, it offers true worldwide compatibility. This has only previously been achieved using 35 mm film and then only since the early 1930s, when the world, which was already moving to a film width of 35 mm, finally agreed to use the same perforation as well.

24P stands for 24 fps scanned progressively. This involves scanning sequential horizontal lines of information within the frame rather than the more traditional television method of scanning all the even-numbered lines and then returning to the top of the picture to scan the odd-numbered lines until all the information within a single frame has been read.

The combination of a frame rate of 24 fps and progressive scanning is vital to the success of this format being taken up worldwide. This is because it echoes the cinema film standard of 24 fps, where a rotating shutter is used in both the camera and the projector. The act of almost instantly switching on and then switching off each frame of film creates a motion blur on the frame which, when projected, is perceived by the human eye very much as that eye would have perceived the motion in real life. A not often understood factor in the 24P HDCAM system is that in addition to scanning progressively the camera, unlike a traditional television camera, switches its imaging chips on to receive an image and then switches this function off before the image is read out for recording. It therefore creates a frame-by-frame motion blur almost exactly like the film system, which as we have seen appears almost the same as the eye would have perceived the original action.

HDCAM simply stands for the recording format used. Again it is accepted as an international standard. The two parts of the standard, 24P and HDCAM, now come together to be an internationally accepted exchange format from any country to any other country. There are several reasons why this standard has become so popular. The main one is that if you simply play out a 24P HDCAM tape it is easy to arrange the signal to be identical to that which would come from a telecine machine running 35 mm film at 24 fps, and every television station in the world has one of those and the necessary electronics to interpret the information into whatever transmission standard they use.

There is one more factor to add to the mix before one has complete international compatibility. Previous high definition formats have used a variety of both vertical lines of pixels and numbers of horizontal pixels in each line. For a single standard to become universal it became imperative that any new standard was formatted in such a way that the mathematics required to convert the original format to any other country's format could be carried out easily and economically using electronic standards converters. A vertical array of 1080 pixels combined with a horizontal array of 1920 pixels fulfils this requirement and this is the layout of the pixels within the HDCAM format.

The outcome of the bringing together of these requirements within the 24P HDCAM overall format means that any television station can receive a tape from any other station around the world and easily, and economically, transmit it. It also means that this tape can be turned into 35 mm film, again easily and economically, for projection in a cinema. As you will find out later in this book, there are very good and provable reasons why an image containing 1080 × 1920 pixels, if written out to film with sufficient precision, is perfectly capable of being converted into a photochemical image on film, especially 35 mm film, and can be projected very successfully in even the largest of cinemas. This now adds a further potential for international compatibility for, just as a story recorded on film has for many years been easy to write to videotape, by using the 24P HDCAM format it is now possible to maintain sufficient image quality to go seamlessly in the opposite direction.

Is not the attempt to achieve all this on tape rather than film simply re-inventing the wheel? No, because there is one more overriding factor we have not yet looked at – costs. While an HD camera kit currently rents for around 130 per cent of a similar 35 mm kit, the acquisition costs can drop dramatically, to something like 1.2 per cent. Yes, there is a decimal point in there and this comparison is based on purchasing the raw stock and simply processing it; no costs for prints or telecine have been included. With the HDCAM tape you can have immediate playback at full HD resolution. This means that a producer might very well save more on stock and processing costs per day than the entire cost of the camera kit; in other words they may make a profit! These are very rough figures and will be looked at in much greater detail elsewhere in this book.

1.1 Electronic projection

Rapidly gaining acceptance is the concept of cinemas using electronic projectors. As this becomes more the norm it will inevitably feed back and make digital acquisition even more attractive. Where the savings when shooting are in stock costs, though the camera equipment is more expensive, so it is with the cinema and the distribution of the prints. A top quality electronic digital projector can cost as much as five times that of a mechanical projector; you will not be surprised to hear that the cinema owners are not too pleased at the cost of re-equipping. The distributors, on the other hand, are very keen, so keen in fact that they are looking at ways to finance the changeover on behalf of the cinema owners.

The attraction lies not just in the savings on print cost, but in the cost involved in physically moving the prints around the world which, it is said, is even greater than that of making the prints. Currently supplying the signal to a digital projector would most likely be a computer server or an HDCAM tape deck. This situation is going to change as soon as the number of digitally equipped cinemas increases. It is currently possible to send a feature film down a fibre optic in real time but the cost of linking all the cinemas in the world looks somewhat prohibitive to me. A more likely solution would be to deliver the information via satellite. Three geostationary satellites would cover a high proportion of the globe. When this solution was first mooted satellite data transmission rates dictated that it might take 8 hours or so to download a 110-minute feature film. This state of affairs meant that a server was still needed at the cinema to store the film. This has two distinct disadvantages, the cost of the server and the fact that it might leave the film more open to piracy. As satellite data transmission rates improve, it will clearly be possible to transmit in real time, thus overcoming both disadvantages.

There is then an additional advantage to the distributor. The cinema will no longer hold the switch to start the film, it will be in the distributor's control and the images will only exist at the cinema in a virtual form.

There is also the question of quality of image. The image from various digital projectors can vary enormously from the exceptional to the downright terrible. The difference is almost solely down to the cost of the projector. My personal favourite is the Barco D-Cine 'Premiere'[R]. The tonal range, clarity and contrast, to my eyes at least, are every bit as good as any film projector. In addition there is no dirt on the picture, no scratches and no picture weave. There are traditionalists who say they miss all this, it is part of the cinema experience. I cannot agree. A 24P HDCAM image that has only ever been in the digital domain projected using the finest available projector is, to me at least, the finest projected image I have ever seen. But I may be biased.

2
Picture quality

2.1 What does HD look like?

Before I go any further I must admit to a bias; with my Director of Photography hat firmly in place, I just love the images created by the HDW F900, particularly when that camera is fronted with Panavision lenses. The images are very sharp with a long tonal range, and the colours are lifelike and true. Whether seen on a monitor or digitally projected there is no dirt on the picture, no scratching and no picture instability such as weave of unsteadiness. If the final product is to be shown from a film print then all the possibilities of print imperfections return, of course.

To be starting with such a high technical standard is a joy for the Director of Photography (DoP) for, if one feels the image too sharp, diffusion filters allow you to reduce it to any degree or look you wish for. If the colours are too bright for the script you are working on, then with filters or by adjusting the in-camera menus this is easily attenuated. And the result of your adjustments is easily assessed on a monitor in real time. Especially when using a 24-inch high definition monitor, what you see is what you get or, to use a favourite phrase of mine, if it looks right it is right.

If you come from a film background then the easiest way to envisage the HD image is to think of the picture you would get shooting on 35 mm Kodak 320 ASA extended range Vision stock and printing to their Premier release print stock. The quality of lenses you deploy will change the image every bit as much as it will on a film camera and again I must admit to a bias; to my eyes and style of shooting, the Panavision range of Zoom and Prime lenses is unbeatable.

2.2 Comparison with 35 mm film

The most notable thing if you are watching HD projected using a state-of-the-art HD projector is the almost total lack of grain. Some people miss this effect dreadfully. If you really cannot cope with such a clean image then you can add grain or what I like to think of as texture in post. It is also possible to add texture in the camera; simply shoot with some gain switched in. I have very successfully shot HD with 6 dB of gain switched in and the resultant image has been much admired. If you are going to film for final delivery then it would be a wise precaution to print a short test, for the effect of gain is more noticeable on the big screen than on a monitor.

2.3 Comparison with anamorphic 35 mm

To shoot HD in the anamorphic 2.4:1 aspect ratio you simply switch the viewfinder marking to show a bright line box in that aspect ratio and compose to it. The image will remain unsqueezed right up to the point in post-production where you make the first film image. At that point the printer will horizontally compress the image to produce a conventional anamorphic photographic image. If you are projecting with a digital projector then a simple switch is all that needs to be set to show the image in the 2.4:1 ratio.

As the HDW F900 camera always records in a 16×9 aspect ratio where the image is comprised of 1080 vertical pixels, the centre section used for anamorphic imaging will comprise of just a little over 800 pixels vertically. There are those steeped in the film tradition who would like to deny the evidence of their eyes and say this cannot possibly produce a sharp enough image. I put it to you they are wrong and believe I can prove it.

The finite judgement of sharpness in the theatre is made by the human eye. The resolution of the human eye is well known, so if the picture on the cinema screen is sharper than the human eye can perceive then the brain will tell the viewer that the picture is sharp. In most cinemas 800×1920 pixels produces an image which more than meets this requirement, hence we perceive it as sharp, as anyone who has seen *Star Wars II* will testify, for this is exactly how it was made.

A counter argument goes that 35 mm film must be sharper because the image has a resolution which is referred to as a 4K resolution, meaning 4000 horizontal pixels, whereas HD only has a little under 2K of resolution. This is true but the 4K film negative, in order to reach the cinema screen, must by printed onto an interpositive; this will then be printed onto an internegative and this will finally be printed onto the release print. That release print will then be projected onto the screen. At every transfer of the image from one piece of film to another, quality will suffer. It can be proved that it is almost impossible to provide an image on the cinema screen using this traditional process which exceeds the equivalent resolution of 1000 lines or a 1K image.

The HD image, on the other hand, while starting at a little under 2K resolution is transferred digitally, that is just re-recording zeros and ones so there is no loss of quality at any transfer point. Hence the resolution being projected is the full 2K image originally formed by the camera, arguably higher than can be achieved photographically.

There are more technical explanations of most of these matters elsewhere in this book.

2.4   Comparison with Super 16 mm

The Sony HDW F900 in both its native form and in the 'Panavized' version produces an image that bears direct comparison with conventional theatrical 35 mm image quality, as we have seen. It therefore has an image improvement factor more or less the same as comparing Super 16 mm to 35 mm.

There are HD cameras which are marketed specifically at high-end television. Sony make the HDW 750 range which, while still using imaging chips having 1080×1920 pixels, which I would consider true HD, uses a 10-bit processor, as against a 12-bit processor in the HDW F900, and has far fewer facilities within them. For instance, they are market specific in that there is a PAL standard version that will only record in the 25P or 50i format and an NTSC version recording in 28.98P, 59.97i and 60i. They can, however, be set up to give both an HD SDI (High Definition Serial Digital Interface) output as well as a PAL, in the European, or NTSC, in the US version. The HDW F900 will record in all eight formats used all over the world. The HDW 750 is a little smaller and lighter and can give a quality of image, when shown on television, which will still compare with 35 mm, but the differences may become apparent when shown on a big screen in a cinema. To date there is no 24P version of the HDW 750 so direct frame rate compatibility with cinema is impossible.

Also available, again specifically aimed at television production, is Panasonic's HDC 20A. This camera records a 16×9 image at 60 fps (frames per second) and this recording can be played back at anything between 4 and 60 fps using very clever interpolation. The camera will only record a full 1080-line vertical resolution in an interlace format. If used in the progressive scan format the vertical resolution drops to 720 vertical lines and this probably limits its use exclusively to television. Like the Sony HDW 750 it uses a 10-bit processor.

All this said, the 20A produces a very attractive image on even the largest monitor and for certain uses the higher frame rate is undeniably useful. My belief is that this camera can hold its own with a comparable Super 16 camera but cannot truly compete with a 35 mm image.

2.5 Comparison with Digi Beta

Frankly there is no contest. In my opinion all the HD cameras discussed above produce a better picture than a Digi Beta camera, the Panasonic noticeably and either of the Sony cameras considerably. Digi Beta cameras are considerably cheaper to either rent or buy so they will be around for use in television for some time yet.

3
Display quality

3.1 HD shown on television

There are some who say there is no point in shooting HD when the finished product is only ever going to be shown on television – I disagree. Just as a film originated on 35 mm looks better on either PAL or NTSC than one originated on 16 mm or Digi Beta, the same is true for HD, as it is a picture of very similar quality to 35 mm. This is known as retaining its headroom.

As an HDCAM tape recorded in the 24P format is rapidly becoming the international exchange format, we can expect a gradual increase in picture quality for prestige programming. It is possible to play a 24P HDCAM tape out of, say, a Sony HDW F500 VTR, where the output is already converted to the PAL or NTSC formats. Even using this simplistic down-conversion the headroom is retained and clearly visible.

I was showing the Panavision HD system to one of the more sceptical line producers I frequently work with. To my delight he rapidly became a fan of the system but right at the end of the demonstration asked if it were possible to see a full HD resolution monitor right next to a standard PAL monitor with the picture down-converted via the HDW F500. As luck would have it there was just such a capability set up in another room for an entirely different purpose. We ran a single tape, the contents of which he had by now seen as a played-out HD image on a 24-inch HD monitor as well as the same film written to both 1:1.85 format and 1:2.4 format projected film.

After staring at two 14-inch monitors right next to each other, one a full HD monitor fed from the HD SDI (High Definition Serial Digital Interface) socket on the HDW F500 and the other a high resolution PAL 625-line monitor fed from the PAL down-converted output on the same VTR, his reaction after seeing every frame was 'well the PAL looks just like 35 mm with lines!'. I rest my case.

3.2 HD written to film and projected mechanically

If the transfer from HD tape to film is carried out with sufficient precision, and the quality of image produced by different companies can vary tremendously, then to all intents and purposes the resultant print will be very similar indeed to the same image having been acquired on 35 mm negative. There are those who will tell you different but I have met few who doubt the quality of HD who have seen the demonstration reels at Panavision.

3.3 HD shown on a state-of-the-art digital projector

The quality of image on a cinema screen from a high-end digital projector showing an image that has never been anything but HD is simply stunning. It looks a little less like film origination than HD written back to film and arguments will go on for years yet as to whether that difference is an improvement or a degradation of the cinema picture quality. I come down firmly in the 'it's better' camp. Maybe that is my training in the BBC, where we were always trying to reduce grain and other mechanical defects of the film process or maybe I, as a DoP, have simply been going in that direction all my working life, but I love the fact that it is very sharp, there is no dirt and dust, no picture weave and far less flicker. All good things to my way of thinking.

I have heard one explanation that purports that the blanking time of a mechanical shutter is preferable for it lets our brain rest. My reply is to ask if I blink 24 times a second will I feel less tired? Nonsense, if that were so I am confident God would have given me that facility. Here's to flicker-free projection I say.

3.4   Digital projectors

Unlike a 35 mm mechanical projector, which is roughly the same size and cost no matter what the size of the cinema, digital projectors come in many more shapes and sizes – and costs. In order to give a sensible comparison I shall compare two projectors from the same manufacturer, Barco, and before going further admit that at the present time I have a personal liking for this company's products.

3.4.1   The Barco D-Cine Premiere® DP 50®

This is a truly top of the range projector capable of filling a screen up to 20 metres (66 feet) wide. It incorporates a Texas Instruments' state-of-the-art 'Dark Chip' Digital Micromirror Device™. Figure 3.1 shows the projector fitted to a Kinoton SK50DC lamphouse. I saw *Star Wars II – Attack of the*

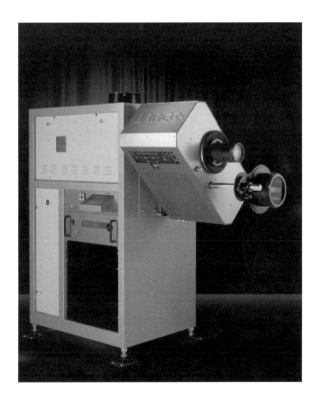

Figure 3.1 The Barco D-Cine Premiere® DP 50® digital cinema projector

Figure 3.2 The Barco SLM R8 digital projector

Clones first projected using this projector head and can assure you it was true cinema quality. It was, in fact, filling the screen at the Odeon Leicester Square.

For those interested in technical specifications it has a resolution of 1280 × 1024 pixels for each of the three channels Red, Green and Blue. It has a contrast ratio of 1350:1 from full black to full white and colour processing has a total bit depth of 45 bits with 35 trillion shades, with a colour gamut 40 per cent better than HDTV – more or less the equivalent of film.

This is a very serious projector capable of the most demanding premiere. The only downside of this device is that it currently costs several times as much as a 35 mm mechanical projector.

The projector is normally fed from a 24p-C server but can take any input via the ACSAR (Alternate Content Switcher and Router).

3.4.2   The Barco SLM R8

This is a much smaller and less costly device than the DP 50. It utilizes Texas Instruments' three-chip DLPTM technology with a powerful 7500 ANSI lumens light output and will comfortably fill up to a 10 metre (33 foot) wide screen. It is very quick to set up; I have seen it giving a superb picture within 30 minutes of being delivered. For medium to small theatres such as many multiplexes this projector is ideal, for it only costs about twice as much as a 35 mm mechanical projector.

It does not have the contrast ratio of the DP 50, coming in at either 450:1 or 900:1, the higher ratio being achieved at a small cost in the intensity of the output. It does have the same resolution however, again 1280 × 1024 pixels per colour.

The SLM R8 can run from any source up to HDTV interlace or progressive scan.

4
Cost implications

4.1 Savings

4.1.1 Origination costs

In order to get a hold on how HD compares with other origination systems it is instructive to add together all the expenditure right up to the cutting room door. Once the material enters the cutting room the variety of processes that may be chosen are so great that direct like-for-like cost comparison is very difficult.

In order to make this comparison I have made certain assumptions, as follows:

1 The unit is required to shoot 5 minutes of cut screen time per shooting day.
2 Costs used in this model include all current discounts based on a 6-day shooting week and a finished product of 110 minutes of screen time.
3 An HDW 750 will rent at a 30 per cent discount on an HDW 900 and the camera is roughly half the total kit cost.
4 HD kit costs are based on using a Panavision camera and lenses; as these are usually at the upper end of the price range, it seemed a more just comparison.
5 It is assumed that the cutting room will require the material to be delivered on a Digi Beta tape. The film models therefore include the cost of telecine to this format and the HD models include transfer from HDCAM tape to Digi Beta.

In Figure 4.1 it can be seen that in all instances there is a saving ranging from only 3.3 per cent when Super 16 mm is compared to an HDW 900 to 72 per cent when shooting 35 mm 4 perf at a shooting ratio of 20:1. In Figure 4.2 an HDW 750 is compared and costs now vary from 13.5 to 74.25 per cent. It is worth noting at this point that nowhere do the comparisons show HD to be more expensive.

4.1.2 Stock savings

The greatest saving is in the origination medium. If we look at the pure cost of picture origination – that is, just negative stock and processing for film as against the tape cost alone – Super 16 mm costs 8.5 times as much as HD and 4 perf 35 mm costs a staggering 32 times as much. And remember at this stage in the process the film cannot be shown, for it is still only in its negative form, but the HD tape can instantly be played at full picture quality.

HDW 900

Shooting ratio	10:1	12:1	15:1	20:1
Super 16 mm	3.3%	6.5%	16%	26%
35 mm 4 perf	63%	65.4%	68%	72%
35 mm 3 perf	55%	52%	49%	46.5%

Figure 4.1 Cost comparison when shooting with an HDW 900 – percentage saving

HDW 750

Shooting ratio	10:1	12:1	15:1	20:1
Super 16 mm	13.5%	16%	23.5%	32%
35 mm 4 perf	67%	69%	71%	74.25%
35 mm 3 perf	60%	57%	54%	51%

Figure 4.2 Cost comparison when shooting with an HDW 750 – percentage saving

4.1.3 Insurance savings

There are some less obvious possible savings. One producer I have met was having to put two VTR (Video Tape Recorder) playback machines into the cutting room as a very quick delivery was required. As this equipment was already paid for, they realized that it was possible to make an exact copy of the day's work every night on wrap. This is known as cloning the tape and is simply a matter of telling the machines to transcribe the zeros and ones on the tape without processing the information, thus making an absolutely perfect copy.

This very astute producer was then able to negotiate with the completion bond company to send them the camera original tapes immediately after cloning and thereby dramatically reduced the cost of negative insurance.

4.1.4 Savings in print costs

Were you making a very low budget movie it is possible to save completely the cost of producing a print. Once you have conformed your HD masters to a single finished tape you have in your hands the highest quality version of the movie you will ever know. Assuming you have not yet found a distributor, which is very common on low budget films, why not hire an HD-capable cinema and show them the conformed tape? It should cost no more than hiring a mechanical cinema, the picture quality will be stunning and only when a distributor has come on board do they need to make conventional prints, and this can be agreed to be at their expense.

4.1.5 Shooting for anamorphic release

Many first- or second-time directors find themselves in the position of wishing they could shoot in the widescreen picture ratio of 2.4:1, but are prevented from doing so by the considerably greater cost of hiring the necessary lenses, which often also increases the lighting budget as they are not necessarily as fast as conventional lenses. With HD these problems disappear. Although the camera will always record an image with an aspect ratio of 16×9 (1.777:1), if you wish to end up with a 35 mm anamorphic image from an HD original you simply switch on the 2.4:1 bright line mask in the camera viewfinder and compose for this. You introduce similar masks onto your monitors both on set and those used in the editing room. When you come to show your finished movie there is a switch on the digital projector to enable it to project only the centre section of the image, the part for which you originally composed. Similarly, if you are heading for a film version, again it is simply a matter of telling the printing machine that you want an anamorphic 2.4:1 master and it will take the centre section of the image and squeeze it to produce an image which looks exactly like it was shot with anamorphic camera lenses.

As to lighting costs you are using exactly the same lenses for HD origination whatever aspect ratio you choose to shoot in. Therefore it is quite possible to shoot an anamorphic picture at an aperture of T1.8. You can therefore, if you so choose, work at far lower set brightness than with a film camera fitted with anamorphic lenses. The camera has, by the way, a limiting aperture of T1.6 caused by the image-splitting prisms; this is described in the more technical section of this book.

You will have realized that as you are not using the full height of the HD image you might well lose picture quality; you are in fact now only using around 800 pixels vertically, though horizontally you still use the full 1920 pixels. Theoretically you do lose picture quality but the quality of the image projected suggests that you don't. In fact, on some screens the appearance of the image suggests that the image is improved. This is because, providing that two pixels are closer together on the screen than the resolution of the human eye, your brain will tell you that the image is perfectly sharp. In almost all viewing conditions that is so because the screen is made wider for the anamorphic viewing, so objects in the picture will be bigger and you may therefore think them sharper.

If you need proof of this phenomenon just buy yourself a ticket to see *Star Wars II*, preferably in a digital cinema. The above technique was exactly how it was produced.

4.2   Added costs

4.2.1   Camera kit rental

It is important to compare the costs of the whole camera kit and not just the camera itself. Even if you are using video assist with a film camera you will not need, say, a 24-inch high definition monitor, but when shooting HD such a monitor can be an invaluable tool both to the director and the cinematographer. They are expensive items and can push up the total kit cost dramatically. As a very rough guide, a top-end HD kit comprising a Panavized HDW 900F, a couple of zoom lenses and a wide angle prime lens, together with a selection of monitors and heads and tripods, will often cost something like 130–150 per cent of a similar 35 mm kit.

Similarly, comparing a Super 16 mm kit with an HDW 750, again with Panavision lenses, the difference is 235 per cent – much more expensive, but you do still get a picture that looks as if it was shot on 35 mm when shown on television.

4.2.2   Editing costs

If you are taking the most common route through the editing process, converting either film or HD to Digi Beta for the cutting room, then the expenditure is not significantly different. Most post houses charge roughly the same to telecine 1 hour of either 16 mm or 35 mm as they do to down-convert 1 hour of HD to Digi Beta.

At the end of the editing session it will probably be necessary to conform the camera masters to the EDL (Edit Decision List). This comes at a not dissimilar cost to negative cutting so little is lost or gained, though it is possible to make savings by grading the HD master at the same time rather than having to have photochemical answer prints.

If you can afford it, it is possible to use an off-line edit suite that can operate directly in the HD domain. In terms of picture quality this is ideal, for as finer and finer cuts are achieved the result can be played out in full HD quality without the need to conform the camera masters; indeed, some sophisticated editing packages can perform most of the grade as well. In practice, editing in full HD format is only common for movies with a very big budget or commercials where the time spent in the editing suite is much shorter and therefore becomes affordable.

4.2.3   Writing out to film

If you decide to write out to film it is important that you make the right decision as to producing either the equivalent of an intermediate negative or an intermediate positive. If you only expect to make a few prints, say six or less, then the advice is usually to go to a negative. If you are making a large number of prints you would probably go to a positive so that you can make a number of internegatives, from which you then make the release prints in volume.

It is most important to make the right decision as the conversion from HD master to a photo-chemical master can be a very expensive process. Most printers take around 2.5 seconds to print each frame, so a 120-minute movie is going to take just a little under 5 days to print. As the printing machines are very expensive you can imagine where the money goes.

There are two forms of printers, one using lasers to write lines of information to the film stock and the other forming the whole image on a CRT (Cathode Ray Tube) and then projecting it onto the film. They produce images with a slightly different character; both can be very good but you will need to test or see demonstrations of both before you shoot and decide which you are going to use, otherwise it will be impossible to visualize the finished picture during shooting.

In general, the post houses using a CRT tend to be a little cheaper.

4.3   A cost comparison example – *Oklahoma!*

I was asked to be the DoP on transferring the National Theatre stage production of *Oklahoma!* to the screen just as HD was becoming commercially available. Unfortunately, as we needed three cameras for the duration of the shoot plus a further two occasionally, using HD became an impossibility as Panavision simply could not guarantee enough equipment at that early stage of its introduction, so we shot it on 35 mm film. This, I thought, was a great shame, for there would have been many advantages with HD both for myself as DoP and to the producers.

For myself I would have loved to have been staring at 24-inch monitors showing the finished product, for I saw many advantages when lighting a huge set, 110 feet across and 90 feet deep, in being able to see the results of my work instantly.

For the producers there would have been two main advantages: firstly, as they needed both a 35 mm print and a tape for international television distribution, the HD master tape would have rendered a much better image than the PAL master transfer after standards conversion to, say, NTSC; secondly, it would have saved them a lot of money. My judgement at the time was that the film version would have looked equally good originated on either medium; now I have much more experience of HD I think it might even have looked better shot digitally.

4.3.1   Stock and processing savings

In 19 days I shot 265 000 feet of 35 mm negative. At the standard prices prevalent at the time of shooting, the cost of the raw stock, processing it and transferring it to a Digi Beta tape for the cutting room would have been about £150 000 ($215 000). The equivalent HD tape cost would have been about £3250 ($4650). So using HD, in terms of stock costs, would have saved £146 750 ($210 000). Put another way, it was over 46 times more expensive to use film.

4.3.2   Camera rental

With the camera rental prices applying at the time, I estimate that the HD camera and monitoring kit might have been £12 500 ($17 900) more expensive than the 35 mm kit.

4.3.3   Additional costs

There would have been an additional cost of making a negative from the HD master in order to provide the cinema print that was required. It must be remembered that, more often than not, there will be little need for photochemical grading as the HD to HD grade may often be done in the same photo finishing house and they will be very familiar with the in-house film-out requirements.

At the time we shot *Oklahoma!*, transferring an HD tape to a film negative was far more expensive than it is now; there were very few post-production facilities that could handle it then, whereas now there is much more competition in the market, which has naturally driven costs down. Still, to be fair, let us look at the costs at the time. *Oklahoma!* had a finished screen time of 180 minutes. Transferring HD to 35 mm negative would have cost £600/minute ($858/minute), so the cost of making a negative would have been £108 000 ($154 440).

4.3.4   Overall savings

All the photochemical costs after that would be identical except that small savings might be made in the lack of the need for answer prints, but let us ignore that. Therefore, even after making a 35 mm negative, the producers would have saved £39 800 ($50 900) on the stock and processing costs going right as far as the cut negative. Today, HD to film transfer prices are roughly half what they were when we shot *Oklahoma!* so, were they making it today, the producers could look to saving something like £79 600 ($101 800).

5
Delivery requirements

5.1 For delivery on film

There are various processes that need to follow the completion of the editing process. If you have been editing from Digi Beta copies, the original camera tapes will have to be conformed to the EDL, thus producing a continuous stream of shots that make up the movie. It is prudent to keep to a minimum the number of times the HD information is re-recorded, so the grading process might be combined with the conform, thus taking out one copying process.

If you have been editing on a platform that has been working in full HD standard and the material was played in from the camera tapes, then the material will in all probability have been stored on a disk array. This means that there will have been a zero loss of quality during the edit and a fully edited version lies in the disk array, thereby removing the need to conform. In these circumstances, and assuming they have the facilities, you might prefer to grade and add all the effects within the same post house directly from the original disk array.

In a very few post houses you might even be able to play out from the edit suite disk array directly into the photomechanical printer, always assuming you have never come out of the HD format, thereby maintaining the necessary quality. If this is practical it is an excellent way to proceed. If this is not possible then one way or another you must arrive at a fully conformed and graded HDCAM tape which contains all the effects and titles, etc. This tape will, most likely, be fed into a disk array associated with the printer for, as we have seen, it takes some 2.5 seconds to print each frame. Pausing each frame on the tape is impractical, so the material must reside on some kind of drive capable of random access.

As we have seen elsewhere in this book, the first photographic copy that is struck can be of various types. If the printer uses a CRT, then most likely the first copy will be made onto slow speed camera negative. If a laser scanner is being used then the probability is that intermediate stock will be used, but then you have the choice of writing either a negative or a positive image.

5.2 Multi-format delivery requirements

If you are not required to deliver a film-out print then it is becoming increasingly likely that any overseas client will prefer that you deliver the product on an HDCAM tape recorded in the 24P format. The alternative is that they will require a tape converted by you to their home standard; this is relatively easy to arrange. Most post houses are both adept and experienced at this form of conversion with absolutely no, or at worst very little, loss of quality or convenience. The thing to watch out for, with certain conversions, is that the time code has gone across successfully. If you know before shooting commences that a foreign version is required, I strongly suggest you make a small test and send it right through the post-production chain.

5.3 HD projection

Most HD projectors are capable of taking an output directly from an HD VTR. This, however, is not an ideal source if many viewings are to take place, as it involves minimal mechanical wear to the tape. Alternatively, you can transfer the material to a hard disk array or transfer it to a server. There is an increasing move to persuade cinemas to accept the movie from a central point with delivery by satellite or fibre optic. These options would only transmit the zeros and ones, not formed pictures, so there should be no loss of picture quality.

As I have said earlier, the greatest single effect on picture quality will almost certainly be the quality of the digital projector.

6
Sales potential

6.1 Multiple standard sales

If you have made the master recordings on HDCAM using the 24P or 25P recording format, then it is relatively easy to produce economically many versions from this master, in many formats. Direct from the Sony HDW 500 VTR, assuming it is fitted with all the conversion cards, you could play out in 24P, 25P, 30P, 23.98P, 29.97P, 59.97i, 60i and 50i. That covers most, if not all, of the television formats around the world. From the same master tape it is possible to print out to film in almost any aspect ratio from 1.175:1 right up to 2.4:1.

Clearly, by originating in the economical and convertible formats of either 24P or 25P using the HDCAM tape format, many markets are opened up which otherwise might have been closed or for which it would have been too expensive to provide a suitable version.

6.2 Multiple venue sales

It is clear that from a 24/25P HDCAM master all television stations and cinemas can receive a version that precisely fills their requirements. There are other venues and display points that should be considered. In-store large screen displays will benefit from the added quality and colour depth of HD. Very large screens or video walls of images are increasingly used for sales presentations; the difference in visual impact on such screens between pictures originated on conventional television formats or even Super 16 mm and HD can be quite startling.

When multiple screens are used the format will fulfil all likely requirements; think of an in-store situation where you might want a video wall at one point in the store but require several conventional televisions around the store. Economics may force you to use domestic televisions around the store but the big screen would be better supplied with true HD. The HDW 500 VTR is capable of giving you all these standards simultaneously.

6.3 Additional sales to HD users

Currently, the USA, Japan and Australia have HD transmission systems and are often prepared to pay a premium for HD programmes. They deem an HD programme to be one originated in true HD or one shot on 35 mm and transcribed through a telecine capable of sufficient quality. With the possible exception of wildlife programmes, they will not accept material originated on Super 16 mm or Digi Beta.

As can often happen, a single additional sale to an HD station can more than finance any extra costs involved in HD origination. Clearly, a prudent producer would try and make the sale before production begins, but as we have seen elsewhere in this book it is quite likely that there are reasons, some even economic, to shoot on HD even without a pre-sell in place. If this is the case then a post-production sale to one of these stations, particularly given the premium they might pay, can be very nearly all profit. The only costs involved are transcribing an extra HDCAM tape and shipping.

6.4   Future proofing

The raw tape stock is unlikely to last physically as long as film, even given that both are stored in ideal conditions. The cost of lengthening the life of an HD tape is very low; you just make a clone every 20 years or so. The cost of preserving film is high for, even if the master negative exists in perfect order, new prints are expensive. I believe the long-term costs of archiving over very long periods will favour HD.

There is always the argument that recording standards may change and they certainly will, eventually, but HD is so easily convertible between standards I cannot see why a copy in some new format could not be made simply and economically. If you want to make a new television copy at full resolution from a film the cost can be considerable, involving both telecine and processing charges.

Part 2

Pre-Production Decisions

7
Production considerations and frame rates

7.1 What is the 'film look'?

If you want HD to look as close as possible to film then the most significant decision you can make is to hire a Director of Photography (DoP) with a film background. No other decision will contribute more than this. The history of film goes back well over a hundred years and this background has created a certain ethic that somehow runs through the veins of a film DoP. Live television is a very different medium and has been going just over 60 years, while digital cinematography has been around a little over 10 years. Hire the people with the relevant experience and hire the best you can afford.

With the exceptionally long tone range recorded by the HDW F900 camera, together with its inherent sensitivity, lighting issues remain the same as if you were shooting 320 ASA film.

All that said, there are many technical considerations that contribute to the audience getting what it perceives as a film experience whether the image is being shown in a theatre or on a television screen.

7.2 Frame rates

7.2.1 A little history

Theatrical film is traditionally shot at 24 fps (frames per second), but at the end of the nineteenth century a taking frame rate of 16 frames per second was becoming common practice. At that time both cameras and projectors were still hand cranked, and most were usually geared such that a constant cranking speed of two turns per second resulted in this frame rate, which was all very convenient. Those in the industry who were beginning to consider themselves artists would have preferred a higher rate, for this would have reduced the flicker on the screen, hence the phrase 'going to the flicks'. The film producers and distributors, on the other hand, were seriously opposed to any increase in frame rate as this would use more film and therefore put up costs. Little has changed.

By 1926, the American Society of Motion Picture Engineers (SMPE, later the SMPTE) Standards and Nomenclature Committee recommended camera cranking speeds as follows: 'Regarding camera speed we recommend as a recommended practice: a camera cranking speed of 60 feet per minute (16 fps), with a minimum of 55 feet and a maximum of 65 feet when normal action is desired, in connection with the Society of Motion Picture Engineers recommended practice of 80 feet per minute projection speed (21 fps)'.

To recommend different taking and projection speeds may now seem ridiculous, but what they were trying to set a standard for was a frame rate that was perceived to be correct on viewing. Try turning the sound off on your television and notice how the action suddenly seems to be slower despite your certain knowledge that it cannot be, so the SMPTE were on the right track.

The result of this recommendation is that, from the turn of the century to the coming of sound on film, the camera frame rate was set at roughly 16 frames per second. When sound recorded optically in synchronization with the picture came in around 1927, the frame rate of 16 fps, or 60 feet of film per minute, was too slow to make an adequate sound recording using the optical recording techniques available at the time. More film passing the sound head every second was needed to enable higher frequencies to be recorded with less background noise. By now, it was known that the flicker apparent in a film projected at 16 fps, or thereabouts, started to disappear above a projection rate of 20 fps. At 30 fps it seemed to disappear completely even on the most demanding scenes, these usually being those with pronounced highlights, as flicker is more discernible in the brighter areas of a scene.

In America the mains electricity has a frequency of 60 cycles per second (cps); therefore, a standard synchronous electric motor there will have a shaft speed of 1440 revolutions per minute. This gives a shaft speed of 24 revolutions per second. The Americans, who after all pioneered the making of the talkies, therefore chose the very convenient frame rate of 24 fps as being almost totally free of any flicker, producing a linear film speed sufficiently high to enable good sound to be recorded with the picture on the same piece of film and being absurdly simple to drive the projectors at a constant speed from a simple synchronous motor. This frame rate (24 fps) is today the world standard for theatrical motion pictures.

Further to the longevity of the 35 mm film format was the international standardization of the perforation on 35 mm film. Prior to 1932, most companies were using film 35 mm wide, but there were many different perforation standards, particularly before the introduction of sound. In 1932, an international standard was agreed that all theatrical films should be produced on 35 mm film with the Bell and Howell perforation. This standard, together with the already agreed 24 fps standard, set the die for the future right up to today. The only change since 1932 has been a very slight modification to the shape of the perforation, that in current use being known as the Kodak perforation.

7.2.2 Audience perception

A frame rate of 24 fps may not be an ideal shooting rate in all circumstances; indeed, there are many who would advocate a shooting rate of 30 fps, but it cannot be denied that our audience has become conditioned to that rate. They have come, if you like, to expect the slight flicker on the cinema screen. When film shot at 24 fps is shown on television in America a 3:2 pull-down standard has to be used in order to increase the origination speed of 24 fps to the television full picture rate of 30 fps (see Chapter 27 for a fuller, technical, description of 3:2 pull-down).

This introduces some technically undesirable motion artefacts, especially in horizontal movement, but the audience seems to have come to expect this and reacts to it as the 'signature' of a high quality film being shown on their television. In Europe, film originated at 24 fps is simply shown at 25 fps, that being the European television full frame rate and corresponding to their 50 cps mains supply. Consequently, the running time of the show is reduced by 4 per cent. Due to the human eye/brain having no shutter and allowing rapid movement to overlap slightly, this being known as the persistence of vision, I have yet to meet anyone who can, visually, discern a 4 per cent change in motion speed.

Unfortunately, there are some among us who can very readily discern a 4 per cent change in sound pitch – those with perfect, or near perfect, hearing pitch. Our hearing is much more sensitive to changes in frequency than our eyes are to change in visual motion speed. This facility is not built into human beings just so that they can better appreciate music, but so that we are very sensitive to changes in tone. This allows us to tell whether an object emitting a constant sound is static, moving towards us, where the pitch will be constantly increasing, or moving away from us, where the pitch will be constantly decreasing. This pitch change with movement is known as the Doppler effect, named after the German scientist who defined the phenomenon.

It is possible when showing a film at 25 fps but which was shot at 24 fps to pass the sound through a frequency corrector and return it to perfect pitch at the new showing rate. This is not a very expensive process but, unfortunately, is rarely carried out.

7.2.3 Traditional cinema flicker

As we have seen, the current standard for the mechanical projection of 35 mm film is 24 fps. And we know that this gives rise to a certain amount of flicker on the cinema screen, but we accept that the audience is happily conditioned to this. Things are just a little less simple than that; they are also a little more elegant. Figure 7.1 shows how a camera shutter is orientated to leave the aperture open during 180° of its rotation and to blank the aperture for the other 180°. This is all very simple and effective for, at 24 fps, it results in an exposure of 1/48th of a second. So, half the time the film is being moved to the next frame and half the time is given over to exposure.

In the cinema projector things are a little different. In the camera, which is usually close to the microphone picking up the sound, the film transport mechanism has to be very quiet. A claw mechanism is usually deployed which might not be terribly fast at pulling down the film accurately but is quiet.

In the projector a prime consideration is to maximize the amount of light reaching the screen. As the projector will almost certainly be in a separate room from the audience, known as the projection box, how much noise it makes is not a prime consideration. What is a prime consideration though is how kind the transport mechanism is to the film and its perforations, for whereas the camera only passes the film once, a piece of print film destined for the cinema may pass through a projector many hundreds of times.

Most cinema projectors use a transport mechanism known as the Maltese cross. It is simply a sprocket wheel attached to a drive shaped a little like a Maltese cross, which is driven by a rotating pin. This arrangement causes the sprocket to rotate intermittently. The advantages of this transport mechanism are that it is very kind to the film, as at least four perforations on each side of the film are engaged with the sprocket teeth at any one time, thus greatly reducing the load on each sprocket, and

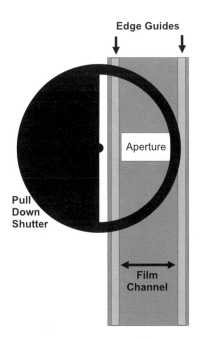

Figure 7.1 Thirty-five millimetre film gate and camera shutter

it can therefore safely pull the film down much more rapidly, usually in one-quarter of the full frame rate, without damaging any of the perforations. It is, however, very noisy.

As the projector mechanism only needs one-quarter of total time to transport the film, the shutter can now be opened for 270° and closed for 90°. This increases the screen brightness by 50 per cent relative to a 180° shutter.

The disadvantage of this arrangement is that having a greater opening time than closed time brings us back to our old problem – flicker. Extending the shutter opening time will considerably increase the apparent flicker.

This is overcome by introducing a very small extra shutter blade, as shown in Figure 7.2, which effectively fools the eye into thinking it is seeing 48 fps despite every two consecutive frames being identical, as the same frame is still in the projector gate. This extra blade is known as the 'phantom shutter'.

All this may seem less than relevant to HD cinematography. It is not, for it is important to understand what the HD 24P format is trying to replicate. Though it would arguably produce a better image, with less flicker, at 30 fps, which the camera is capable of, this would be unfamiliar to our audience. In order to obtain seamless acceptance from the audience, at least until digital projection becomes more common, an identical frame rate and flicker to 35 mm film is very desirable.

Images originated on an HD camera shooting at 24 fps with the shutter set at 1/48th of a second with that image printed out onto film and shown on a mechanical projector at 24 fps in the cinema will replicate the same image originated on 35 mm film shot at 24 fps with a 180° shutter in every discernible respect. Add to this the internationally accepted HDCAM recoding format and one has the same worldwide compatibility that film has enjoyed since 1932.

7.3   When other frame rates may be desirable

All the above applies when the product is destined solely for the cinema. Many other considerations come into play when mixed presentation is desired. For instance, if you are expecting roughly equal returns from a cinema release and showings on European television, especially if you are on a low

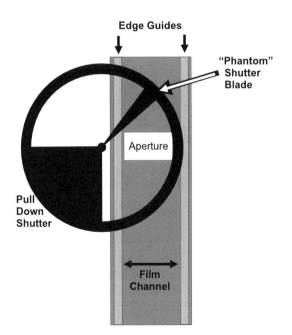

Figure 7.2 Thirty-five millimetre film gate and projector shutter

budget, 24 fps may not be the best choice. In America though, again with half your revenue coming from a television showing, 24 fps would probably be ideal. Let us look at the options.

7.3.1 Low budget European shoot

Frame rate considerations can be much more complicated in Europe than in the US. Almost certainly you will be hoping for an American sale, so eventually you will need a 24 fps version, possibly both for television and theatrical release. Clearly you will need a 25 fps version for European television, but the same 24 fps theatrical version is as correct there as in the US.

Despite all the different frame rate versions you will need, the greatest influence over your shooting rate may well be which non-linear editing suite you intend to use. While the ideal editing suite would be non-linear working exclusively in the 1080-line HD standard, these are very expensive. A more economical approach would be to down-convert your camera tapes to Digi Beta or Beta SP, thus making huge savings on the rental cost of the record/playback machine in the cutting room, and edit on a non-linear machine working in the 25 fps PAL format. This is probably the cheapest option overall.

There is a problem, however. While some suites in Europe can cut at 24 fps, most will only run at 25 fps. If you have shot at 24 fps you will almost certainly encounter few problems digitizing your picture and sound into the machine at 25 fps. But be warned! There is a strong likelihood that while the machine has coped with the time code differential playing into the machine when you have finished your cut, the EDL (Edit Decision List) and the output time code may both be complete nonsense. The only way to be sure is to make a test long before you start your shoot. If the output is less than ideal, one complete solution would be to shoot at 25 fps, which is totally compatible with European edit suites, as they are equipped to work in this format whether the origination was on film or PAL standard tape shot at 25 fps.

If you decide to shoot at 25 fps, then as we have seen your audience will not be able to tell any difference in the picture and, at worst, you may have to pay for a pitch conversion to the soundtrack. This pitch conversion is still not likely to be as expensive as the other options.

7.3.2 Low budget US shoot

Compared to your European counterparts, decisions are much easier here. Again, cost considerations will probably dictate that you down-convert your camera master tapes to Digi Beta or even Beta SP, but as virtually all US non-linear edit suites accept a 24 fps input with a 3:2 pull-down conversion, and can output images, sound and time code successfully, you are unlikely to encounter problems.

You will therefore end up with a conformed 24 fps HD tape. For sales to the European PAL market you have a couple of options. You can electronically standards convert directly from the HD-conformed master to a Digi Beta PAL tape – the Sony HDW F500 desktop recorder will do this if fitted with the correct board – or if you are going to a film version you can telecine either the negative, the intermediate or the print at 25 fps. Again, the sound pitch can be easily and relatively cheaply corrected if you wish to do so.

7.3.3 Big budget productions

If you can afford it, the absolute ideal is to cut your movie on a non-linear edit suite capable of remaining in the 1080-line HD format at 24 fps with progressive scan. Your pictures on the monitors will always look superb and your standards conversion problems are now virtually non-existent. You can cut at 24 fps and, using the Sony HDW F500 desktop recorder fitted with appropriate conversion boards, you can output in virtually any format you wish. You will, however, need deep pockets!

7.3.4   Thirty frames per second?

If your product is intended solely for the US television market, whether it is to be transmitted on Digital HDTV (High Definition Television), Digital SDTV (Standard Definition Television) or analogue NTSC, you might like to consider shooting at 30 or 29.97 fps, still in the progressive scan format. This will produce results virtually identical to the way very high quality television commercials are shot in the US – on 35 mm film running at 30 fps – thus removing the 3:2 pull-down motion artefacts.

The cost of film stock has prohibited narrative US television being shot this way, but a 20 per cent increase in tape cost, an increase of £1.25 or $1.75 per minute, is so small as to be an irrelevance. The increase in film costs, just for negatives and processing with no print or telecine transfer, would be £50 or $75 per minute of screen time.

7.4   Progressive or interlace?

There is a school of thought that says if you are only going to show your product on television, whether in the US or the UK, you are better off shooting HD in an interlace format. With very few exceptions, such as possibly in sport, I strongly disagree.

The main thrust of the HD revolution is to make the images appear to the audience to be as high a quality as they expect from a film original, for this they think of as quality programming. We have seen that production values, especially the quality of lighting and composition, must be as good as you would expect from a 35 mm film product. The one thing that will never look like film if you originate in an interlace scan format is the motion artefacts. These are only the same if you originate in the progressive scan mode.

Our lay audience may not be able to describe what is different between an interlace image and a progressive scan image, but they will certainly know there is a difference and they have been conditioned to regard the film/progressive scan artefacts as superior and to have added value.

If you have the slightest chance of going to a film print do not, whatever you do, shoot in interlace. It looks dreadfully inferior on a cinema screen. See Chapter 27 for a technical explanation.

8

Production considerations relating to the type of production

Apart from cost considerations, the greatest influence on your decision as to whether to shoot IID, and how you decide which of the eight available frame formats to use, will be the type of production you are on. Sport, for instance, when destined solely for television transmission might best be shot at 60i or 50i (US or Europe direct television compatibility). Anything with a likelihood of reaching the cinema screen should be shot at 24P or in Europe possibly at 25P. Already we are seeing differences between the US and Europe, and these differences are not just technical, the type of programmes and films made either side of the Atlantic can be very different. Therefore, at the risk of repeating myself I will treat these two markets separately.

8.1 Shooting in the USA

8.1.1 Theatrical productions

Many television theatrical productions in the US still use 35 mm film. This will undoubtedly change somewhat, but at what rate and when is very hard to predict. The options if you want to go to HD are almost exclusively between 24P and the native television standard of 60i. If you are going to have a theatrical release 60i is not really a viable option. If you think you will be making a theatrical print and a television version it is nearly always best to shoot at 24P (or 23.98P) and make a 3:2 pull-down version for television, for this is the current norm even when shooting film.

Figure 8.1 gives some of the reasons why you would wish to stay with 24P when shooting for even a limited theatrical release.

Some very low budget films are made in the US using either Super 16 or Digi Beta. If shot on Digi Beta it is more common to use a European PAL camera as the 25 frame rate of PAL solves some of

Theatrical	24P	60i	Reasons
Cinema film	Definitely	No	Total compatibility with 35 mm film
Cinema film + heavy TV sell-through	24P or 23.98P	No	Total compatibility with 35 mm film + easy transfer to TV
Cinema short	Definitely	No	Total compatibility with 35 mm film
Cinema short with TV sale	Definitely	No	Total compatibility with 35 mm film
Cinema commercial	Definitely	No	Total compatibility with 35 mm film
Cinema + TV commercial	24P or 23.98P	No	Total compatibility with 35 mm film + easy transfer to TV

Figure 8.1 Frame rates for theatrical release when shooting in the USA

the problems of getting an interlace image onto film – when shot this way they simply run 4 per cent slower in the cinema. 60i NTSC origination and print-out to film is nothing like as successful. Both these routes still have the inherent motion artefact problems of an interlace image, as discussed in Chapter 7.

8.1.2   US prime time television productions

Totally unlike Europe, a large proportion of US prime time television production has historically been originated on 35 mm film, albeit often using a three-perforation pull-down camera rather than the conventional four-perforation pull-down used in the cinema, as this reduces the stock and processing costs by 25 per cent. This convention has several advantages; in particular it facilitates telecine transfers direct to any television standard without the need for electronic standards conversion (NTSC 60/59.94 Hz for US and 50 Hz for PAL in most of Europe). Shooting on film is also seen as a sure way of future proofing a programme; no matter what formats or conventions arrive in the future it will always be possible to retrieve the master negative from the archive and put it through an appropriate telecine machine outputting in that new format.

There is another possible option for the future which is not, as yet, common practice. There is a very small increase in cost difference between shooting HDCAM at 24P or 30P (see Chapter 7), so a new choice comes into consideration. For prime time television where no theatrical release is envisaged, a substantial increase in perceived picture quality can be obtained at minimal cost by shooting at 30P (or perhaps 29.97P). This is new territory and needs careful consideration.

8.1.3   US commercials

Television commercials shot on film in the US are conventionally shot at 24 fps or, if they have really high production values, 30 fps. The latter rate is desirable as it removes the 3:2 pull-down issues and the motion artefacts inherent in that transfer process. When shooting on film the increase in stock costs can be prohibitive (see comparisons in Chapter 7), while with HDCAM the real cost increase is negligible. Hence there is a strong argument for shooting HDCAM commercials at 30P or 29.97P in order to be even more compatible with the NTSC transmission format.

In one commercials arena HDCAM has a severe drawback. It will not run at high speed and cannot be ramped (changing frame rate during a shot); 30 fps is the highest true shooting speed the camera is capable of. It is possible to shoot at 60i and, in post-production, double up the lines on each field to make them each into a vertical 1080-line frame. However, technically you do lose half the vertical resolution though to the human eye it does not seem to be quite as much.

There are now some very sophisticated post-production techniques that are capable of taking a full resolution 24P or 30P master and interpreting it as anything up to and sometimes beyond 90 fps very convincingly. Some can even achieve very acceptable ramping. To wish to go down this route you would probably have to have some other, high priority, reason for shooting on HD in the first instance. A lot of blue screen plus some high speed might be a case in point.

8.1.4   Other US productions

The film-originated sitcom must be very vulnerable to a conversion from film to HDTV. Stock costs are high relative to total production costs. The multi-camera shooting approach lends itself to HDTV more readily than film; just think of the increase in quality of the video assist – it would be full resolution HD finished product. Lighting costs will remain roughly the same; remember the camera is fundamentally a 320 ASA device, though with experience my guess is that DoPs may find themselves using a little less fill light because of the characteristics of the camera. Lighting techniques in all other respects can remain exactly as they are.

8.1.5 What frame rate to choose

Apart from scripts intended solely for theatrical release, and these should almost certainly be shot at 24P, there are few absolutes here. There are, however, many near certainties. In Figures 8.1–8.4, I have set out my 'best guess' as to the correct decision, based on current practice, together with the reason for my thinking. The figures cover four main areas of production, which are:

- theatrical productions (Figure 8.1);
- broadcast release-only productions (Figure 8.2);
- cable-only release (Figure 8.3);
- US syndication-only release (Figure 8.4).

8.1.6 Potential cost savings

Prime time production costs, in particular, are steadily rising and have been for some time now. This has forced some productions to shoot outside the US in an effort to curtail these costs. HDTV offers some real savings and might just keep some productions in their native land.

The HDCAM recording medium offers substantially lower costs than motion picture negative, together with a complete saving on processing and telecine charges.

There are other, perhaps surprising, savings that can be made. Because of the instant playback available, sets can be struck immediately a scene is finished, thus saving studio or location rental charges and possibly construction labour costs. Master tapes can be cloned every night (clone = digit-to-digit transfer, an exact digital copy) and the master tape can then be lodged with the picture's insurers, perhaps saving some of the cost of negative insurance.

If extensive blue or green screen work is envisaged, this can be carried out in real time, if required, and is in any case likely to be both cheaper and more successful than if originated on film. Most likely this was part of the motivation for George Lucas to shoot *Star Wars II* on HDCAM. It was he, after all, who brought Sony and Panavision together, thus creating their joint venture to produce the more advanced Panavision version of the camera.

8.2 European productions

The 35 mm television market does not exist in Europe. Here sitcoms do not abound and are never shot on 35 mm. Film for television is usually shot on 16 mm, most often Super 16, and this is how the majority of high-end television drama is shot within Europe. Major feature films are in a very similar position to the US, but the low budget feature industry looks quite different.

If you look at Figure 8.5 you will first notice how very different it looks from Figure 8.1; likewise compare Figure 8.2 with Figure 8.6. Both the definition of the kind of films and programmes shot and the likely shooting formats are quite different. This is a reflection of the different markets either side of the Atlantic.

Broadcast	24P	60i	Reasons
Made for TV movie	24P or 23.98P	Unlikely	Total compatibility with 35 mm film, use 3:2 pull-down
One-hour prime time drama	24P or 23.98P	Unlikely	Total compatibility with 35 mm film, use 3:2 pull-down
Half-hour prime time sitcom	Possibly	Possibly	Difficult call – check with broadcaster
Sports programme	Poor results	Very likely	Motion artefacts better with 60i for this subject
Network news magazine	Probably not	Most often	60i traditionally used here – better with stock footage
Documentaries	Sometimes	Sometimes	Subject and broadcaster dependent
Wildlife and natural history	Possibly	Preferable	High speed shooting of animals might affect decision
Reality specials	Very unlikely	Very likely	Tradition dictates 60i
Soap opera	Possibly	Preferable	Tradition and compatibility dictate 60i
Local news	Very unlikely	Most likely	Compatibility dictates 60i

Figure 8.2 Frame rates for broadcast release in the USA

Cable	24P	60i	Reasons
Cable one-hour drama	24P or 23.98P	Some	Total compatibility with 35 mm film, use 3:2 pull-down
Cable half-hour sitcom	Few	Very likely	Difficult call – check with broadcaster
Cable 'do-it-yourself' series	Unlikely	Very likely	Common practice
Cable sport	No	Definitely	60i traditionally used here – better with sports motion

Figure 8.3 Frame rates for cable release in the USA

Syndication	24P	60i	Reasons
Syndicated 'action' hour	Unlikely	Normal	Common practice
Syndicated talk show	Unlikely	Normal	Common practice
Syndicated game or dating show	Unlikely	Normal	Common practice
Syndicated court show	Unlikely	Normal	Common practice

Figure 8.4 Frame rates for syndication when shooting in the USA

8.2.1   European feature films

With a few exceptions, European films with budgets in excess of £4 million usually shoot on 35 mm; in the main this is likely to remain so for some time, but there is a slow but significant interest in 24P developing. Pictures budgeted between £1 million and £4 million are definitely moving towards 24P as an origination medium. It should be noted, however, that pictures with a £4 million budget usually have a distributor attached before principal photography commences and therefore have to have the cost of a film print in that budget. While HD can still be attractive here, the cost differential between HD and film is not as significant as might be expected, as the cost of going to print can sometimes absorb some of the savings that can be made using HD 24P for origination.

With films having a budget between £600 000 and £1.4 million matters are very different. Low budget European film makers rarely have a distributor attached before shooting. It is common for a film to be at the final cut stage before the producers find a distributor. Many of the producers working in this area have quickly realized that HD camera tapes are, as far as the images are concerned, finished product. It is increasingly common for a film to be shown to prospective distributors as a conformed HD tape either on a large high quality television or by hiring a major cinema which is equipped with a top of the range digital projector and inviting a group of prospective distributors to the viewing. On, say, a Sunday morning hiring, such a venue is not prohibitively expensive. Sometimes 500 or 1000 feet of selected scenes are printed out to film to convince the distributors of the quality of the product, but as distributors become more familiar with the HD 24P format this is needed less and less.

Figure 8.5 shows likely origination mediums and the reasons for such decisions with respect to European feature films.

8.2.2   European television

Major 1-hour or 90-minute television dramas in Europe have, in the past, been traditionally shot on Super 16. A very small number are shot on Digi Beta and in the UK no more than one a year will go to 35 mm. Some one-off productions and some 1-hour series are being shot on 24P and have been very successful. The costs analysis involved is sometimes complex with a major foreign sale to an HD outlet, arranged before production commences, being a strong driving force for going the HD 24P route. Figure 8.6 shows the likely origination medium for various television productions and some of the likely reasons for such decisions.

When Sony introduced the television-specific HDW 750 the picture began to change. Suddenly it was possible to put together a budget that came in cheaper than one catering for a Super 16 shoot and get picture quality comparable with a 35 mm shoot. Naturally this had attractions and UK producers

Theatrical	35 mm	Super 16	24P/25P	Reasons
Cinema film over £6m	Definitely	Very unlikely	Possibly	35 mm total compatibility with cinema
Cinema film £1m – £4m	Probably	Unlikely	Possibly	Increasingly moving to 24P
Cinema film around £1m	Less likely	Possibly	Very likely	Costs make good sense on 24P
Cinema short	Possibly	Unlikely	Very likely	24P makes good economic sense
Cinema commercial	Probably	No	Possibly	Slowly moving to 24P
Cinema + TV commercial	Probably	No	Possibly	Increasing interest in 24P

Figure 8.5 Origination for theatrical release when shooting in Europe

Major television	35 mm	Super 16	24P/25P	Reasons
Drama – £1m+/hour	Rarely	Very likely	Possibly	Foreign sales driving some to 24P
Drama less than £1m/hour	Never	Very likely	Possibly	Some moving to 24P, quality vs cost
Comedy hour	Never	Possibly	Possibly	Some moving to 24P, quality vs cost
Comedy half hour	Never	Possibly	Possibly	A few moving to 24P, quality vs cost
Sport	Never	Unlikely	No	Traditionally always PAL TV
Soaps	Never	No	Never	Always studio PAL TV
News and current affairs	Never	No	Never	Studio + Digi Beta + DV

Figure 8.6 Origination for prime time television when shooting in Europe

started to seriously consider moving Super 16 productions to HD and some productions that had, up to then, been originated on Digi Beta have also moved across to HD.

8.2.3 Performance shows

This is an emerging market in Europe, especially in the UK. There is a definite trend to take major theatre pieces out of London's West End or The National Theatre and record them for television and sometimes even give them limited theatrical release. It is an area with which I have been lucky enough to be involved. Two examples show how this market really should go to HD 24P.

8.2.3.1 Oklahoma!

Oklahoma!, a UK National Theatre production, was shot on 35 mm. I shot 265 000 feet of 35 mm in 19 days using three cameras. The savings on HD would have been very significant. The show was on 35 mm because it had been pre-sold to several HD broadcasters around the world and they would only pay the HD premium if we originated on 35 mm or HD. A theatrical print was also required. Unfortunately there was not enough HD equipment available at the time as it was only just coming onto the market.

8.2.3.2 The Merchant of Venice

The UK National Theatre production of *The Merchant of Venice* was shot on Digi Beta. I created some very significant 'looks' for this production, something film would have been far less good at and at which HD 24P would have excelled. Unfortunately the initial budget precluded the HD option at the time.

When we commenced shooting there seemed no prospect of a theatrical release. When the picture had been fine cut and graded the UK producers hired the Princess Anne Theatre at BAFTA (British Academy of Film and Television Arts) in London's Piccadilly for a cast and crew viewing with some extra selected guests. After the viewing the American co-producer decided to make a 35 mm print from the Digi Beta master for limited theatrical release in the US, which made it even more disappointing that it had not been possible to shoot it on HD. Such is life!

8.3 Equipment

Before I go any further with this chapter, I must confess a strong personal preference for Panavision equipment. The convenience and familiarity that their modifications and accessories bring to me, with my strong film background, and the sheer quality of their lenses mean that the Panavision HD system will always be my first choice. That said, I will try and be objective.

More technical descriptions of the Sony 900 and 750 series cameras and the Thomson Viper can be found later in this book.

8.3.1 Cameras

8.3.1.1 Sony and Panavision

The Sony HDW F900 and its Panavision derivative can be considered the first generation of HD cameras that can seriously compete with 35 mm film and remains for many cinematographers their favourite. The quality of the pictures and the universality of the on-board HDCAM recording format mean that it will remain for some time the camera of choice for many cinematographers. The F900's 12-bit processor means that for the big screen it still wins on the picture quality against price argument, even when compared with Sony's excellent HDW 750 series cameras.

The Panavision version of Sony's F900 camera, while coming with a premium price tag, does constitute a considerable step forward in both colour rendition and convenience, together with the considerable increase in lens performance when used with the Panavision Primo Digital Lenses.

The Sony 750 series cameras are perhaps the natural choice for a project which will never reach the big screen, for they are capable of pictures indistinguishable from the F900 when shown on a cathode ray tube. The saving in cost makes the 750 series very attractive in this arena. The reduction in size and weight also contributes to the attractiveness of the 750 for many television productions given their somewhat different shooting styles. In addition, the fact that a down-converted standard definition output can be incorporated within the camera in addition to the expected HD SDI (High Definition Serial Digital Interface) output further enhances the attraction of this camera for television production.

Figure 8.7 shows a Sony HDW 750 fitted with a Canon zoom lens and Figure 8.8 shows a Panavision 900F with a $4\frac{1}{2}$:1 Primo Digital Zoom.

Figure 8.7 The Sony HDW 750 with a Canon lens

Figure 8.8 The Panavision HDW F900 with a $4\frac{1}{2}$:1 Primo Digital Zoom

8.3.1.2   Panasonic

Panasonic's AJ-HDC27V camera is an interesting concept. It will only record full 1080-line high definition images in an interlace format, though it will record in the 720-line format in progressive scan. It will not, therefore, record in the 1080 × 1920 format at 24P, which is the norm for big screen presentation. It does, however, have a considerable advantage in one particular parameter; it will give you pictures at any frame rate from 4 up to 60 fps (frames per second). It does this by always recording at 60 fps and interpolating whichever frame rate you choose during playback.

I am not deeply familiar with this camera but have had a chance to test one briefly and am very taken with the quality of its variable speed interpolation; there is no doubt that it works. As most of my HD work has been at 24P or 25P, the lack of what I consider to be full high definition pictures in progressive scan is disappointing and, to my eyes at least, there seems to be a certain lack of colour depth compared with the Sony cameras. In the television arena there could be considerable advantages from using this camera for certain shoots; sport comes to mind in particular.

8.3.1.3   Thomson

Thomson have a camera they have christened the Viper. It is capable of very high picture quality and can output a totally uncompressed signal which can be an advantage if a lot of post-production is envisaged. There is a considerable downside, however, particularly if you wish to shoot like a film camera – there is no on-board recorder. With this camera you give up the convenience of the camcorder layout in order to achieve the uncompressed output.

I am sure there will be a future for this concept, but for the regular film and television productions I work on it must be limited.

8.3.2   Lenses

Lenses for use on HD cameras are, in the main, sourced from two separate parts of the industry. There are those that come from the manufactures who traditionally supply the video world and those that are more familiar with the film industry. Both the look and function of lenses from these two very different backgrounds often betray their heritage. It is common for a lens from the video world to be described as being 'film style' but do not be deceived – many of them have characteristics a dyed-in-the-wool film technician would find totally unacceptable. For a further description on this matter you can refer to Section 14.1 in the chapter on lenses.

8.3.2.1 Manufacturers

From the video world Canon and Fujinon probably lead the field, both offering good lenses specifically for the HD market. Both produce zoom lenses and Canon have a range of prime lenses; they are the FJ5, the FJ9, the FJ14, the FJ24 and the FJ35, where the number indicates the focal length of the lens in millimetres. The FJ5 has a maximum aperture of f1.7, with all the others having a maximum aperture of f1.5. Fujinon have a range of eight prime lenses which include focal lengths of 5, 8, 12, 16, 20, 34, 40 and 54 mm.

From the film world the most prominent manufacturer must be Panavision, which has produced a complete and fully matched set of lenses that includes four zooms and six primes. They are currently:

Zooms:

- A 4.5 times zoom ranging from 6 to 27 mm with an aperture of T1.8.
- A 4.5 times zoom ranging from 25 to 112 mm with an aperture of T1.9.
- A 9 times zoom ranging from 8 to 72 mm with an aperture of T1.9.
- An 11 times zoom ranging from 9.5 to 105 mm with an aperture of T1.6.

Primes:

- A 5 mm with an aperture of T1.8.
- A 7 mm with an aperture of T1.6.
- A 10 mm with an aperture of T1.6.
- A 14 mm with an aperture of T1.6.
- A 20 mm with an aperture of T1.6.
- A 35 mm with an aperture of T1.6.

Also available are a set of six prime lenses from Zeiss which have a configuration and quality you would expect from such a manufacturer that has a long reputation for excellence. Their specifications are:

- A 5 mm rated at f1.7/T1.9.
- A 7 mm rated at f1.5/T1.6.
- A 10 mm rated at f1.5/T1.6.
- A 14 mm rated at f1.5/T1.6.
- A 20 mm rated at f1.5/T1.6.
- A 40 mm rated at f1.5/T1.6.

8.3.2.2 Primes vs zooms

If we accept that to produce images for large screen projection we must be able to resolve a circle of confusion of one pixel, or very nearly one pixel, then if a lens meets this requirement, or very nearly meets it, there will be no discernible difference in image quality whether it be a zoom or a prime lens. In these circumstances size and weight may determine your choice. If you are going to need both a zoom and some prime lenses, then you will have to be very careful to ensure that both the quality and character of the images match.

Not many of the lenses available to the HD cinematographer meet the ultimate near one pixel resolution and this, to my eyes at least, can be discerned on a cinema screen.

8.3.3 Preferences

What follows must be a very personal view and I am sure you will not be surprised to find I favour the Panavision lenses; these, though, can only be rented and their quality commands a margin on the rental price. The Zeiss lenses are also very good and consequently are also very expensive. At the time of writing I understand Zeiss have no intention of adding a zoom to their range. If you are from the video world or trying to keep your budget down, my own choice would be for a Canon zoom.

9
Crewing

There is an unfortunate misconception rife among some producers that if you shoot digital HD you can work with a much smaller crew than with film, which is also, of course, HD in its way. To make the judgement simply on the recording format is, in my view, foolish and comes from looking at the history of the HD tape medium from the wrong perspective.

Historically, video shoots have used smaller crews. This is because they have been conceived from their beginnings as low budget productions and, had the decision been made to shoot them on film, it too would have been done with the smallest crew possible.

There is another significant and unfortunate result of these misconceptions. With some rare exceptions tape has not, in the past, been scheduled for many productions that would have had even the slightest chance of affording film. As a result, even Digi Beta has rarely been given the chance to show its true potential as, with the lower budgets it is usually confined to, the quality of the design input is often so poor, the daily minutes of screen time shot so high and the crew so small that it becomes impossible to produce a high quality product no matter what you are recording on.

If you subscribe to any of the above opinions of low budget tape productions you must change them when shooting HD. With HD the recording medium is irrelevant to these arguments, for it is the picture quality that is the key technical contributor to the crewing decisions. The quality is as high as 35 mm and therefore all crewing must relate to previously gained 35 mm experience. The HDW F900 kit is usually bigger and heavier than a Digi Beta, though the HDW 750 camera kit comes in much nearer to the same weight.

9.1 Should the DoP operate?

In my opinion, not if you want your digital output to look as good as possible. The viewfinder on the cameras is usually poor compared with a film camera and therefore I believe that it is essential that the DoP stays back at a correctly set up HD monitor in order to judge what is being recorded. There are better HD viewfinders coming on stream so this may change. The new Panavision full HD progressive scan colour does improve matters in this respect.

9.2 Do you need a focus puller?

Operators with a television studio background are used to pulling focus for themselves. Allowing them to continue to do this on an HD shoot can be very dangerous indeed. Those of us who are trying to produce really good images from HD are usually working at very wide apertures in order to reduce the depth of field to something that looks similar to that expected on film. Once this shorter depth of field is achieved, the focus pulling difficulties become the same as for 35 mm film and a fully trained and experienced focus puller becomes essential. More often than not this desire to reduce the depth of field, and have softer backgrounds, comes not only from the DoP, but is also a requirement of the director.

9.3   Do you need a loader?

There is no job for a traditional loader but there is a vital job for a slightly differently trained camera assistant. Fortunately, many very good film loaders are just as skilled and useful on an HD shoot. Tapes still have to be changed, labelled and report sheets prepared for the cutting room. Still more importantly, the colour monitor will have to be set up, organized and lined up. Most of my camera assistants who perform these tasks are more than able to line up the monitor and I have come to rely on them to do so. As I would not necessarily have the time to do it, my camera assistants will check the line-up every time the monitor is moved and after every break.

If you are on a multi-camera shoot then the logging of the tapes becomes vital and a camera assistant can end up the busiest person on the set.

9.4   Naming the camera assistants

Within a year of the introduction of the Sony HDW F700, the Guild of British Camera Technicians (GBCT) suggested to its members that the current naming of the camera assistants as Focus Puller and Clapper Loader should revert to the older names of First Assistant Cameraperson (AC1) and Second Assistant Cameraperson (AC2). This, I believe, was both sensible and significant. The GBCT saw that HD was a reality and that many of its members would be working in this area, and renaming their grades would help them to gain work within the new parts of their industry.

It is not often that one sees an established industry guild look forwards rather than hang on to the past as furiously as possible and I, for one, commend them for an almost unique foresight.

9.5   Do you need a clapperboard?

My answer is definitely yes. It only takes the slightest error in the camera, the play-out machine feeding the off-line editing suite, the edit suite itself, the conform suite or in the creating and reading out of the Edit Decision List (EDL) for a shot, or whole scene, to go completely out of sync or, even worse, end up cut into the wrong place. If a film-style clapperboard is used there is always the visible shot number to refer back to and the physical clapper to re-sync to.

I have to admit that I doubt machines' ability to, reliably, count. This lack of faith has saved many a production considerable amounts of money by them being able to go back to the clapper to regain sync. Some old ways are still the best!

There is another reason to use a clapperboard which is just as important. Most technicians are so tuned to knowing a take starts with calling the number and banging two bits of wood together that they don't really go quiet or, more importantly, really start to concentrate, until they hear the board. It pumps up the adrenaline and you will find you are going for far fewer takes if you use a clapperboard than if you do not. That can be a big saving.

Actors find the same to be true; to a film-trained or experienced actor the moment to perform simply has not come until the board has gone on.

9.6   Do you need a dolly grip?

Definitely. The modern style of shooting usually involves a very mobile camera and the grip, or dolly grip in the US, is the person to provide this quickly and smoothly. They also provide all the usual toys and accessories one expects on any shoot. A good grip's van is an Aladdin's cave and a treasure trove of solutions to problems. They also do all the usual and useful things like having the required camera support needed for the next shot already set up and that can really speed things up.

9.7 Sound

The manning requirements for sound hardly vary at all between film and HD. The route chosen for post-production will dictate whether or not the sound is recorded on the HD camera tracks alone or if a second recording is to be made, in which case this is usually recorded on a portable DAT (Digital Audio Tape) recorder. When shooting HD it is usual for the DAT recording to be the master with the camera tracks as backup, so there will usually be a cable between the camera and the recordist.

Clearly the recordist, more properly referred to as the mixer in the UK, will not be able to operate the mixing desk, the DAT recorder and the microphone, so the absolute minimum sound crew will nearly always consist of a mixer and a boom swinger. A third person on sound, often known as the sound engineer, can be a great boon as they can swing a second boom and greatly speed up the turn round to a new set-up.

9.8 Electricians

A popularly held misconception is that HD cameras need less light. This is a fallacy. The baseline equivalent film speed of an HD camera is usually 320 ASA to tungsten light, the same as one of my favourite film stocks.

The DoP will frequently be lighting to balance with existing sources such as daylight or practical lamps within the set and then exactly the same amount of light will be required no matter how you photograph the image. This said, I am often using a lens setting around one stop wider on video than I might for Super 16 and two and a half stops wider than for 35 mm. This is to obtain roughly the same depth of field purely for artistic reasons. The differences will be obtained by the choice of film speed in the film camera, the sensitivity setting on the HD camera and with neutral density filters, behind the lens with HD, and in front of the lens in both mediums.

When all these considerations are taken into account, it becomes clear that the same number of electricians are likely to be needed and that their number will be dictated more by the script and the way you intend to shoot it than by what you are recording the image on.

Part 3

Preparing for a Shoot

10
Camera preparation prior to the shoot

10.1 Accessing the in-camera menus

1 Switch the camera on and cap the lens. Note that, unlike film lenses, the iris ring on a digital video lens goes past the smallest aperture to a position usually marked 'C'. This stands for 'capped' and is fitted mainly to enable a quick and effective black balance to be performed. It is just as useful in capping the lens to make reading the menu on a monitor easier.
2 To display the in-camera menu in the viewfinder, hold the Menu switch down and move the Display switch to Menu. You will have to start with the Display switch set to OFF.
3 Hold in the page selector wheel and push the Menu switch upwards against the spring loading. When you release the Menu switch, the TOP MENU file page will be displayed in the viewfinder.

The image in the viewfinder should now look like that in Figure 10.1.

N.B. If you want to view the menus on a colour monitor you will have to use the triple RGB cable to feed signal to the monitor; a black and white image may be obtained with a single cable coming from the Y socket.

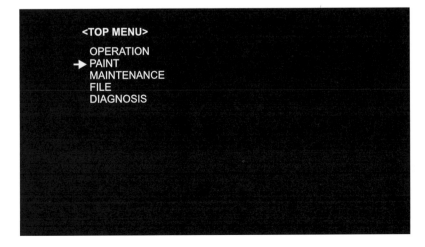

Figure 10.1 Main File Menu

10.2 Resetting the camera to the standard settings

Before preparing the camera it is usually easiest to first reset the camera to the supplier's standard settings.

1 With the TOP MENU page up, rotate the page wheel until the arrow is pointing to PAINT and click the wheel.
2 The arrow will be pointing at the page number – click the wheel to change the arrow into a question mark and then rotate the wheel until you arrive at page P13.
3 Click the wheel to turn the question mark into an arrow and rotate the wheel until you have the arrow pointing at STANDARD, as in Figure 10.2.
4 Click on STANDARD and you will get a flashing sign on the second line down saying RECALL OK?. Click again and the recall will be carried out and the second line will read RECALLED. You have now reset all the menus to the supplier's standard.

Now carry out exactly the same procedure in the Operator Menu.

1 With the TOP MENU page up, rotate the page wheel until the arrow is pointing at the OPERATION and click the wheel.
2 The arrow will be pointing at the page number – click the wheel to change the arrow into a question mark and then rotate the wheel until you arrive at page P9.
3 Click the wheel to turn the question mark into an arrow and rotate the wheel until you have the arrow pointing at STANDARD.
4 Click on STANDARD and you will get a flashing sign on the second line down saying RECALL OK?. Click again and the recall will be carried out and the second line will read RECALLED. You have now reset all the menus to the supplier's standard.

10.3 Setting the frame rate

1 Bring up the TOP MENU and rotate the page wheel until the arrow is pointing at MAINTENANCE and click on it.
2 The arrow will be next to the page number; click on this and it will turn into a question mark. Rotate the page wheel until you come to page M7.
3 Now click the wheel again and the question mark will turn back into an arrow. The screen should now look like that in Figure 10.3.

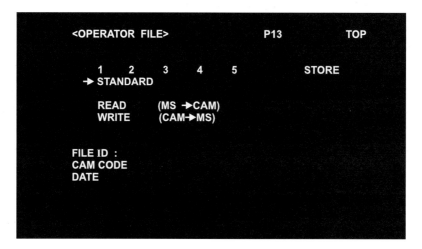

Figure 10.2 Operator File

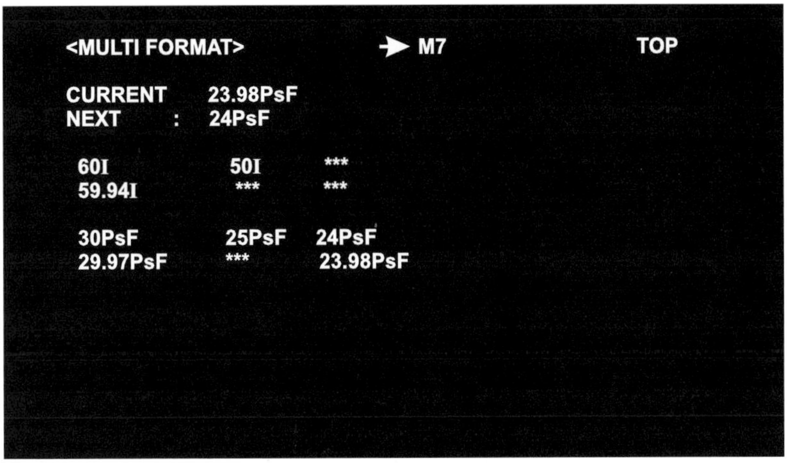

```
<MULTI FORMAT>              ➤ M7              TOP

CURRENT     23.98PsF
NEXT    :   24PsF

60I         50I       ***
59.94I      ***       ***

30PsF       25PsF     24PsF
29.97PsF    ***       23.98PsF
```

Figure 10.3 Multi-Format Menu

4 Click the wheel to turn the question mark into an arrow and rotate the wheel until the arrow arrives at the camera recording format you want. Let us assume it is 23.98P, shown on this page as 23.98PsF.
5 Click on 24PsF and it will now be shown on the line NEXT.

The same holds true whatever frame rate you wish to go to.

1 You now have to turn the camera off and then back on.
2 Hold the Menu switch down and click the Display switch down to get the menu back on the screen.
3 Hold the wheel in and click the Menu switch up and release it to get back to the TOP MENU. Now move the arrow to MAINTENANCE and click the wheel. As page M7 was the last page looked at, this page will come up and you should now see CURRENT 24PsF as the second line on the page. The camera will now record in the 24P format.

N.B. You should check with the production as to what format they wish to shoot in. If you cannot find this out, both my and the Panavision default setting is 24PsF.

10.4 Setting the shutter speed

The shutter on both the Sony and the Panavision HD Digital camera is not calibrated as an angle measured in degrees but is marked as a fraction of a second, much like a still camera. If you wish to set the camera up as having the equivalent of 180°, then the number under the fraction should be twice the picture taking rate. So if you set the camera up at 24P, to get the equivalent of a 180° shutter you must set the shutter at 1/48.

1 Go to the TOP MENU page and click on PAINT. Now click again to turn the arrow into a question mark.
2 Spin through the pages until you arrive at page P12.
3 Click again to turn the question mark into an arrow and turn the page wheel until the arrow is next to the exposure, as in Figure 10.4.
4 Click the wheel to turn the arrow into a question mark and rotate the wheel until the shutter speed you wish to set is showing.

You have now set the shutter speed.

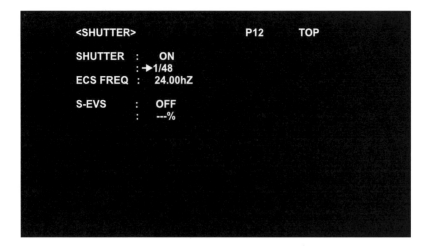

Figure 10.4 Shutter

10.5   Equivalent shutter angles

As the shutter speed in the Sony HD camera is set very like a still camera and film technicians are more used to thinking in terms of a rotating shutters angle of opening the equivalent are as below.

Equivalent shutter angles in degrees

1/Speed	24P	25P and 50i	30P and 60i
Off	360	360	360
32	270	N/A	N/A
48	180	N/A	N/A
50	N/A	180	N/A
60	N/A	N/A	N/A
96	90	N/A	N/A
100	N/A	90	N/A
125	69	72	87
250	34	36	43
500	17	18	22
1000	8	9	11

N.B. Both my and the Panavision default settings are 24P with a shutter speed of 1/48, as this sets the camera up to create pictures that look the same as a 35 mm camera running at 24 fps with a 180° shutter.

10.6   Setting the viewfinder markings

1   Open the TOP MENU page and click on OPERATION, then click to change the arrow into a question mark and scroll through the pages to page 3.
2   Click to change the question mark to the arrow and set the arrow next to MARKER; click to the question mark and set the line to ON.
3   Click the question mark back to an arrow and set the first four lines as in Figure 10.5.
4   If you know what markings the operator prefers or the format the production is going to be shooting as its primary aspect ratio then you can set these. Bring the arrow down to ASPECT MODE and click to the question mark.

5 As you rotate the wheel you will see a number of preset formats, which you can choose from. They are 16:9, 15:9, 14:9, 13:9, 4:3, VAR H, VAR V, VISTA1 and VISTA2. The first five aspect ratios deal with all the most common television formats. VAR H allows you, using the next two lines, to adjust the horizontal lines in the viewfinder. VAR V adjusts the vertical lines in the viewfinder. Unless you know the exact number of pixels that represent an aspect ratio, these lines are best adjusted to the same kind of chart you would use for a frame leader. It is perhaps best to leave this to the crew to prep just as they would for film when shooting a frame leader.

Panavision usually use the default of 16:9 with a centre cross, as shown in Figure 10.5. Check with your camera operator as to what they prefer.

If you refer to the menu section at the back of this book, you will see all the parameters that can safely be set by the camera crew, together with a detailed description of both the parameters of each line on each page of the menus and a figure showing how the viewfinder will look as you set the page.

10.7 Recording on a memory stick

You can record all your settings on a Sony memory stick in both the Sony and the Panavision versions of the camera. Unlike the Camera Control Card used in the Digi Beta camera, which can only record one set of parameters but records all of them at a single record command, the F900 requires you to record separately the Operation and Paint menus to a given file. However, you can record up to five combined files on one memory stick.

If you refer to Figure 10.2, known as the <OPERATOR FILE>, you will see the top line has numbers 1–5; these are the five combined memories that can be recorded. You must use this page to record the Operator File to the designated number you chose. The Paint File must be recorded separately; you do this by going to page P13, known as the <SCENE FILE>, and recording it to the same file number.

My habit is to record both the Operator and Paint File loaded by the supplier to file 5 and my pre-shoot settings to file 4. If I make any alterations during the shoot I start recording at file 1, thus keeping new files as far away from my safety files as possible.

10.8 Black balance

A black balance should also be carried out at the beginning of every day. To perform a black balance, simply cap the lens and press the white/black balance downwards and release it. After a few seconds

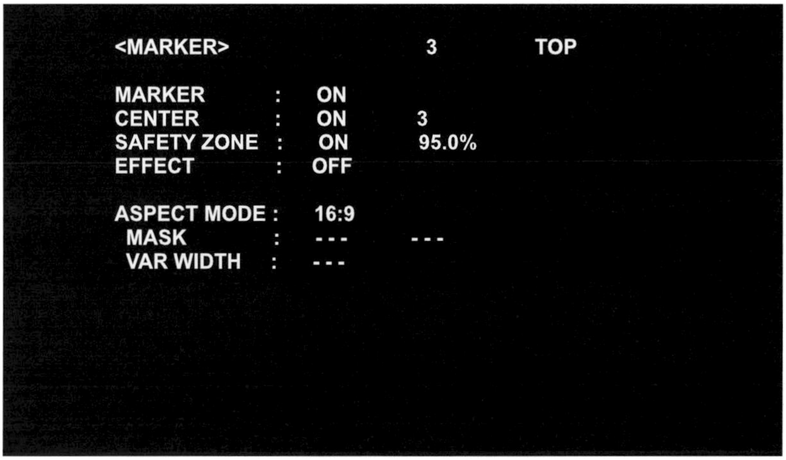

Figure 10.5 Viewfinder Marker

you will see the picture bounce; wait a couple of seconds and it is safe to open the aperture. Your black balance is now complete.

10.9 Lining up the monitors

A monitor should be lined up every time it is switched on and every time the lighting environment around the monitor changes. I strongly recommend you line up to SMPTE (Society of Motion Picture Engineers of America) bars. The alternative, EBU (European Broadcasting Union), bars require a meter to set them properly, whereas the SMPTE bars are designed to enable a very accurate 'eyeball' line-up.

A full description of how to accurately line up a monitor using either form of bars is contained in Chapter 15.

10.10 Setting the back focus

10.10.1 Zoom lenses

1   Set the lighting to give a correct exposure with the lens wide open. It is quite acceptable to deploy the ND filter wheel to achieve this.
2   Put a star chart (Figure 10.6) at around 6 feet, or 2 metres, away from the camera.
3   Zoom right in and focus the lens in the normal way. If you can possibly do so, check all the focus adjustments on a monitor, with the chroma taken out, so you have a black and white picture.
4   Adjust the lens to wide angle and rotate the back focus ring until the star chart looks sharp.
5   Zoom in and adjust the lens focus.
6   Zoom out and adjust the back focus.
7   Repeat steps 5 and 6 until no further improvements can be made.
8   Lock the back focus ring.
9   Run through steps 5 and 6 again to check the back focus ring did not move when you locked it.

N.B. You may have to go through steps 5 and 6 several times before the focus is correct at both ends of the zoom without any refocusing being necessary.

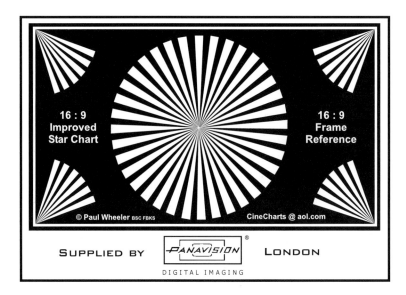

Figure 10.6 The improved star chart

10.10.2   Prime lenses and very wide angle zooms

Set up the star chart at a convenient distance which is marked on the lens scale and set the lens to this mark – this should be no closer than the minimum focus plus 6 inches. Alternatively, focus the lens and the back focus as above.

All the lenses being tested should have their back focus checked before going out on a shoot.

10.11   Cables

All the cables, both mains and video, should be plugged up and checked for continuity. It is a good idea to wiggle every BNC plug to check it is still sound, as these plugs are probably the most unreliable item on any digital shoot. It is a good idea to equip yourself with an appropriate crimping tool and some spare BNC plugs if you are going to be away from base for any length of time – people do have a habit of tripping over monitor leads and ripping the cable out of the plug.

10.12   Accessories

If you are familiar with the kind of lens hood supplied with, say, the sort of zoom lens that normally goes with a Digi Beta camera, then I must advise you that this is simply not adequate for the quality of images an HD camera is capable of. On a bright day, with some cloud in the sky, it is quite likely that you will be able to darken your shadows by around half a stop by deploying a film-style matte box. This is a result of the superior flagging now in place removing the sky flare.

If you are using a native Sony camera, film-style accessories, including matte boxes and follow focus units, can come from a variety of manufacturers. Arri, Croziel and some others manufacture such equipment, so you must make yourself familiar with whatever your hire house has supplied. The Panavision accessories are either identical or very similar to standard film equipment; this is quite intentional, to allow film-trained camera assistants to smoothly move across to the new camera and check the equipment in the usual way.

This is the end of the pre-shoot camera check.

11
'Top of day' camera assistant checks

It is wise to carry out a 'top of day' check every shooting day. This is not only the professional approach, but will contribute to your peace of mind. Experience has shown that while these cameras are unfamiliar to many on the unit, a certain amount of prodding and poking may happen behind your back. This must be discouraged, but a wise precaution is to guarantee the camera is perfect at the beginning of each day.

1 Put all spare batteries on charge if they have not been on charge overnight.
2 Build camera as you expect to need it for the first shot of the day.
3 Put a fully charged, or the battery holding the best charge, on the camera.
4 Switch the camera on.
5 Perform an Auto Black Balance.
6 Check the Gain switch is in the correct position (usually L–0 dB).
7 Check the white balance (usually PRESET).
8 Check, and adjust if necessary, the back focus on the first lens of the day.
9 Check the frame rate – you can do this by simply holding the Menu switch to STATUS and the setting will appear in the viewfinder.
10 Check the shutter speed by moving the Display switch to ON; the setting will appear in the viewfinder. After checking reset the switch.
11 Load a new tape and rest the time code *or* regen the time code if you are continuing with an existing tape.
12 Check with your sound mixer that they are plugged in and happy with the gain settings and record 30 seconds or 1 minute of bars and tone.
13 Line up the monitors you will be using at the start of shooting using SMPTE bars.
14 Check the Output switch is set either to CAM or DCC, whichever your DoP prefers.

Until you are thoroughly familiar with your daily checks, you might like to use something like the check list shown in Figure 11.1, where a tick can be put in the last column when each check is complete. This is particularly useful on a shoot with a big crew, where there may be two of you who might carry out the daily checks, or on a multi-camera shoot. Whoever completes the check can leave the check list with the camera to show the checks have been carried out, by whom and when. This can remove the chance of unnecessary duplication of effort.

My own crew's preference is to build and check the camera before going to breakfast, so the first member to arrive on set gets on with the job and puts the completed check list under the camera handle, switches the camera off, puts a polythene bag over the camera and goes to eat.

TOP OF DAY CHECK L:ST

AC.................................... DATE........... T:ME............

ITEM	CHECK	USUAL	CHECK
1	Batteries on charge		
2	Build camera		
3	Put charged battery on camera		
4	Switch camera on		
5	Auto Black Balance		
6	Check gain switch	L	
7	Check white balance setting	PRESET	
8	Check back focus		
9	Check frame rate	24PsF	
10	Check shutter speed	1/48	
11	Load tape and reset time code or regen	Code	
12	Record Bars and Tone		
13	Line up monitors		
14	Check OUTPUT switch	DCC	

Figure 11.1 Top of day check list

12
Troubleshooting

12.1 Stating the obvious

Forgive me if some of the solutions listed below seem obvious, but I can readily recall times when a camera, mechanical or digital, has seemed to fail at an extraordinarily embarrassing moment and panic has set in. In a state of panic it has, on one occasion, taken me a full 5 minutes to realize that the lead leaving the camera was not actually plugged into the battery. Hence if you have need to grab this book in order to obtain help with a problem the obvious is also here – hopefully you will then realize the lead needs plugging in a little quicker than I did.

The HDW F900 camera is proving to be very reliable; therefore, if you seem to have a fault do try and troubleshoot it yourself, as a touch of finger trouble may well prove to be the answer. If you have been through all the troubleshooting checks and things are still amiss, then more often than not there is little you can achieve on location. Your best repair kit is your mobile 'phone – ring your supplier, they may have good advice, and if things can't be made to work, will almost certainly ship you a new camera immediately.

I was at Panavision London recently when there seemed to be a problem with one of their HD cameras that could not be solved on location. Within 2 hours, a new camera body was on its way travelling as hand luggage with one of their young engineers who, despite having to fly the length of Europe followed by a long Jeep ride the other end, had a new camera, perfectly set up to the DoP's requirements, in the hands of the crew an hour before the on-set call time. That's service! The irony was the problem turned out to be a little lack of experience on behalf of the crew; no matter, as the camera was still fairly new and at that time these things were to be expected.

12.2 Problems and solutions

Problem: No image on the monitor.

Solution:

1 Have you switched the HD SDI adapter on?
2 Is the monitor powered correctly – does the standby light glow?
3 Is the monitor set to the correct channel?
4 Check all cable connections.
5 Is the BNC cable of sufficient quality?
6 Try another video cable.

7   Try using the output from the Y, Ph or Pr sockets on the side of the camera. If the image is good you may need to change the HD SDI adapter.

Problem: The monitor is showing coloration in the corners of the image.

Solution: Degauss the monitor – there will be a small button somewhere on the monitor to do this.

Problem: No image in the viewfinder, but there is an image on the monitor.

Solution:

1   Is the eyepiece cable correctly inserted into the camera?
2   Is the camera powered correctly?

Problem: No image through the Miranda or Evertz down-converter.

Solution:

1   Is the power LED alight – if not, check power cable connections.
2   Check video cable connections.
3   Check power and DIP switches on the down-converter.
4   Check the monitor (see above).
5   If the cable connection is OK it is just possible that the internal camera fuse is blown – if you suspect this call your supplier, it is not user replaceable.

Problem: Camera will not power up.

Solution:

1   Check power cables and connections.
2   Check battery voltage – try another battery.
3   If using the mains converter, check the power supply is on.
4   Did the camera overheat and shut off? If it did, let it cool down – this may take 20 minutes or so – and then press the reset button under the rear of the camera. Make sure the fan extracts are unblocked – they are near the top handle.

Problem: Camera will not record.

Solution:

1   Is the camera powered correctly (see above)?
2   Is the tape cassette write protected? Check that the red tab is flush with the cassette case and not pushed in.
3   Is the humidity warning on display in the viewfinder? If so, dry out the camera and press the rest button under rear of camera.
4   Go into the diagnosis menu and see if anything looks amiss – DO NOTHING – consult your supplier with your findings.
5   There may be another internal problem – consult your supplier.

Problem: Monitor is too bright when using the component Y, Pb and Pr inputs.

Solution: The monitor is probably not terminated – if it has a switch deploy it; if not, fit termination plugs to the video out socket.

Problem: Monitor is green when using the component Y, Pb and Pr outputs.

Solution: The monitor is probably configured for an RGB signal rather than a component Y, Pb and Pr signal – reconfigure the monitor.

Problem: Monitor shows a single pixel as a bright and constant colour.

Solution: Perform a black balance repeatedly, holding the black balance switch down for at least 3 seconds, until the pixel disappears. It might help to turn the monitor brightness up to be absolutely sure the problem has gone away – it may still glow at higher monitor brightness; keep operating the black balance until it disappears. If it won't disappear consult your supplier.

Problem: Image is vignetting on one side and/or blue flickering band at the top of the screen.

Solution: One of the internal filter wheels is almost certainly not perfectly in its indent position – check both internal filter wheels.

Problem: Image has excessive blur when panning.

Solution: The shutter is almost certainly switched off – make sure it is switched on and at the right shutter speed. Probably, the shutter switch on the camera control panel has been moved.

Problem: Image looks soft – this might only be noticeable on a 24-inch monitor.

Solution: Check the back focus on the lens. This will most likely show up if you have zoomed in, eye focused and zoomed out; the image will go soft as you zoom out.

Problem: Footage marks on lens are no longer accurate.

Solution: Check lens back focus.

Problem: The camera will not accept external time code.

Solution: Is the time code set to F-Run? If not, set it to F-Run.

Problem: No audio signal level on camera VU meter.

Solution:

1 Check cable connections.
2 Is the input switch situated above the XLR input socket on the back of the camera at the proper setting – mic/line?
3 Check the audio in switch – it should be set to rear not front.

Problem: The Lens Ret – i.e. record preview – function on the assignable switch is not working.

Solution:

1 Is the tape cassette write protected? Check that the red tab is flush with the cassette case and not pushed in.
2 With the Panavision camera check the switch is correctly programmed – Page 8 marked <OTHERS> in the Operation menu.
3 Was the last take at least 3 seconds long? It has to be for Lens Ret to function.

Problem: White balance is not functioning correctly – AWB: NG will appear in the viewfinder.

Solution:

1 If LEVEL HIGH appears in the viewfinder, the exposure level is too high. On a Sony camera with a conventional lens with a hand grip, switch the lens to Auto Exposure and try again. With a Panavision camera, set the level of the white card to approximately 70 per cent – you can do this using the zebra function or, better still, get the DoP to take an incident reading immediately in front of the card and use this reading as the stop on the lens.
2 If COLOR TEMP LOW or COLOR TEMP HIGH appears in the viewfinder, then you are not using the appropriate colour correction filter in the filter wheel. Try different filters until white balance operates successfully.

3 If LEVEL LOW appears in the viewfinder, there is simply not enough light reaching the camera head. Either open the iris or add more light to the subject. Do not solve this problem by adding gain.

4 If AWB: WHITE PRESET appears in the viewfinder, then the white balance switch on the side of the camera is set to PRESET – move it to the A or B position, where an auto white balance can be performed.

Problem: The audio is not in sync with a down-converted image.

Solution: The down-converter takes a few milliseconds to carry out its job, so you need to insert an audio delay box into the audio line. This problem usually only presents itself when using a down-converted image for playback.

Part 4

The Shoot

13
Lighting and exposure for HD

13.1   Equivalent ASA speed or EI rating

I check the speed of a Panavized F900 in exactly the way I would when testing a film stock's ASA or EI rating. Note that the numbers will be the same.

When checking a film stock's ASA speed, I set the camera up facing an 18 per cent reflectance grey card and make a range of exposures, noting the setting on my meter for each one. Then I ask the laboratory to make me a middle of the range one light print. Whichever exposure most exactly matches the tonality of the original grey card I deem to be the correct rating for that particular film stock.

With any HD camera my approach is the same but the technique a little different. I set the 18 per cent grey card up as before and, close by, set up a carefully lined up 24-inch monitor. Making sure that the card is evenly lit, I adjust the exposure until the grey on the monitor exactly matches the grey of the card. Now I take a reading of the card with my Pentax digital spotmeter and set the reading in the viewfinder on its scale, then I adjust the ASA setting on the meter until the aperture shown is the same as that on the lens. The ASA setting on the meter is now showing the equivalent ASA speed of the camera. Every time I do this with any version of the Sony HDW F900, I arrive at an equivalent ASA of 320.

13.2   Tonal range

There is much discussion as to the length of the tonal range of HD cameras; I have a very simple test. Using a Kodak 18 per cent Grey Card Plus, which has a black and a white patch both sides of the grey, as shown in Figure 13.1, I light it evenly to a brightness that gives a perfect exposure with the lens set at, say, T4 – a stop I know works well for this test – and have the image up on a carefully set up 24-inch monitor. Without touching the lens setting I now reduce the lighting level while watching the monitor and keep on reducing the level until the grey area on the card is only fractionally lighter than the black patch next to it. I now take a spotmeter reading on the grey area; this will be the lower end of the camera's tonal range. Again, without making any adjustments to the lens, I now increase the lighting level until the grey area of the card is only fractionally darker than the white patch next to it and take another reading on the grey area of the card; this will be the upper end of the tonal range. The number of stops between the first reading and the second reading is the tonal range.

It is important in the above test that you have just the very slightest difference in brightness on the monitor between both the black and the white patches and the grey area of the card, for if they are exactly matched you might be at the limit, or you might be far beyond the limit, and you won't be able

Figure 13.1 The Kodak Grey Card Plus

to tell, as either situation would look the same on the monitor. Just before the limit the camera is still, just, recording detail and this point can be thought of as definitely within the tonal range.

Sometimes when I demonstrate this test to colleagues I have to repeat it a second time, as they simply cannot believe the result. The tonal range of a Sony HDW F900, by my test, is 11 stops.

Now, those 11 stops are from limit to limit and the characteristics of the camera, particularly as set up by Panavision, are similar to a film emulsion in that there is a straight line section of linear response over most of the range, but there is certain amount of roll-off at both the extremes of black and white. I have spent some time trying to grasp where these roll-offs start and stop; this involved changing lighting levels minutely in the stop and a half from pure white to pale grey and at the other end of the scale from pure black to dark grey, taking readings with my spotmeter all the while. My conclusion is that you can safely work on the basis that there is a nine-stop linear section of tonality with around a stop of roll-off at each end. Very like a well-known modern film stock, which must contribute, in part at least, to the pictures from the camera looking so very like film.

13.3   Lighting ratios

Many cinematographers, especially those from a film background, are used to thinking through a lighting scheme by relating their ideas to the concept of a lighting ratio. A lighting ratio is a simple enough thing; it is a number given to the difference in brightness between one part of the scene and another.

If you have taken readings of two parts of your set and the difference between them is one stop, what would be the lighting ratio between them? As it requires twice as much light to increase an exposure by one stop, the lighting ratio will be 2. If the difference had been two stops the lighting ratio would now be 4. This is because every stop increase in brightness doubles the amount of light required and therefore doubles the lighting ratio.

As we have seen, the F900 camera can photograph a tonal range of up to 11 stops, so if you refer to Figure 13.2 you will see that the total lighting ratio of the F900 is 2048 from maximum white to minimum black. Figure 13.2 also shows how the progression from a single stop of brightness difference giving the expected lighting ratio of 2 moves through the different stops of differential. As we have seen, each change of one stop doubles the lighting ratio.

```
┌─────────────────────────────────────────────────────────────┐
│          Lighting ratios relating to difference in exposure    │
│                                                               │
│    1  stop difference in exposure = lighting ratio of 2        │
│    2  stops difference in exposure = lighting ratio of 4       │
│    3  stops difference in exposure = lighting ratio of 8       │
│    4  stops difference in exposure = lighting ratio of 16      │
│    5  stops difference in exposure = lighting ratio of 32      │
│    6  stops difference in exposure = lighting ratio of 64      │
│    7  stops difference in exposure = lighting ratio of 128     │
│    8  stops difference in exposure = lighting ratio of 256     │
│    9  stops difference in exposure = lighting ratio of 512     │
│   10  stops difference in exposure = lighting ratio of 1024    │
│   11  stops difference in exposure = lighting ratio of 2048    │
└─────────────────────────────────────────────────────────────┘
```

Figure 13.2 Lighting ratios relating to difference in exposure

The lighting ratios you choose to use when lighting for HD should be exactly those you would use for film. If the camera can photograph it, so can you. There is to my mind, however, a more elegant way to light for HD – light to the monitor.

13.4   Lighting to a monitor

If you are about to execute some fairly sophisticated lighting, then I would strongly recommend you work to a well set up 24-inch monitor. An argument goes that if the camera works with 11 stops of tonal range, and even the very best cathode ray tube will be hard pressed to display six stops of tonal range, how can you trust the monitor? Well you can. Both the camera and the monitor have within them circuits to subtly squeeze all the camera's ability into a shorter range with sufficient cleverness that the human eye/brain combination, when looking at a high grade monitor, will believe it is seeing the full 11 stops of tonal range in a perfectly natural way. Believe me, it works. I have lit several pictures using HD now and have always lit to the monitor using my exposure meter for nothing more than lining up the monitor's contrast level and, in whatever medium they were eventually displayed, the pictures were always exactly as I expected them to be.

There is a great joy in working to a monitor; it is a bit like painting – instead of doing mathematics while staring down a spotmeter I am freed to literally paint with light. Every mark I make on the set will instantly appear on my canvas, the monitor's screen. It is hard to describe the freedom I felt when I first started working this way; it was very liberating. Instant gratification I suppose.

13.5   Highlights and shadows

There is a misconception about that blames 'video' for the poorer handling of highlights than film in some circumstances and with some cameras. Very often it is not the image being recorded on video that is the influencing factor, but the fact that you are working with a positive image rather than a negative one. Those of you who have shot reversal film or still transparency will be familiar with a similar image, one where the shadows seem to look after themselves more than when using a negative/positive process, but where more care must be taken with the highlights, and so it is with any video camera – they shoot a positive image.

So whereas with film you would probably spend more time reading the shadows with your meter to establish that they will be recorded just as you wish, you must get into the habit with HD of walking back to the monitor and checking your highlights first.

13.6   Exposure

13.6.1   Using a monitor

There is an absolutely sure-fire way of getting your exposure spot on. Light the set by eye and, when you have all your keys, cross lights and backlights to your liking, walk back to your monitor and with one hand on the lens aperture ring adjust it until you think your highlights are perfect. Now complete your lighting by adding your fill light until you are equally happy with the shadow detail. How could it be simpler?

13.6.2   Using a meter

On the other hand, I had one colleague, let us say he was of the old school, who was about to shoot a picture with a young director. I had spent some time with him explaining HD and he was very enthusiastic about the picture quality and how the cost savings might allow more young directors to get their films made. He may be old school but he is certainly not against progress. After much thought he confessed to me he hated monitors so much that even when shooting film he refused to look at the video assist, what was he going to do? I assured him that the camera was very stable in its equivalent ASA speed and he could safely assume it to be 320 ASA to tungsten light and if he lit with his exposure meters in his usual fashion all would be well, and it was. The young director came back at the end of the picture and expressed the opinion that the DoP must be a genius for the pictures were terrific, but he had done it without once looking at a monitor. How times change.

So here are two very different approaches to exposure control; both work perfectly so use whatever works for you. I will be sticking to my monitor, for me that is much more fun.

13.6.3   Auto exposure

Most HD zoom lenses have a side handle much like traditional video lenses, on which there is usually both a button and a sliding switch associated with exposure. The sliding switch normally has two positions, auto and manual. If left on auto the camera will continuously adjust the exposure to its own liking. If set to manual you can simply grab the iris ring and set it to your preference, or if you press the button on the hand grip it will give you a one-time-only auto exposure which might be a very good starting point for making your own assessment.

To my mind most video cameras, including the Sony HDW F900, tend to overexpose when set to auto, which is curious as this will exacerbate the video highlights problem. There is a page in the menu where you can give the auto exposure control a bias and I tend to set this to reduce the exposure by around one-third of a stop.

The Panavision version of the HDW F900 is not set up to have any auto exposure facility at all, for their lenses do not have this facility, so you will have to work to the monitor or use an exposure meter in the traditional way.

13.6.4   Exposing using a waveform monitor

Before I describe how to use a waveform monitor I must confess I am not a fan of them. On the two occasions I was persuaded to have one on set I thought my lighting was not as brave as it normally is; the waveform monitor was making me more cautious. I understand what they do and respect those that like using them, but they are definitely not for me.

On the screen of a waveform monitor you will see a graph where the vertical component is the signal level and the horizontal component is the position across the width of the scene. It is not a single line graph, for it is filled in with the energy levels of the vertical components of the picture. There are two horizontal lines on the screen, one near the top and one near the bottom, which represent the voltages of peak white and peak black.

The general idea is to adjust your lighting and exposure to keep the highlights under the top line on the screen and the shadows above the bottom line on the screen. One tends to come to think that any part of the display that is outside these limits must be an error. This is not necessarily so.

When I am lighting for film I am conscious that some parts of the scene will be too bright, and some too dark, to have detail in them. Knowing which parts of the scene will exceed the ability of the film stock and handling them in an artistic way is part of my art. I know I can ignore the top and bottom line on the screen of the waveform monitor, but for some reason that is psychologically very hard to do.

It is particularly distressing when you have a beautiful picture on the monitor and someone with too little knowledge spies your waveform monitor and expresses the opinion that you are overexposed because a few spikes go above the top line. For me, the waveform monitor stays back in the stores.

14
Lenses

14.1 How to choose a lens

There are many parameters that define a good lens from a bad one. For high definition cinematography, where there is a mixture of both film and video backgrounds, the most important include: resolution (that is, what is the smallest dot in the scene that can accurately be recorded); contrast (does the lens have a short hard tonal range or a long gentle one?); colour rendition (this breaks down into two separate parameters, the overall colour hue of the image and edge fringing); and finally breathing (which describes the effect of an image size change when the lens focus is racked).

14.1.1 Resolution

There are many ways to define the resolution of a lens, but the simplest is to consider the same parameter that is used to compute depth of field charts, the circle of confusion. The circle of confusion does not exist until we choose it. Typically, for 35 mm cinematography using spherical lenses, a circle of confusion of $\frac{1}{1000}$ of an inch, or 25 microns ($25\,\mu$), is used.

Before we go any further, let us define a circle of confusion. The correct circle of confusion is the diameter of the largest dot on the recorded image that will still look sharp to the audience in the most taxing presentation venue in which that picture will ever be shown. The principle is that if you try and photograph an infinitely small dot, how large would you allow that dot to grow as it becomes less well focused on the image plane and at what size will it appear to the audience to be out of focus.

If you are going to show your images in a large cinema, say in a capital city, this will be a very taxing presentation on the parameter of resolution. As we have seen for regular 35 mm cinematography, $\frac{1}{1000}$ inch ($25\,\mu$) is considered adequate. Next we must consider the difference in recorded image size between the 35 mm frame and the area of the HD image chip. The 35 mm frame is 2.5 times larger than the HD chip, so for a dot on the HD chip to seem to be as sharp on the same cinema screen as one projected from a 35 mm print it must be 2.5 times smaller, i.e. $\frac{1}{2500}$ inch or $10\,\mu$. There are only a few lenses that can achieve this.

14.1.2 Contrast

This is a difficult subject for perceived resolution; that is, how our eye/brain combination assesses sharpness can be materially affected by the contrast of the image. A very contrasty lens might give you a picture on even a 24-inch HD monitor that looks very sharp, but if that image is expanded to a large cinema screen the lack of resolution that has been masked by the excessive contrast will now be very apparent.

14.1.3   Perceived sharpness with regard to contrast

The eye/brain combination perceives sharpness quite differently from the way we might measure resolution on a lens-testing bench. Perception is an impossible thing to measure yet we, as cinematographers, need to get a grasp of how our audience will see our work and need to know if they will consider our pictures to be sharp.

Increasing the contrast of a scene will, most likely, increase the perceived sharpness of the scene. That said, it might also reduce the artistic value of the scene or even take it away from the cinematographer's initial concept of the scene as represented in the script. A cinematographer might wish to show a scene with a reasonably high resolution but having a gentle, low-key feel to it. To do this, the cinematographer needs lenses that have a very long tone range and a gentle contrast, but still appear sharp.

Let us look at some of the sharpness we perceive in a scene as against the actual resolution of the image. In Figure 14.1, we have two nearly identical images; don't study them too carefully, but at a glance, which do you think is the sharper? I would guess you chose the bottom one. WRONG! All the images for this example were taken on my Nikon CoolPix camera; the top picture was downloaded at 300 dots per inch (DPI) and the lower picture at 75 DPI – the difference is the top picture has a much lower contrast than the bottom picture – contrast has fooled you into thinking the resolution is higher when the contrast is higher.

Now look at Figure 14.2. Which do you think is sharper here? I guess you will again choose the bottom picture. Both pictures were downloaded at 300 DPI. Again, it is the contrast of the bottom picture that makes it look sharper.

Don't look at Figure 14.3 until you are holding the book at arm's length and then try and decide which picture is sharper. My guess is you will think they both look the same. Now bring the book to your normal reading distance, normally 10 inches or 25 centimetres; if you look at the top of the gate you should see a jagged line in the bottom picture but a true and straight one in the top picture. Both pictures have exactly the same contrast, but the top picture has a resolution of 300 DPI and the bottom a resolution of 75 DPI proving, I hope, that viewing distance is also a critical factor.

The conclusion from all this is that a lens that appears sharp may not be so; it is therefore important that you measure resolution and judge contrast – separately.

14.1.4   Colour rendition

14.1.4.1   Overall colour bias

All makes of lenses tend to have an individual character; some are cold and clinical, some are warm and gentle, and some are utterly neutral. Most of the time my own preference is for a neutral lens, for I can then add the character I require scene by scene with the aid of filtration.

Perhaps the simplest way to discover the difference in colour bias between different manufacturers' lenses is to mount them on the camera and line them up at the standard 18 per cent grey card we use in the film world. Fill most of the frame with the card and set the correct exposure. Having first lined up the monitor correctly, can you now see any colour difference between the card and its corresponding image on the monitor? You should easily be able to tell the difference between warm, cold and neutral lenses using this simple test.

14.1.4.2   Colour fringing

This is a phenomenon almost unheard of with any lens from the film world built in the last 30 years. Unfortunately it is all too commonly found on even some of the most recent video lenses. The reason is twofold. Firstly, the film DoP is used to paying considerably more for their lenses than the equivalent video cameraperson, so there are the financial recourses available to film lens manufacturers to design out the problem. Secondly, until the advent of HD a video image was very rarely shown on a big screen and consequently the problem was not immediately evident on a normal size television screen, though it can nearly always be detected if you look closely.

Figure 14.1

14.1.4.3   What is fringing?
If you look closely at a hard edge on a picture on a television screen and find that it is not totally pure, but there appears to be single or multiple coloured lines around it, this is fringing. It is caused by the lens being unable to bring all the colours in the visible spectrum into focus at exactly the same place.

For HD cinematography, a lens showing even the slightest hint of fringing must not be accepted.

14.1.5   Breathing

Breathing is when the image size changes when the lens focus is changed. It is very common indeed with most lenses used for television video camcorders and almost unheard of with film lenses. Again, the

Figure 14.2

acceptable cost of the lenses is the main contributing factor. A Director of Photography working in film is very unlikely to accept a lens that shows even the slightest sign of breathing, but a news cameraperson using a camcorder where the image is moving much of the time will hardly notice the effect.

Unfortunately there are a number of lenses purporting to have been designed specifically for HD, most of them coming from established video lens manufacturers, that show not just slight but considerable breathing. This, to me, is wholly unacceptable.

14.1.6   Focusing a lens

Before you can successfully focus any lens on an HD camera, you must have assured yourself that the back focus is correct by carrying out the procedure described in Chapter 10. You will have done this using a star chart, as shown in Figure 10.6 in that chapter.

Figure 14.3

You may be tempted to use this chart as a target when carrying out eye focuses at various distances – this is unwise. Though it looks like a perfect image to focus on, experience has proved this not to be the case. I recently had a complaint from a crew that one of the Panavision Primo Digital zooms they had with them was not focusing to scale. The lens was immediately swapped out and I put it on the lens test bench; it focused very accurately to scale and the definition was above specification, so what was going wrong? I telephoned the unit and found that, quite sensibly as things stood at that time, they were using the star chart as a focus aid when making eye focus checks through the lens. The next thing was to repeat that with the rejected lens, so I set up the lens on a camera back at Panavision, back focus checked it at around 6 feet and then very carefully set the star chart up at 12 feet and did an eye focus. The scale showed 11 feet 9 inches, exactly what the crew had been getting.

Time for greater minds to be brought to bear on the problem. I asked Panavision's head of camera maintenance to focus the lens; it came up at exactly 12 feet. Puzzling. Asking a number of technicians in the building to focus the lens proved that less than one in five got it right and those that did all had considerable experience of using various lens test charts. Your average crew member, embarrassingly including myself, always came up with something near 11 feet 9 inches. Not one of us focused long and this I cannot explain.

I spent the next few days pondering this and driving everybody in the building mad by asking them to go through the same routine with all kinds of charts I wanted to try. Eventually I came to the conclusion that because the star chart was of such high contrast, what we were seeing was a function of apparent sharpness being influenced by the contrast of the image. Incidentally, we were all getting the same results whether we focused through the viewfinder with or without the peaking turned on and even on a 24-inch monitor.

After some days I came up with the chart shown in Figure 14.4. During all my testing I had decided that because the pixel layout in the camera is made up of horizontal and vertical lines, straight lines might be confusing the result. I had also come to the conclusion that the target must be of a low contrast nature whilst still being easy to judge focus on. Further, prior to all this, I had never used the peaking control on the viewfinder, as I found it disturbing during normal photography, but was rapidly coming to the conclusion that with the right chart for eye focusing it could be an advantage.

If you set a camera up on what is now known as the annular focus target (Figure 14.4) and wind the peaking in the viewfinder up to maximum when you focus the lens, you will see the peaking move up and down to the top and bottom of the finest set of rings you can resolve at any given distance. When the peaking effect is at its closest top and bottom you are in perfect focus at any distance. The peaking effect is unlikely ever to form a perfect and complete circle. This chart can, therefore, safely be used for eye focus checks and, using the same technique, can be used as a back focus chart.

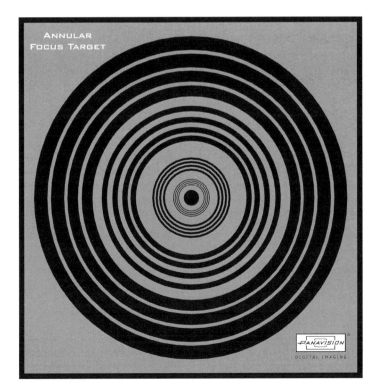

Figure 14.4 Annular focus target

This in no way negates the use of the star chart for setting the back focus, it still works perfectly well, but if you want a chart that can be used for back focus and general eye focusing on the set then the annular rings are a better bet.

14.1.7 Comparative focal lengths

Because the dimensions of the chip in a video camera are considerably smaller than the frame size on 35 mm film, the focal length required to obtain an identical shot will be shorter for the HD camera. In fact, a ratio of 2.5 times is correct, making a 25 mm lens on a 35 mm camera to have the same field of view as a 10 mm lens on the HD camera. The ratio of 2.5 times will become familiar to you, as it applies to many of the comparisons between these two formats.

To compare HD to Super 16 mm, the ratio is roughly 1.33. Figure 14.5 shows the lenses that will obtain the same horizontal angle of view on 35 mm anamorphic lenses, 35 mm spherical lenses, HD lenses and Super 16 lenses.

14.2 Depth of field

One of the signatures of the video look is, in comparison to 35 mm film, a considerably greater depth of field. Depth of field is a function of two variables, the focal length of the lens and the aperture being deployed. This part of the video look comes about because, to obtain the same field of view, the focal length of the lens on a video camera using a $\frac{2}{3}$-inch chip, such as Sony's F900, the focal length will be 2.5 times shorter than the lens required on a 35 mm camera. It is possible to get the same depth of field by using a wider aperture; in fact, you will need to set the lens $2\frac{1}{2}$ stops wider so T4 on the 35 mm camera will have the same depth of field as T1.6 on the $\frac{2}{3}$-inch chipped video camera. Figure 14.6 shows the apertures required to obtain the same depth of field on 35 mm anamorphic lenses, 35 mm spherical lenses, HD lenses and Super 16 lenses.

14.3 Calculating depth of field

The simplest and probably the best way to calculate your depth of field is to use a proprietary slide rule designed for the job. In my opinion, the HiDef Kelly Calculator designed and manufactured by the Guild of British Camera Technicians (GBCT) is one of the best available. It comes with compre-

35 mm 2.4 : 1	35 mm 1.85 : 1	HD 16 × 9	Super 16 1.78 : 1
25	12.5	5	6.75
30	15	6	8
35	17.5	7	9.5
40	20	8	11
48.5	23.75	9.5	13
50	25	10	13.5
70	35	14	19
100	50	20	27
125	62.5	25	34
135	67.5	27	36.5
175	86.5	35	47.25
360	180	72	97
524	262	105	142
560	280	112	151

Figure 14.5 Equivalent focal lengths

35 mm 2.4 : 1	35 mm 1.85 : 1	HD 16 × 9	Super 16 1.78 : 1
2.8	2	0.8	0.9
4	2.8	1.1	1.3
5.6	4	1.6	1.8
8	5.6	2.2	2.8
11	8	3.2	3.5
16	11	4.4	4.8
22	16	6.4	7

Figure 14.6 Apertures to obtain the same depth of field

hensive instructions, the cover of which is shown in Figure 14.7, and if you are familiar with earlier Kelly calculators you will not be surprised to discover that it works in exactly the same way. In the HD version, one side of the calculator functions with imperial measurements, as shown in Figure 14.8, and the other side works in the metric system, as shown in Figure 14.9. To avoid confusion, the solid part of the scale is gold on the imperial side and silver on the metric side.

Using the Kelly could not be simpler; you choose the appropriate focal length of lens you are using and find it on one of the circles. Rotate the top disc until the arrow aligns with the distance set on the focus barrel of the lens; this is inscribed on the under disc, and either side of the original arrow the distances that can be considered to still be in focus will be adjacent to the aperture you are using.

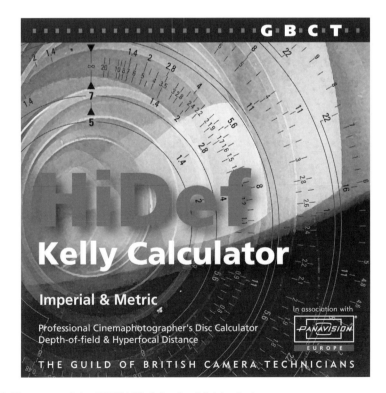

Figure 14.7 The cover of the GBCT HiDef depth of field calculator

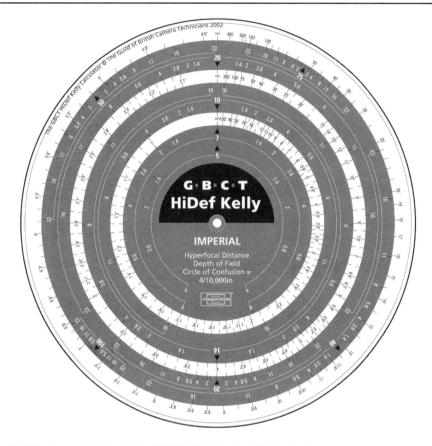

Figure 14.8 The imperial side of the GBCT HiDef depth of field calculator

There is a considerable amount of additional useful information in the instructions that come with the Kelly Calculator; I have been using the film versions since I was a focus puller and swear by them.

14.4 Neutral density filters

One of the two filter wheels at the front of the HDW F900 camera contains a clear glass plus three neutral density filters, or ND filters as they are always referred to. A neutral density is one that will reduce the amount of light passing through it without changing the colour at all.

On the Panavision 900F the nomenclature is: for filter 1 – Clear; for filter 2 – 0.6, 2 stops; for filter 3 – 1.2, 4 stops; and for filter 4 – 1.8, 6 stops. This is all very logical, for a density of 0.3 reduces the amount of light by exactly half. On the Sony version of the camera, the filters are the same but, very confusingly for a person from a film background, they are labelled: 1 – Clear; 2 – 1/4 ND; 3 – 1/16 ND; and 4 – 1/64 ND.

To keep the lens on the HD camera aperture $2\frac{1}{2}$ stops wider than the 35 mm equivalent requires the use of ND filters; this is why the camera has three ND filters on a wheel within it. These filters are of a sufficiently high quality that you should have no hesitation in using them in appropriate circumstances. If even deploying the six-stop filter leaves you with an unacceptably small stop, then there is absolutely no problem in using extra ND filters in front of the lens just as you would with a film camera.

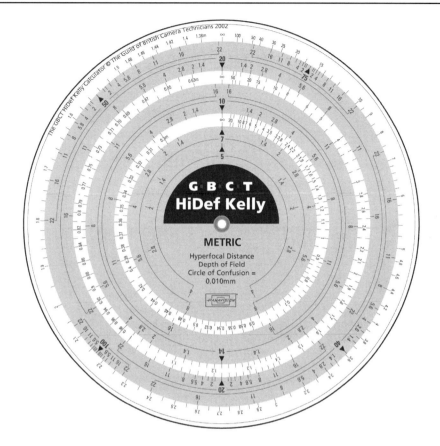

Figure 14.9 The metric side of the GBCT HiDef depth of field calculator

14.5 Limiting apertures

All optical devices have the equivalent to an aperture – that is, there is a limit to the amount of light they can pass. This is true of the splitter block in the Sony F900 camera's beam splitter that is used behind the lens to break up the image into red, green and blue light, as described in Chapter 25. The limiting aperture of this block is f1.4 or T1.6.

This means that if a lens with a wider aperture than T1.6 is used then the exposure will never be more than T1.6, for this is the maximum amount of light the block will pass.

14.6 Filtration

14.6.1 Colour correction

All the filters you might use to correct or adjust the coloration of the image with a film camera will give you exactly the same results in the final image. I am not entirely happy with the Sony colour correction filters and, when shooting in daylight, frequently leave the clear glass in place on the colour correction filter wheel, marked 3200K, and put a Wratten 85 filter in front of the lens. This, it seems to me, makes the resultant image look even more like film, which is what I am used to.

14.6.2 Diffusion

Diffusion filters are another matter entirely. Again, this is influenced by the smaller area of the HD chip as against the 35 mm frame. The strength of diffusion you must use to gain the effect you desire is relative to the area on the camera image, so just as you would use a lighter filter on Super 16 than you would on 35 mm, you must be lighter still on HD. My experience is that Super 16 requires roughly half the diffusion that you would use on 35 mm and HD requires a little less than half that which you might use on Super 16.

Curiously the diffusion filters I regularly use on Digi Beta, which has the same size chip but with far fewer pixels, does not have the same effect on HD. My favourite filter when shooting Digi Beta is a 1/4 white Tiffen Promist. With this filter on an HD camera it appears to be much stronger, so I drop to a 1/8 Promist. I gather various filter manufacturers are bringing out lighter strength diffusion filters than they have offered in the past to give cinematographers working with HD greater control over the image than traditional film filters would allow.

It should be noted that the effect of diffusion when judged even on a 24-inch monitor will not correspond to the same effect when shown on a large theatrical screen. If you are only shooting for television then it is perfectly correct to judge your filtration on a 24-inch monitor. This is not a safe practice if the pictures are going to be shown theatrically. If you are shooting your first HD picture and you are fond of diffusion, then it is essential that you shoot some tests and have them post-produced in the same manner as the final delivery system.

15
Monitors

If, like me, you choose to light to your monitor then this chapter might just be one of the most important you ever read. Setting up monitors is not difficult or particularly time consuming, but for someone from a film background it can, at first, be a little daunting.

15.1 What kind of monitors are available?

15.1.1 Cathode ray tube monitors

There are three monitors using CRT (Cathode Ray Tube) technology most commonly offered by a supplier. They all come with a 16 × 9 screen, for which the dimension of the diagonal of the picture will be 9 inches, 14 inches or 24 inches. The early HD CRT monitors were all interlace scan only and the picture therefore stuttered slightly when the camera was panned rapidly if you were shooting progressive scan pictures. This effect is never recorded, it being a function of having to display a progressively scanned picture on an interlace scan monitor. More recently, true progressive scan monitors are coming into use and with these the stuttering picture never appears. Not surprisingly, the progressive scan monitors are more expensive.

15.1.2 Liquid crystal display monitors

LCD (Liquid Crystal Display) monitors most commonly have a screen diagonal measuring 6 or 7 inches. They are usually attached to the camera either on top of it, replicating the viewfinder on a studio television camera, or on some kind of flexible arm to enable the focus puller to see the picture the camera is recording. Though they are often interlace devices they rarely exhibit the stutter shown on CRT monitors, as the difference in their technology masks this effect. They are usually lightweight and quite pleasant to look at, though I would hesitate to judge lighting or sharpness on one.

15.1.3 Plasma screens

Plasma screen technology allows for large screens, often with a screen diagonal measuring between 42 and 61 inches. They can be very attractive to look at providing you are not too close. They are very slim but do not quite have the quality of picture of a large CRT screen. They are also expensive.

15.2   Lining up your monitor

One must take great care in lining up your monitor, especially if you are going to judge your lighting via your monitor; fortunately this can be carried out both quickly and accurately.

The camera will usually generate either EBU (European Broadcasting Union) or SMPTE (Society of Motion Picture and Television Engineers of America) colour bars in order to enable you to line up your monitor. The object of the exercise in both cases is to get the colour bars correctly displayed by adjusting the brightness, chroma and contrast controls. EBU bars really require some sort of meter capable of reading the screen brightness, though in an emergency they can be lined up reasonably by eye. SMPTE bars, on the other hand, can be more reliably lined up without a meter, for they were designed so that an 'eyeball' line-up would be reasonably accurately. It is still possible to increase the reliability of your line-ups if you can measure screen brightness accurately in some way, even when using SMPTE bars. With most HD cameras you can choose in the menu whether you wish the camera to generate EBU or SMPTE bars when the external switch is thrown to the bars position.

I used to favour EBU bars, but since working more extensively with HD, where SMPTE bars are more often used, I have changed my mind and now feel much more comfortable lining up to SMPTE bars.

15.2.1   An SMPTE line-up

The first parameters to set are brightness and contrast. Find the red bar and looking slightly below it find the three narrow vertical grey bars. If at first you can't find them, then increase the brightness until they appear. Switch the monitor to blue only. You now need to reduce the brightness until the middle bar just disappears, leaving only the right hand of the three little bars still just visible. The three small bars should now look something like Figure 15.1.

Towards the lower left-hand segment of the screen you will find a white square. Using the contrast control, adjust this square until it just bleeds into the adjoining areas, now back off the contrast control until this effect just disappears. This is often described as reducing it until it ceases to 'glow'. Or you can use some exposure meters to set contrast (see below).

With any television format, the brightness and contrast controls are never wholly independent of each other, so you may well have to go through the loop of making adjustments to both controls until you find you are no longer making any more changes.

The third parameter to set is chroma. On the screen you should see four vertical white bars with three much darker bars between them. If chroma is incorrectly set, this part of the screen may look

Figure 15.1 SMPTE colour bars with 'blue only' switched on – correctly set up

something like Figure 15.2. Below each bar you should be looking at a much smaller and rectangular section to the bar. Ignore for the moment all the other portions of the screen.

What you have to try and achieve is a situation where all seven long bars match, as near as possible, the smaller rectangular sections below them. The control we are going to adjust is chroma. Adjust the control until you have the best possible match between the large vertical bars and the smaller sections below them on all seven bars. When you have successfully done this, the screen should look something like Figure 15.1; in other words the smaller rectangular sections have effectively disappeared.

When you are satisfied with your result, switch off the blue only control – your line-up is now complete.

15.2.2   Lining up using EBU bars

First, set the monitor to underscan. Using the brightness control, adjust the right-hand black bar to match the density of the surrounding unused screen area. Now switch the monitor to blue only. Using the chroma control, adjust the second bar from the left again until the density of the bar exactly matches the surrounding screen density. Using the contrast control, adjust the extreme left-hand bar, which is white, brighter and brighter until it just appears to 'glow', then back off just a little until it stops glowing. You can set the contrast with some exposure meters (see below). Switch off the blue only control. Switch the camera back to picture and your monitor should be perfectly lined up.

Monitors should be lined up a few minutes after being switched on and every time the lighting environment surrounding the monitor changes.

15.3   Using an exposure meter

If you have an exposure meter that can cope with a flickering image, such as a Cine Meter II or a Spectra Combi II, place it with its flat disc attached over the extreme left-hand white bar on EBU bars or the white box bottom left on SMPTE bars and adjust the contrast till the meter reads 27 foot candles. The same trick works with a Seconic L508 Cine with the dome retracted, but the correct reading with this meter is 54 foot candles. The difference in reading is caused by the way meters behave when faced with a scanned picture. To find out if your meter should read 27 or 54 foot candles, simply do a careful eyeball line-up and place your meter on the appropriate part of the screen; it will now read very close to either 27 or 54 foot candles. From now on, set your screen contrast to the appropriate value nearest to your test reading.

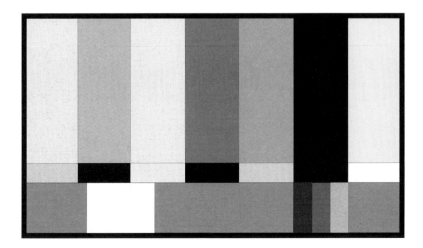

Figure 15.2 SMPTE colour bars with 'blue only' switched on – incorrectly set up

15.4 Cabling your monitor

How you cable your monitor may not seem important; in fact, it is vital to your success.

15.4.1 Single coaxial cables

Most HD cameras either deliver an HD SDI (High Definition Serial Digital Interface) output signal or can easily be fitted with an adapter to make this output available. The advantage of using an HD SDI feed is that you only need a single coaxial cable between your camera and your monitor. The disadvantage is should you want to see menu information on your monitor, HD SDI will not deliver it; it only delivers picture.

When feeding HD SDI signals down a BNC (Bayonet N Connector) cable, the standard cable used in most broadcast applications is not of sufficient quality to reliably transmit a complete signal, except where the cable is very short. It is unfortunate that the HD industry has, in the main, continued to use BNC connectors; they were never designed for the rigours of location work and therefore are rather unreliable. We hang a hundred thousand dollar camera on the end of a plug costing a buck – I, for one, find this ridiculous.

15.4.2 Triple coaxial cables

Alternatively you can, certainly on the Sony F900, take a three-core coaxial cable out of the three BNC plugs on the side of the camera labelled Y, PR and PB. Down this cable you can send both the picture and all the menu information. The disadvantage is that the cable is some 20 mm or $\frac{3}{4}$ of an inch in diameter and quite stiff. If you wish to see menu information but do not require a colour image, you can use a single coaxial cable between the sockets on both the camera and monitor labelled Y. This will give you an HD black and white image with the menu if you need it. This configuration can be very useful when hand holding, especially with the Sony F900, as you can now dispense with the HD SDI adapter box, thus saving both weight and size.

15.4.3 Termination

If you are simply feeding one monitor directly from the camera, this should not be a problem. If you are looping from the camera to one monitor and then on again to another monitor, understanding termination is vital. The simple rule is that the last monitor in the line must be terminated. This may, on some monitors, be automatic, may be done with a simple switch or you may have to put a termination plug onto the Video Out socket of the last monitor on the line. If you don't, the danger is you will see a different image on each monitor and quite likely none of them will be correct.

15.4.4 Serial monitors

Even if you get your termination right, the number of monitors hung onto a single camera output can disastrously affect the quality of the image. Do not accept an image amplifier between any source and the monitor you, the DoP or LD, are going to watch. They may claim to be transparent – that is, adding no changes to the image – but believe me I would never stake my reputation on it.

15.5 Best practice

The monitor the DoP or LD is going to watch should come from a single output on the camera; no other monitors should be fed from this output and no monitors should be fed down line from the DoP's monitor. This rule should never be broken.

Choose another output from the camera or HD SDI (High Definition Serial Digital Interface) converter for any other monitors and do not be swayed from this opinion. I have let this happen in the past and it was a disaster; please learn from my experience.

16
Colour balance

16.1 White balance

If you are using a Sony F900 camera in either its native Sony form or the Panavized version, there are three positions for the switch on the side of the camera that determine which form and setting of white balance you are using. The positions are labelled Preset, A and B. With the switch at Preset the camera will set the white balance to its own internal setting. You can create your own white balance on position A or B by switching to them and operating the white balance switch on the front of the camera.

16.2 What is white balance?

Digital video cameras are set up to show a colour correct image when the scene is lit with tungsten light. The nearer of the two filter wheels to the camera body, situated just above the lens mount and on the operator side of the camera, contains three filters and a clear glass. The filter wheels and the associated descriptive plaque are shown in Figure 16.1. With the clear glass in place, the overall effect is to make the camera have the same colour balance as tungsten balanced film. The other positions give various colour corrections, the values of which are shown in Figure 16.2. This wheel places a coloured filter between the lens and the image splitter block, just as one would put, say, a Wratten 85 filter in front of a film camera lens in order to have the correct colour balance when shooting under daylight with tungsten balanced film.

The cross filter has no effect on colour. It is the equivalent of a light four-point star filter.

16.3 ND filters

The filter wheel farthest from the camera body deploys four filters which have no effect on colour but only affect exposure. The value of these filters is shown in Figure 16.3.

16.4 A warning!

With the exception of zero ND and the star filter, each position on both the ND and the colour correction wheels will have an independent white balance written to it. This means that if you have white balanced at zero ND and you swing the filter to an ND 0.6 you will now have the last white balance setting you made when you used an ND 0.6 filter. This function can be switched off; see the menu section at the end of this book.

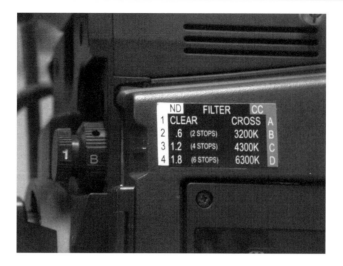

Figure 16.1 The filter wheels with the Panavision version of the indicator plaque

Position A	Cross filter
Position B	Balanced for 3200°K
Position C	Balanced for 4300°K
Position D	Balanced for 6300°K

Figure 16.2 Internal camera filter wheel settings for the wheel nearest to the camera body

	Sony	**Panavision**
Position 1	CLEAR	CLEAR
Position 2	1/4 ND	0.6 (2 STOPS)
Position 3	1/16 ND	1.2 (4 STOPS)
Position 4	1/64 ND	1.8 (6 STOPS)

Figure 16.3 Internal camera filter wheel settings for the wheel farthest from the camera body

16.5 Setting the white balance using a white card

Having chosen the filter in the filter wheel that most accurately reflects the light you are working under, select either position A or B on the Preset selector, fill at least 70 per cent of the screen area with a white card or paper which is illuminated by the primary source of light you are working under and press the white balance switch on the front of the camera. In just a couple of seconds you should see in the viewfinder 'White Balance OK'. The camera has now electronically given you the best possible colour balance for the conditions you are working under. Until you make another white balance on the A or B setting you have chosen, the camera will always give you the same colour set-up every time you switch to your chosen position.

It is important that you have a correct exposure when you carry out a white balance as the camera is set up to make the correction in this mode, otherwise you may get a message in the viewfinder telling you the brightness is too low or too high and the balance will not have been set.

Be careful what white card or paper you use to white balance. Office papers that are sometimes called 'high white' or something similar are, in fact, tinted a little blue to give them a whiter appearance and this may affect your white balance. If you use one of these papers you may find your scene looking a little warmer than you expected. This can be attractive but you need to be aware it is happening.

16.6 Setting the white balance using a coloured card

One way to make any video camera show an image that does not have the same colour cast as the original scene is to white balance to a card or paper that is not white. I don't use white balance very often but should you, perhaps, wish to warm up the overall look of a scene you might white balance to a pale blue card. The white balance process will remove the blue from the set-up and the overall result will be warmer by the same factor as the card was cool. The reverse is true if you use a pink card; the result will be cooler as the pink will have been removed. Green and yellow, or indeed any colour, can be used in this way and the result will be a colour change diametrically opposed to the colour of the card you are using. I find colours other than pink and blue of very little use unless I still have a green cast from fluorescent lights after doing a standard white balance, when balancing again to a very pale green card can sometimes help.

You can easily obtain pastel-coloured thin card in almost any colour from art shops; they usually come in large sheets but are not expensive and easily cut to standard office paper size. I always carry a folding clipboard with me in which I keep my coloured cards, several white cards, for they are used so often they get dirty, and my star chart for setting the back focus. As the clipboard has a folding cover, it keeps everything clean and dry, and can easily be folded backwards so that it can be propped up if I am white balancing or setting my back focus when on my own. If you choose to use a cover like this, make sure you use a black one. When the paper is clipped to it some of the folder will be in shot; the colour of the folder may then affect the white balance.

16.7 Setting the white balance under fluorescent lighting

With any digital camera I rarely use the white balance facility, for I prefer to stay on Preset and occasionally use filters as if I were filming. The exception to this rule is when I am filming under fluorescent light. Here I find the best way to white balance is, having checked all the fluorescent tubes are the same make and specification, to take the white card quite close to a tube and balance it there. This is to make sure that no spurious light that may have picked up some other colour from reflection of another surface is being allowed to influence the setting.

16.8 The outer filter wheel

The filter wheel farthest from the camera body has no effect on colour; again, it has a straight-through position with the other three positions having neutral density filters of varying strength in them. This is to allow you to keep the lens working at a reasonably wide aperture when filming under bright light. At first glance you might think that using as small an aperture as possible, and thereby getting a great depth of field, would be a good idea. This is not always a good thing for two reasons. Firstly, some lenses do not perform at their best at very small apertures; the Panavision Primos are an exception to this rule, as often they are at their best at the wide end of the aperture range. Secondly, one thing that most film people dislike about video is that everything seems sharp and it is impossible to separate the foreground from the background using discriminatory focus. Deploying these neutral density filters can overcome both these problems. The strength of the Neutral Density (ND) filters is shown in Figure 16.3.

It should be noted that in the ND column on the descriptive plaque, Sony and Panavision use different values. Sony list the NDs as 1/4, 1/16 and 1/64. The filters are identical but Panavision use the film standard values of 0.6, 1.2 and 1.8, which are the actual densities of the filters. Figure 16.1 shows a Panavision camera.

16.9 Black balance

Pushing the same switch as is used for white balance in the opposite direction operates the black balance. You should black balance the camera first thing every morning and whenever you change the position of the gain switch on the camera. It is also a wise precaution to carry out a black balance if the camera has experienced a large change in temperature, though this is probably being hyper-cautious.

17
Playback

17.1 Don't use the camera for playback!

Although HD cameras are usually capable of playing back a tape, I strongly advise you never to do this. In absolute extremis, perhaps, but that does not include the director wanting to see a printed tape or any continuity problems. The VTR on the camera is primarily designed as a record unit and without tedious precautions will assume that is your requirement and happily record over any material already existing on the tape. Believe me, I know!

If you absolutely have to use camera playback and it is only needed for reviewing a few seconds, say up to 30 seconds, of the last take then hold the Ret button down until you are that far back and then let it go. The camera will now safely replay and re-sync the time code at the end of the scene. I do not advise rewinding more than about this length.

If you need to go back further then it is essential that you first eject the tape, push the record inhibit slug on the cassette down to the safe position, re-insert the cassette and rewind to where you wish to replay from. Having replayed satisfactorily you must now ensure that you have reached the end of the last recording on the tape. Do not be hurried in this, as it is only too easy to think you are at the last take when in fact you have just viewed the one before it. If you are wrong you are about to erase a printed take.

You now have to remove the cassette from the on-board VTR (Video Tape Recorder), enable the safety slug and return the cassette to the camera's VTR. There are now two ways to re-establish time code sync. If you are using a Sony camera you can open the time code door and switch to Regen and re-sync as per the handbook. There is an easier way which I use very successfully: very carefully play the tape to the end of the last take with your finger on the stop button. If you can stop the tape either side of the last frame to an accuracy better than 5 seconds, then all you need to do is press the Ret button and 99 times out of 100 the camera will re-sync very happily.

I must repeat, please do everything in your power not to replay via the camera. If a senior person, say the producer or the director or even the DoP, if you are one of his team, insists you do it pluck up the courage, tell them of the risks, and make them understand it is entirely their responsibility if something goes wrong. I cannot tell you how many associates I know who have lost a great take by poor playback discipline.

A much safer option is to arrange for a second recording to be made in parallel on a separate recorder linked to the camera via an HD SDI lead. This second recording can not only give you a backup tape, but will also allow you to play back without touching the master tape in the camera. There are several options which I discuss below.

17.2   Using the Sony HDW F500 VTR

The Sony HDW F500 VTR is a superb piece of kit; its front control panel is shown in Figure 17.1 and here it is rack mounted. You can record a backup master tape using the HD SDI (High Definition Serial Digital Interface) cable from the camera and in the same format as you have the camera set to, and play back in almost any format providing the VTR has all the appropriate extra boards fitted. For instance, if you are making your primary recordings in 24P, or any other of the formats available in the camera, and are in Europe, then you can record an identical backup in 24P and play back to cheaper monitors in 625-line PAL. If you are in America, again if you are recording in 24P, or again in any other camera format, you can playback in 525-line NTSC.

What you cannot do, however, is to get an output from the VTR in a different format from that which it is recording in simultaneously with that recording. It will not work as a real time standards converter. Its standard conversion will only work in the playback mode.

The downside of this very clever VTR is it is expensive; both the purchase and rental cost are very similar to a camera body.

17.3   Using DV for playback

A very economical way of providing playback is to use a high-end DV (Digital Video) record/player. These often come cased with a 9-inch monitor and a controller. You need a fairly sophisticated version, otherwise it may not successfully record the time code coming from the camera. As DV recorders work in either the PAL or NTSC recording format, you will have to order the model appropriate for the playback monitors you will be using and will need an additional piece of kit, a down-converter. A down-converter changes the HD signal format into either a PAL signal or an NTSC signal, and they are discussed later in this chapter.

DV recorders have started to be used in the film world for high quality playback, so the playback team will probably be familiar with them anyway. There is possibly an additional saving to be made here, for the signal from DV is of sufficiently high quality for many picture editors to accept it as the input medium for their off-line editing suite. As converting an HD tape to Digi Beta or Beta SP costs around six times the purchase price of the HD tape, very considerable savings can be made here. As I say, if you are going down this route you must use a high quality DV recorder that can handle the full HD time code, otherwise you will have great problems with your EDL (Edit Decision List) coming out of the off-line edit suite.

Figure 17.1 The Sony HDW F500 VTR

17.4 Using two DV recorders

The idea of using the DV playback tape as the cutting room supply copy can be further improved by having two DV recorders on set and getting the playback team to transfer, during the shooting day, just the circled or printed takes from the primary DV machine to the secondary DV machine. If they become proficient at this, then by the last take of the day they should have only one take to transfer, so it hardly adds to their working day.

You now have a tape for the cutting room with only the circled or printed takes on it, which will save the cutting room a lot of time digitizing the day's rushes and the original tape can stay on set for reference. The original tape also provides a backup if any damage should occur to the cutting room copy. This is a nice safe situation as you also have the camera HD master safely stored as well. DV to DV transfers are of very high quality, so there should be no discernible difference between the DV master and the cutting room copy.

A further refinement of this technique is discussed in Chapter 23, Section 23.1.

17.5 Down-converters

The job of a down-converter is, much as its name implies, to reduce the picture sophistication and associated data flow rate of the HD signal to the less sophisticated and lower data flow rate of a domestic television standard. Some models can be switched between standards so that they will output either PAL or NTSC. Few, if any, will output both standards at once, but it is hard to envisage a situation where you might need this. Some have to be purchased or rented in a single standard only, so you must be careful to specify your required output standard at the time of ordering.

The configuration of the down-converter can vary from a large rack-mounted unit through a small box handy for location work, right down to a tiny unit that fits on the side of the camera. There is usually a trade-off between size and weight and the quality of the resultant picture; as a rough guide, the bigger the box the better the picture.

17.5.1 The Evertz down-converter

The Evertz down-converter is a medium-sized unit capable of very high quality output and can be switched to give either a PAL or an NTSC picture from an HD source. It has the advantage of being of a convenient size and can be powered from batteries or a mains supply. Figure 17.2 shows an Evertz unit together with its associated power supply. On the front cover can be seen two cross-cut and knurled nuts which allow removal of the panel, usually with finger pressure, but if they are too tight it is perfectly acceptable to use a screwdriver. Behind this panel are a row of DIP switches which allow you to set various parameters for the unit, including which standard you would like the output to be conformed to.

17.5.2 The Miranda down-converter

The Miranda down-converter takes a very different approach. The whole object of its design strategy is to give as small a unit as will adequately do the job. The success of this strategy is borne out by the fact that it is an ideal unit when hand holding or fitting the camera to a Steadycam rig. Figure 17.3 shows a Miranda fitted to a Sony HDW F900 camera. As you can see, it is so small it does not even cover all the sockets on the side of the camera.

The Miranda down-converter will only work in the standard specified; it is not, therefore, switchable between standards. It can be purchased or rented in either PAL or NTSC as its output.

There are a number of sockets on the back of the unit. Indeed, the unit is so small the five BNC sockets take up nearly the whole of the area of the rear plate. From these sockets can be tapped a straight-through loop of the input that is the same as the three-wire camera output or a composite signal in the ordered format, which as we have seen will either be PAL or NTSC. There is also a luminance-only signal which enables a high quality black and white-only signal to be taken; this is particularly useful when the unit is used in association with a Steadycam rig.

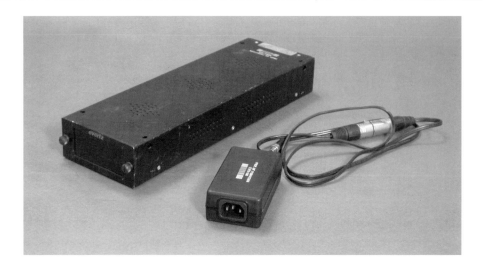

Figure 17.2 Evertz down-converter with power supply

The Miranda down-converter may, at first glance, seem an ideal unit and in many ways it is, but it has to be said that the downside of designing so small a unit is that the picture quality, while adequate for many applications, does not compare with, say, an Evertz converter.

There are, of course, many other units available, but I have cited these two as they are both typical and popular with crews.

17.6 Sound delay lines

If you are using down-converted images from an HD camera then you will, most likely, find that the picture and sound are not in sync on playing back. This is because the picture down-converter takes a

Figure 17.3 A Miranda on-board down-converter

few milliseconds to do its work on each frame. The picture will, therefore, arrive at the playback monitor later than the sound. The sound, of course, has had no need to be converted in any way, so arrives in sync with what would have been the original HD image, hence the discrepancy.

The simple solution is to delay the sound by exactly the same period of time the down-converter is delaying the picture. Fortunately a device to do this job already exists and goes by the title of a sound delay line. The delay any picture down-converter causes is usually written up in its instructions and as sound delay lines nearly always have a simple method of varying the delay time, it is little problem to set up the sound delay to match the picture down-converter being used. Once this has been done and checked during preparation for the shoot, it is most unlikely that it will ever need adjusting again.

17.7 Playback packages

Some rental houses are putting together playback kits which include an appropriate DV recorder and both a down-converter and a sound delay line in a single box. Many playback technicians have put together their own assembly of parts that fulfil all these functions very well indeed. It is prudent to have the whole playback package assembled and checked with at least the main camera before shooting commences. Simply running the camera and playback kit in record mode for, say, 20 minutes and putting a clapperboard on every minute will establish if the HD picture, the down-converted picture and the playback sound are all remaining in sync.

18
Shipping

18.1 It's not ENG!

Although HD cameras tend to look a little like the earlier generation of ENG (Electronic News Gathering) cameras, they are very different and have to be treated accordingly. The Sony HDW F900 is virtually the same size as, and has all the switches in the same place as, the generation of Digi Beta cameras that preceded it, namely the DVW 790. The HDW F900 has even been described as a Digi Beta on steroids, a not totally unfair comparison.

With any HD camera we are dealing with a camera capable of recording an image of massively greater resolution. Curiously the NTSC system delivers almost exactly the same data rate per second as the PAL system. This is a result of the limiting transmission bandwidth available to both systems at their inception. NTSC has to transmit 525 lines of information 30 times a second; 30 complete frames per second derives from their 60 cycles per second mains supply frequency. So $525 \times 30 = 15\,750$ lines per second. PAL has to transmit 625 lines 25 times per second, the local mains here having a frequency of 50 cycles per second. So $625 \times 25 = 15\,625$. Remarkably similar figures given the gap of the Atlantic Ocean, caused by very similar limitations on the amount of data that can be economically transmitted.

Now let us compare a single frame and its resolution. For simplicity I am only going to use the PAL model; the figures for NTSC are very similar. A single PAL image, where the image does not use all the lines transmitted in either the PAL or the NTSC systems, is actually made up of 594 pixels vertically by 1038 pixels horizontally, giving a gross single frame a resolution of 616 572 pixels. Compare this with HD, where the true vertical resolution is comprised of 1080 pixels and the true horizontal resolution is made up of 1920 pixels, giving a gross resolution of 2 073 600 pixels. Gross picture resolution is therefore nearly 3.5 times the resolution of a domestic television. So an HD camera is having to work 3.5 times harder per frame than an ENG camera. To keep it in perfect working order, it therefore deserves much more respect.

18.2 Shipping lenses

ENG cinematographers are used to shipping their cameras with the lenses mounted on them, although the more careful do try and take them as hand baggage. As we have seen elsewhere in this book, to be able to fill a large cinema screen and cause the audience not to question how the image was recorded when they are used to watching 35 mm film, the HD lenses should be able to approach a resolution of 2.5 times that of the 35 mm camera lenses. As we have seen above, the camera itself must be able to record 3.5 times the gross resolution. Put these two factors together and no matter how strong the lens mount, the camera/lens combination is unlikely to perform to maximum specification if they have been shipped attached to each other.

The largest of the Panavision zooms weighs 8.5 kg or about $18\frac{3}{4}$ pounds; just think of the bending forces involved on that lens mount should the camera, with the lens attached, receive a blow. A sensible technician will ship the lenses separated from the camera body, just as film technicians have always done.

18.3 Transit cases

There is a curious divide between the case and padding philosophies either side of the Atlantic. In America a professional shipping case will, as often as not, be made from resin-coated plywood lined with soft foam. This is a great case with a lining that allows the equipment to float about to some extent, but as the foam is always quite thick between the equipment and the case wall the equipment can never receive a harsh blow. Europeans, particularly the British, take a different approach. Their cases are, as often as not, ribbed aluminium and filled with high density foam that very snugly fits the equipment. The philosophy here is that you do not allow the equipment to move, but any significant blow will almost totally be absorbed by the high density foam.

I have worked extensively with cases following both patterns and am confident that both types protect the equipment equally well. As I come from the UK you will not be surprised that I slightly favour the European aluminium case with its high density foam. It does not offer any greater protection than the US version, but the foam lasts a lot longer and the case/foam combination does lead to slightly smaller, and therefore easier to handle, cases.

18.4 Camera set-up when shipping

I have shipped both Digi Beta and HD cameras all over the world for many years and have never found that the shipping procedure alters the camera menu set-up. That said, I always take the precaution of writing the set-up to a card or memory stick, so that should I find the need to re-programme the menu it is the work of moments.

I have been in the situation where I have programmed a card or memory stick on one continent and shipped just myself and the programme to another continent and then loaded the programme into a locally supplied camera. My experience is this is a safe and reliable procedure.

18.5 Size and weight

If you compare a full feature film camera kit with a similar HD kit, the individual boxes may be of different weights but the whole shipping manifest is unlikely to show much change. But note I said camera kit. If your team want to have full HD monitoring facilities, and I would heartily recommend they do, then your monitor shipping weight will almost inevitably be more than a black and white video assist kit. My favourite 24-inch monitor, in its case, weighs around 87 pounds or about 40 kg! But worth every pound, or kilo.

18.6 Batteries

You will need more batteries than if you were shooting with a 35 mm film camera. There are two reasons for this: firstly, any digital device tends to be power hungry and, more importantly, you are consuming power just to make the viewfinder work, whereas with a film camera it consumes virtually no power when in the equivalent of a standby mode.

On-board batteries are very convenient, but even large and efficient ones will only last between 1.5 and 4 hours, depending on how much recording you make in any given time. Often overlooked is the simple expedient of using a block battery, just as we often do with film cameras. Remember video cameras are nearly all 12-volt devices. A good 12-volt block battery will run a Sony HDW F900 all day in all but the most arduous circumstances, so if you are in a studio or even on location but will spend most of the day on a dolly the block battery may be your answer.

19
Multi-camera shoots

In Europe, especially in the UK, big multi-camera shoots are not common. There is a small market for performance films – that is, taking subjects originally presented on the stage and transferring them to the screen – but it is limited. There are a few rock concerts shot with up to 10 cameras but again this is a very small market.

In the USA matters are very different. Traditionally, sitcoms have been shot on 35 mm, most frequently with a camera having a three-perforation (3 perf) mechanism as against the traditional four, which as stated earlier saves 25 per cent of the stock and processing costs. The market is so significant that Panavision has developed a camera exclusively for this market. It is 3 perf, as one would expect, has 2000-feet magazines and usually carries a big, long range, zoom; 2000 feet of 35 mm film is heavy so the issue of the weight transfer from the front of the magazine to the back during a take becomes important. To overcome this, between the camera base and the tripod head there are two wedged plates slotting together with a lead screw arrangement so that the camera operator can smoothly move the camera fore and aft to re-balance the camera during a take.

This camera is often mounted on a studio-style pedestal with all the cabling brought together in a loom. A loom is simply a sheath, usually made of nylon, which encases all the necessary cables so there is only one tail coming from each camera.

It is this multi-camera television market that is embracing the HD philosophy faster than any other. The reasons are simple. There is little difference between the rental cost of an HD camera and a specialist 3 perf 35 mm camera. If you add the cost of 5000 feet of 35 mm raw stock to the negative processing cost and further add telecine time to transfer it to tape for editing and then compare that total to the purchase price of a 50-minute cassette of tape, you find the film cost is around 50 times that of the tape, a powerful argument in this market. Add to this the fact that in going over to HD there is no discernible change in picture quality, given a good DoP.

Things on set get simpler too; tape changes are only needed after 50 minutes of recording time as against a little over 20 minutes for even the specialist film cameras. Wiring looms can be made up in exactly the same way. Instead of having to look at a video assist monitor, the director is now viewing finished product in full HD resolution and colour depth. Recording stock weight transfer problems become a thing of the past, as the weight of the tape is negligible and it travels from the top to the bottom of the cassette during recording, so there is no fore and aft weight transfer as in a film camera.

19.1 Synchronization

Synchronization of the time code between many pieces of equipment has to be very carefully thought out, especially if you are using Sony or Sony-derived cameras. The problem is very similar to that experienced with the earlier Digi Beta cameras. Put simply, the problem lies in the fact that for ease of writing to the tape the total image is recorded in two blocks; this is more convenient and produces a higher tape writing speed. Time code, on the other hand, is written as four groups of two numbers, the groups representing hours, minutes, seconds and frames. A complete frame is the smallest unit it can handle. When you stop recording the tape may come to a halt on either block of the picture information being laid down on the tape. This is not a problem as the recorder will start recording seamlessly on either a first block or a second block, so the picture will be continuous. The time code, on the other hand, can only progress in whole numbers of frames. It is therefore possible to restart recording where the time code has, in effect, made a jump forward in time equivalent to half a frame relative to the picture information. This is not a drawback if you are recording picture and sound on a single camera, but is a crucial matter if you are using two or more devices which need to be synchronized via their time code. Even two identical cameras cannot be relied upon to stop and start with greater accuracy than a time space interval of half a frame.

Therefore, the only solution is somehow to lock the time code of every piece of equipment together with frame accuracy.

19.2   Time code on location

If you are reasonably static on location, it is possible to link up all the various sound and camera devices by running cables from time code out of one device and daisy-chaining BNC cables to time code in the next device, taking time code out of that device to the time code in the next device and so on. If you do this you will need to make sure that all but the first device is set to use external time code. In these situations the sound master will more often than not be something like a DAT (Digital Audio Tape) recorder, in which case this is usually used as the master time code source.

19.2.1   Lock-it boxes

Film crews traditionally hate cables, so though the above solution is very reliable, the necessary cables will be most unpopular. There is a very elegant and not very expensive solution. Each device on set should be given an external time code generator. The version I use nearly all the time is called a lock-it box. Roughly the size of a packet of 20 cigarettes, these boxes are extraordinarily reliable and very easy to use. Most often the lock-it box will be attached to the camera using a pad of Velcro, very convenient.

Usually, the sound department will look after the lock-its and synchronize them all together at the beginning of the shooting day, then hand them round the unit as required. They are more than reliable enough to need no attention until the day's wrap, when they are returned to the sound department to have a power check and be restarted the following morning. It is claimed they will hold sync for up to a week, but good practice suggests a fresh sync up every day is prudent.

19.2.2   Script boy

There is a further refinement to this system. A device known as a script boy can be given to the script supervisor, or continuity as they used to be known. It consists of a clipboard with a time code generator just like the lock-it, with the addition of a time code display on the top of it. A simpler solution I have seen used recently was a digital watch, in this case a G Shock, which the sound mixer was able to set by hand every morning with an accuracy of within a second, usually more than good enough for the notes sent to the picture editor.

19.3   Time code in a studio

Film crews must now abandon all hope; in a studio situation with more than one camera there are going to be so many cables that the sensible approach is to go down that route and get really well organized.

The number of cables can easily mount up and a list might look like this:

Power
BNC HD SDI monitor cable
BNC time code in
BNC time code out
Genlock in
Genlock out
Remote camera control cable
Audio channel 1 in
Audio channel 2 in
Audio monitoring

You can have more; the monitor could be from the three-core socket instead of or in addition to the HD SDI single socket.

The solution to all this is to make up a loom for each camera long before shooting commences. Many suppliers will already have this available, so it is very much worth asking.

On a long or many-camera shoot, it is also quite the norm to have a mains-driven time code generator and run every single piece of equipment from it, including sound department.

Although a nylon-sheathed loom cable may be an inch in diameter (25 cm), it is at least now the equivalent of a single cable and much more crew friendly.

19.3.1   Genlock

One cable we have not discussed is that labelled Genlock. Strictly speaking you only need to run this cable if you are cutting in real time via a control suite. Genlock ensures that all the cameras will open and close their electronic shutters at exactly the same moment. This can be important, for if you cut in real time between one camera and another, imagine what would happen if you left one camera just as its shutter was about to open and cut to the incoming camera just as its shutter was about to close. You would have a totally blank frame.

By daisy-chaining the Genlock out to the Genlock in of the next camera, you have all the shutters working in perfect synchronism.

19.4   Menu set-ups

19.4.1   The Sony RM-B150

Many lighting directors from a television studio background like to have remote control over the camera set-up. I do not, but that's a matter of taste and background. There is a remote control box for the Sony HDW F900 and it goes under the title of an RM-B150, illustrated in Figure 19.1. The problem with using an RM-B150, as I see it, is that you can only control the image from each camera by referring to the monitors, which seems a shame when you have all those nice digital pages in the menus. Now engineers from a television studio background do this with amazing precision, but it frightens me to hell.

The RM-B150 is capable of controlling many of the picture parameters, such as brightness, gamma, black levels, etc., and has a remote run/stop. It controls all but the run/stop with rotary knobs with little guide as to the extent of their effect. It should also be noted that having made changes using the RM-B150, if you now unplug the unit it leaves the camera with all the settings you have made; the camera does not go back to any previous setting.

Television studio practice allows for small differences in exposure and colour correction from camera to camera; this is not the case in film. A film DoP, if shooting with several cameras, will either light the set for a perfect match, my preference, or give each camera a separate exposure setting. Neither route is 'correct'; they are simply the result of different experience and training.

Figure 19.1 The Sony RM-B150 remote control unit

19.4.2 Using memory sticks

I am sure it will come as no surprise to you that I prefer to have all my cameras set up to exactly the same parameters so that I can match the monitors by adjusting my lighting. That is not to say that I may not use slightly different set-ups from scene to scene, but I try very hard never to make any changes during an individual scene. This is because I have a hang-up about lighting and picture continuity in general, which comes from my film background, where shots within a scene might very well have their order on the screen rearranged in the cutting room, so I try very hard to ensure that they will all match no matter what the order. If you are more used to working in a studio where a live cut is made, then you are much more certain of the eventual cutting order and need not acquire my neurosis.

My technique is simple; I set up the main shot, usually something like a master wide and, using the camera's menu, set this camera to my preferred look. I will then record the settings to a memory stick and using the stick load these settings onto all the other cameras. As a precaution I will keep an eye on the leading actors' close-ups during rehearsals to make sure my settings and the make-up do not conflict in any way. In these circumstances the majority of my lighting will almost certainly have been done in advance of shooting and I will have considerable control over the lamps via a dimmer board. My aim is always to have set the lighting for the whole scene well before rehearsals are over and not touch anything at all during the scene.

19.5 Matching lenses

The ideal is to have all your lenses from a single good quality manufacturer so that no adjustments between cameras is ever called for. If you source your cameras and lenses from Panavision, you can be absolutely sure of a perfect match between all zoom and prime lenses, and no adjustments whatsoever will be needed. My apologies to other manufacturers, but experience has led me to favour the Panavision Digital Primo lenses; they suit my style and are utterly reliable.

If you find your lens set does not match in image quality and look, there are things you can do about it but, usually, you will be bringing the look of your better lenses down to the quality of your worst lens. If you look carefully in the Sony HDW F900 menus in the section named Operator, you will find a page labelled Lens File. Here it is possible to assign individual settings to several different lenses.

The problem is that to make a sharp lens match a softer lens you either have to reduce the image enhancement of the better lens and/or bring up the electronic image enhancement of the poorer lens so much the image acquires all the bad characteristics of the look of poor quality video, so why are you spending so much money on an HD kit?

Personally I would not accept a lens set that did not match perfectly without any adjustment within the camera.

20
Hazardous conditions

There are many myths about video cameras in general, and HD cameras in particular, regarding their vulnerability to the elements. Most of this is nonsense. If you think of the amount of electronics packed into a modern film camera, what makes an HD camera more susceptible to hazardous conditions? Very little.

There are a couple of cut-out switches in the camera to protect it from abuse. It will stop if the humidity surrounding the tape record drum becomes too high, and it has to be very high indeed for this to happen. A film camera would probably be equally in trouble. This safety trip is a wise precaution, for if the humidity surrounding the tape drum ever reaches a critical point the tape will, eventually, stick to the drum. You don't want this to happen as it is not a field serviceable condition. The camera is going to need a whole new tape drum and that is going to be very expensive. I have been associated with a long-term shoot where a Panavized Sony camera was up a Scottish mountain in a gale for some considerable time; sensible precautions were taken, exactly as you would with a film camera, and there was never the slightest suggestion that the camera was threatening to shut down. There was a real chance that the crew would have to though!

There is a heat overload cut-out switch as well; this is mainly to protect the computer processors from overloading. I have never experienced or heard of this tripping out. I have been associated with an HD shoot in the Moroccan desert where the temperature was 110°F in the shade – the cameras worked perfectly.

20.1 Resetting the trips

If you look under the camera at the rear on the operator's side you will see a small hole; this is the reset button. If the camera has tripped out then press a small, blunt object such as the end of a paper clip into this hole. The camera will not restart immediately. You need to take it where it is drier or cooler, depending on why it has tripped, and wait for the conditions to change. Removing the cassette and leaving the door open can help matters. The camera will come back to life when you press the reset some 20 minutes later.

Treat an HD camera with the respect you would give a high quality 35 mm camera and you are unlikely to have any problems. Nevertheless, let us look at the precautions you might like to take.

20.2 Water

Please ignore the old adage 'water and electricity don't mix'; the adage should be 'water and electricity mix only too well'. In fact, they attract each other. If there is the slightest sign of rain, keep the rain cover handy. If you are going into a very humid environment take the camera and lenses in some hours before you need to use them and let them normalize. Keep a hair-drier handy in these circumstances to speed things up – but not on full heat please! All just as you would with a film camera.

20.3   Heat

Referring to the above, don't put the rain cover on unnecessarily, it can cause a heat build-up, as the fans cooling the computer processors won't get their heat away as efficiently. If sound have insisted, as they often do with the quietest of cameras, that you cover it with something to make it quieter, take that something off as soon as the take is finished; remember the front-end processors are working full time just to give you a picture in the viewfinder. This is one difference from film.

If you were shooting on a very hot exterior location you would be very foolish not to put an umbrella up over a film camera to ensure that the film stock did not reach temperatures that would change its characteristics; please do just the same with an HD camera even if the reasons are different.

20.4   Cold

It is traditional to 'winterize' a film camera if it is going to an extremely cold climate. HD cameras probably survive cold better than film cameras. HD lenses will need just the same attention as film lenses. The biggest problem might be cables; they can become very brittle in the cold, especially BNC cables. Check out a few different makes of coaxial cable in a cold store to find the one that will survive.

Batteries in extreme cold are always a problem. Two remedies come immediately to mind. One is putting a DC supply cable into the camera and keeping the battery on the other end of it inside your clothing. Alternatively, if you are shooting more formally, say on a tripod or a dolly, then before you leave home have some 12-volt block batteries clad in 1- or 2-inch polystyrene and then have an outer case made for them in plywood. In really freezing conditions, you could have a double thickness polystyrene layer underneath the block battery and mount a 12-volt car headlamp bulb under it as a heater. Your battery will run down somewhat faster, but while it has a charge it should be lively enough to keep the camera running.

20.5   Dust

All the usual precautions apply, such as protecting your lenses, setting up wind breaks where possible, perhaps using the rain cover to protect the camera, etc.

There is one both essential and simple protection an HD camera needs over a film camera. The most vulnerable parts of the HD camera, with regard to dust, are the tape transport mechanism and the record head drum. Very fortunately the gaps around the cassette loading door are not used in any way as cooling ports, so, if you are in a dusty, gritty or dirty environment, simply put some gaffer tape over the gaps between the camera body and the cassette loading door.

20.6   Gamma rays

Now this is a bit sci-fi but bear with me, it could be important. One of the few things that can kill a pixel on the imaging chip is a gamma ray hitting it smack in the middle. At ground level there is very little chance of this happening; the Earth's atmosphere absorbs or reduces the chances by a very large factor. On the other hand, if you are flying the camera at an altitude anything above 30 000 feet, gamma rays are much more prevalent. I have only known of one occasion where a camera has suffered gamma ray damage after flying and only one pixel was affected.

In all my time with both Digi Beta cameras and HD cameras, I have only known one moment when several pixels were destroyed at the same time. Curiously over a 24-hour period a camera in London was fine before lunch and after lunch had several dead pixels. The following day I had a telephone call from a crew in Prague in Czechoslovakia saying there were a couple of dead pixels. Very strange: was there a sun spot that day or something? Who knows.

A pixel normally dies switched on, so you will see a bright spot on the screen. It will be of the colour relating to the chip it is on. Fortunately there are several ways to get rid of this bright spot. If you have missed it during shooting, and because it will always be in exactly the same place in the picture area, it is easy to eradicate in post-production. If you spot it before turning over then there is a 90 per cent chance you can quickly solve the problem. Hold the black balance switch down for at least 3 seconds. The camera will now perform an extended black balance and an auto pixel check. This might take up to a minute. The camera has a sophisticated memory circuit in it and if it finds a dead pixel it will, for the rest of the life of the picture head block, take an average of the eight pixels surrounding the dead pixel and assign this average to the dead pixel's output. The memory is sufficient to cover for up to 40 dead pixels. I have never known a camera reach anything like that number of dead pixels, but should it do so the only solution then is to change the prism block and the three receptor chips.

If the auto pixel check fails to clear all the dead pixels, and you are only likely to be in this position if the pixel has only partially failed, which will give a dull coloured glow on the screen, then the pixel memory correction can be initiated manually. I am not going to go into the whole procedure here, but if you need to do it in some distant part of the globe, then ring your supplier and they will happily guide you through the process. If you are on your mobile 'phone, make sure you have a fresh battery; it is not difficult but it is tedious. It's very like playing an old computer game, you have to line up a vertical line and a horizontal line exactly over the pixel in question. With two million plus pixels per chip, this can take a while and there is no scoring system so it can be a thankless task.

21
Camera supports

Tripods and tripod heads should be chosen in much the same way as you would for a film camera. This means that for a Sony HDW F900 you should have the quality and strength you would use for a 35 mm camera and for the Sony HDW 700 range or a Panasonic HDC 20A you could go down to the slightly lighter equipment you might use for a fully equipped Arri SR3. Unless we are going to be taking the kit into difficult locations, my preference is to always go for the 35 mm type supports, as they are usually much more robust and generally nicer to use.

21.1 Fluid heads

Any fluid head that is robust enough to take easily the weight of your chosen camera in its heaviest configuration, say with the biggest zoom and the on-board battery attached, will suffice. That said, I have a personal preference for underslung fluid heads where the tilt bearing is level with the optical axis. These are usually of a dog-leg or 'L' configuration. My favourite is the Ron Ford Baker Fluid 7; it has been going for many years and has been in continuous development, so the current model will comfortably support an F900 in any configuration. I still own a Mark 2 F7 and I will happily put up an F900 with anything but the 11:1 zoom on-board.

Cartoni have introduced a head of similar configuration to the Ron Ford Baker Fluid 7 which they have christened the Lambda. It is more easily adjustable than the F7 and pays for this by being slightly larger and heavier. I have recently used one and was very impressed.

21.2 Geared heads

There is much discussion about the value of a geared head. Certain DoPs I know dislike the use of geared heads; they express the view that such a mechanical device produces a camera movement that is not hand made or personal enough – I disagree. The whole principle of the 'boat' on a geared head is that you can both rotate and tilt the camera where the centre of both movements is the nodal point, or optical centre, of the lens. The human eye is a ball rotating in a spherical socket where the centre of the ball remains in the same place, thus never moving up or down, left or right of the optical centre of the eye, just like the camera on a well set up geared head.

If those DoPs that dislike the use of geared heads could be persuaded to watch a monitor when the camera was operated by a truly skilled operator using a geared head, I think some of them might change their view. That said, the skill of the operator and their talent for the task will be much more in evidence when using a geared head than when on a fluid head. Talent will out, never more so than with he, or she, who cranks the handles.

Underslung or dog-leg fluid heads are capable of the same centring of the lens nodal point, but nearly always the need to balance the head puts the nodal point ahead of the pan centre.

All geared heads have a certain feel to them which makes different operators prefer different makes of head. I am happy to use an Arri geared head, preferring a Mark 1 to a Mark 2; I have used a Panahead extensively and like it a lot. On a job some years ago I had been using an Arri head for some weeks when it needed to go back to the hire company for some minor adjustment that was unwise to carry out in the field. The company rang me to apologize for not having a spare Arri in stock and asked me if I would take a Mitchell Lightweight just for a couple of days until they could get the Arri back to me? I said yes, of course. I didn't return the Mitchell until the end of the job. Four weeks later I had bought my own Mitchell Lightweight. When I operate myself the sheer joy of driving a head you love and are familiar with is a very special pleasure.

21.3   Remote heads

You should treat remote heads just as you would with a film camera, with one proviso. Not all the suppliers of cranes and remote heads are fully up to speed with the requirements of HD cameras. Sometimes they forget that whereas most film cameras run on 24 volts, nearly all HD cameras run on 12 volts. The cabling is also very different; the BNC lead that is usually used for the film camera's video assist is unlikely to be of sufficient quality to be able to handle the data stream associated with an HD signal. You will probably get a picture, but not a very good one, especially if it is a long crane and therefore needs a long cable run.

Even the stop/start plugs and cables are different; zoom and focus may or may not be compatible. All these things must be checked long before you arrive on the set.

Remote heads are usually controlled by either a joy stick or a pair of wheels emulating the controls on a geared head. The operator's viewfinder is now a television monitor. From what I have said about my affection for a geared head, you will not be surprised that I prefer the wheels. Indeed, if an operator chooses the joystick I think the camera movements often look a bit 'clunky'.

If my operator is under pressure when the crane comes out, I sometimes offer to do the crane shot for them 'just to take the pressure off a little', which is, of course, just an excuse. I love little more than flying a camera through three dimensions while 'ackling the 'andles'. And it does massage my pride to show the younger members of the crew that some of the older members of the crew can still enjoy themselves.

21.4   Underwater

Underwater cinematography has much the same problems whether you are using a film camera or an HD camera. I have done it myself and would now always give the advice – bring in a specialist. In the end, a skilled underwater cameraperson will save the production time and money and make a difficult shot look easy.

Housings need to be looked at carefully. Most HD cameras are a very different shape to film cameras; for a start they tend to be longer, so this should be looked at well in advance of the shoot. A number of manufacturers now have dedicated HD housings that work very well.

21.5   In the air

I have seen a Sony HDW F900 very successfully mounted on several fixed wing and helicopter mounts, including the Wescam. In the end there were very few problems. Again, the power supply voltage must be looked at in advance. It is a very good idea to make sure you can balance the camera correctly well before the shooting day. HD cameras can have their centre of gravity in a very different place from many film cameras. This can apply to the left and right dimension, as well as the fore and aft. On the test day it is wise to take along a selection of sliding base plates, especially an extra long one, just to make sure you get a good and balanced fixing.

21.6 Motion control rigs

With most motion control rigs you will have no problems other than the balance and voltage ones discussed above. There is, however, one fascinating piece of equipment available which, unfortunately, I have not as yet had the chance to try out. Panavision have a device they have named the Panahub that fits on the non-operator side of their version of the Sony HDW F900. It will combine a large number of data streams; it can not only lay down all the lens data including zoom setting, focus and aperture, but can record many of the data streams from the axis controls of a motion control rig. Two of the four soundtracks available on the record tape are used, so instead of recording sound on them it records meta-data (meta-data = data about data).

In theory, at least, this would mean that you could record a take, go away for several weeks and, providing you have the nodal point of the lens in exactly the same place on the rig, replay the tape and teach the motion control rig to carry out exactly the same shot as you took all that time ago. What an exciting prospect that might be.

22
How HD affects other crafts

In general, if most of the other crafts on set treat HD as a 35 mm shoot all will be well. There are a few instances, however, where certain specific matters are different, so let us look at them craft by craft.

22.1 Art and design

In the main, sets and set dressing will need to be every bit as good as for 35 mm; the resolution of HD is as good so, if a join is going to show on 35, it will show on HD. Colours are much the same but, if you are shooting with any HD video camera other than a Panavision one, you will have to watch deep or dark reds as they tend to come through in the equivalent density but coloured orange. The Panavision camera will record a perfect deep or dark red, so you have no need to worry when using that camera.

There is a very slight tendency to moiré patterning just as there will be with any CCD (Charge Coupled Device) pixel-driven imaging system, which includes virtually every video camera. Textures having very fine regular detail should therefore be camera tested at an early stage.

Very pure whites can be a slight problem especially when put next to, or in, a very dark colour. But this is something to keep a watch on even with film.

So, in general, there are few problems for art and design.

22.2 Costume

I have experienced a few problems with our friend moiré patterning on some costumes. Some loosely woven cloths can, at certain distances and size of shot, start to shimmer in the classic moiré patterning manner. Any materials you think might be even a slight problem should have a camera test before you make up the garments. Some check patterns will also have the same problem. Costume designers who are experienced in working in television will have little problem overcoming these effects as they will be familiar with them, but designers who have only ever worked in film would be well advised to have some camera tests shot.

It should be noted that these problems are likely to be less than if you were shooting on Digi Beta due to the closer density of the pixels on the camera chip.

Dark or deep reds can be a problem just as for art and design, as they are for all video cameras with the exception of the Panavized Sony camera.

22.3   Make-up and hair

The problems here are different from the previous crafts as there are few colour or moiré issues, but there is a problem with using lens diffusion. It is quite common, say with a hairpiece mounted on a net, for the Hair Designer and the DoP to work closely together to ensure the net does not show. With HD there is less the DoP can do to help, for a diffusion filter that works on a 35 mm camera will be far too strong for the rest of the image on an HD camera. Any form of diffusion on HD has to be very light as it has a greater effect and this makes it very difficult for the DoP to find that subtle level of diffusion where the lace will disappear but the rest of the scene will not look false.

The same applies to the treatment of wrinkles on an actor's face; something can be done but it is usually less than can be achieved with a film camera. That said, there is a skin tone diffusion control in the Sony HDW F900 which can help a little, but it is very subtle. Unfortunately all the artificial definition enhancement is turned off in the Panavision version of the camera, so this function now has little or no effect, for you cannot turn down something if it has already been turned off!

The only solution the DoP has in these circumstances is to pay greater attention to the lighting, so allowances must be made to give them a little more time in this area if the make-up problems are to be adequately addressed.

22.4   Sound

Sound has roughly the same problems on HD as with most film shoots, although you might say the camera crew are going to perceive a problem with the sound department. It is more than likely that the cutting room, and the producer, will insist that the floor-mixed sound be fed back to the camera and be recorded on at least two of the camera's four soundtracks. This is for two reasons. The cutting room will most likely prefer to take their first soundtrack into the off-line edit suite directly from the videotape, as this is much quicker and they will almost certainly be conforming the DAT tapes later. Secondly, the producer will see the soundtracks on the videotapes as a worthwhile backup of the DAT tape should there be a problem at a later date.

As most camera crews look upon extra cables coming out of the camera as a curse something worse than a bad cold, much patience and forbearance must be brought to bear.

22.5   Script supervision and continuity

The most obvious difference here is that whoever logs the shots will be working to time code numbers rather than footage numbers. On many of the shoots on which I have worked, at the end of every printed take the focus puller calls out the focal length of the lens, the focus settings, the aperture and possibly the number on the footage counter. Surely the simplest thing is for them to simply replace the footage reading with the time code? It is not always as simple as that, for on most shoots the time code display will be showing the time of day plus the frame number and will be running continuously. There is a pause button on the time code readout, but it requires some deft finger work to hit that button as well as shutting the camera down after a take. It cannot be arranged to happen automatically.

As I have suggested elsewhere in this book, the solution might well be a simple digital watch set as near as possible to the same time of day as the camera, which the person logging the shots can glance at on cut. A better solution might be to get them a script boy, which is a clipboard incorporating a time code generator that is locked to the camera every morning and has a screen to display the numbers. This can also be fitted with a pause and restart button so that immediately the button is pressed from a stopped condition the time code automatically catches up jumping, as it were, the lapsed time during its off period. This device replaces the traditional stopwatch very elegantly.

22.6   The second assistant cameraperson or ex-clapper boy

Although not strictly another craft, as they are very much an integral part of the camera crew, I think special mention should be made here of a few of the changes to their responsibilities that have come about with the introduction of HD. The biggest problem they sometimes have is, as they are now in charge of the setting up, lining up and cabling of the essential monitors, they can easily be run ragged by other crafts persuading them to run extra monitors. It should be understood that it is an onerous and responsible task to make sure that both the director and the DoP have the monitors that they want when and where they need them, so the second assistant will be quite busy enough getting monitors ready for these two senior heads of department, especially if there has been a big camera move, without other crafts prevailing upon them to supply extra monitors for their convenience.

The practice I like is for the second AC to cable, from a single primary source on the camera, a feed for the monitor the director and DoP will be using. When this is done a second feed, totally independent of the one already fed, is supplied for anyone else to tap into. If the DoP allows it, then the second AC can rig a single monitor on this secondary feed for continuity, make-up, wardrobe, etc. to share. It must be understood that anything beyond the first monitor on the second feed is nothing to do with the second AC; they will simply be too busy. If any other craft wants their own monitor, they must find the labour to daisy-chain it from the first monitor on the secondary feed.

All this might sound a bit complicated but bear with me for, as I describe in detail elsewhere in this book, if a monitor is plugged into the DoP's monitor and that monitor is faulty or unterminated, then this can lead to the DoP lighting quite incorrectly, hence monitor cabling discipline is essential.

Part 5

Examples of Shoots

23
Some pictures that made it to HD – and why

23.1 *The Children of Dune*

Some 4 or 5 months before the shooting of *The Children of Dune* was due to commence, one of the producers came to Panavision in London to talk about the possibility of shooting with the Panavision HD camera. I was there in my capacity as an associate of Panavision. After something like a 2-hour presentation I had the impression that he was convinced he wanted to shoot on HD, but the producer made it clear that economics would be the deciding factor.

The previous series, *Dune*, had been shot on three-perforation 35 mm, so we knew where the extra expenses would be and where the economies could be made. Although the equipment was going to be a little more expensive than 35 mm, over the shooting period that was planned, something like 4 months, the economies on stock and processing were going to be huge. So we progressed to the point where we all agreed in principle that HD was the answer, that they would make sizeable savings and there would be absolutely no loss in quality when compared to the previous series.

However, given the size of the project, the leap of faith required to change from a tried-and-tested system to a brand new camera and, of course, competition from other potential suppliers, the decision to switch to HD and to use Panavision cameras and lenses went right to the wire.

Before the final decision was made I went with Peter Swarbrick, the Head of Digital Imaging Panavision Europe, to Prague with a camera kit for some camera tests with the DoP and his crew. My personal opinion, strictly as a fellow DoP and not as an associate of Panavision, is that no self-respecting DoP would commit to using what to him was a brand new camera without pointing it in anger himself. I would not have done so.

Fortunately the green light came about a week before principal photography was due to commence. Panavision shipped the kit, and I went to Prague on a support mission a couple of days before shooting was due to start. We had agreed the camera set-up they were going to use some time before; it was to be the standard Panavision set-up with the small changes Panavision recommend when only going to television and they were going to shoot at 23.98 frames per second, the primary commission being for an NTSC station. Two days before shooting, I set up the cameras in the Panavision Prague offices and meticulously went through both cameras' menus to be absolutely certain that there was no difference between them and that both were at the agreed settings. Then we shipped them to the studio. Peter Swarbrick and his assistant, Alex Golding, had both checked the cameras before shipping, but with a 4-month schedule ahead of us we were taking no chances. I wanted to walk on the set knowing that when I said the cameras were set up correctly I was taking the responsibility. I was, after all, going to be there for a week so there would be no getting out of it if there were any discrepancies.

23.1.1 Rushes requirements

There were unusual requirements for rushes on *The Children of Dune*. It was part of the package that low resolution rushes would be sent over land lines from Prague every night to both New York and Los Angeles. To facilitate this, a company called Picture Pipeline, who at that time specialized in compressing and encoding images for exactly this purpose, already had a link from the US to and from Prague. This was needed so that producers in both US locations could approve the material and the picture editor could start work in one of them, then once a week rough cuts could be sent back to Prague.

The original plan was to drive the day's rushes from Prague to Hamburg, where the HD tape would be down-converted to Beta SP. The same driver, having had a little sleep, would drive both sets of tapes back to Prague, so that the down-converted copy could be transmitted to the US. We got into discussions as to whether it would be prudent to make an HD clone of the rushes at the same time, as everyone was very nervous of the then plan to send a package of the only rushes tapes back to the US on a once-a-week basis.

23.1.2 An extended playback facility

It seemed to me things were getting too complicated and money was being spent in the wrong areas. I proposed that a better investment would be to add to the playback requirements an HD VTR (Video Tape Recorder) so that a clone of the camera master could be recorded simultaneously with the take being made. This could be done very simply by taking a direct feed from one of the HD SDI (High Definition Serial Digital Interface) sockets on the camera and linking it directly to the VTR. Playback department would then be responsible for starting and stopping the HD VTR at the same time as they started and stopped the DV playback recorder that was already booked for the shoot.

Matters progressed in a very interesting manner from here; it was pointed out that the DV copy was perfect for inputting to the Picture Pipeline equipment for transmission to the US. It was quickly established that the playback operator was happy to provide two DV rigs and would dump the printed takes from the primary machine to the secondary machine during the shooting day.

This proved to be an ideal set-up for this production. Every week the master HD camera tapes could be safely sent to the US in the secure knowledge that a clone was in a safe in the production offices in Prague. Almost as soon as wrap was called on set there was a DV tape of only the printed takes available to be sent via Picture Pipeline to the US, which meant they would receive them many hours earlier than if they had been sent on a round trip to Hamburg for transfer. An added bonus was a better deal on the picture insurance as there were, in effect, two copies of the master negative which would never be in the same place at the same time.

23.1.3 The equipment list

The equipment list varied a little over the shooting period, but the one shown in Figure 23.1 is more or less what they ended up with. The 9:1 zoom with its range of 8 to 72 mm only became available around a third of the way through the shoot and Panavision sent them one as soon as possible. I gather it became their lens of choice, which is hardly surprising as Panavision designed it primarily as a studio lens and the whole of *The Children of Dune* was shot in a studio; even the exteriors of the Planet of Dune were built in a studio.

23.2 Birthdays

Birthdays could not be a more different project from *The Children of Dune*. It is an 8-minute short intended for UK cinemas and to be shown at film festivals in order to progress the young team's careers. There was simply not enough in the budget to shoot on 35 mm and as it was intended for cinema presentation it would not have been made if HD had not been available. On this occasion I agreed to be the DoP as I liked the director, Chris Atkins, and his company Stage 2 Screen. He had also written the script, and it gave me the opportunity to shoot without making any concessions to trying to make HD look like film. I would light like film but would use no diffusion and would not

---

The Children of Dune
Equipment List

Cameras:
2 × Panavision HD camera bodies with full accessory kits
(A further camera body + viewfinder only to be held at Panavision Prague offices)

Lenses:
1 × 6 : 27 mm T1.8 Primo Digital zoom
1 × 25 : 112 mm T1.9 Primo Digital zoom
1 × 8 : 72 mm T1.9 Primo Digital zoom

1 × 5 mm Primo Digital prime lens
1 × 7 mm Primo Digital prime lens
1 × 10 mm Primo Digital prime lens
1 × 14 mm Primo Digital prime lens
1 × 20 mm Primo Digital prime lens
1 × 35 mm Primo Digital prime lens

Control units:
1 × RM-B150 camera control unit

Monitors etc:
1 × 24-inch HD monitor
2 × 14-inch HD monitors
2 × 9-inch HD monitors
Trolley for 24-inch monitor

Many BNC leads of various lengths

1 × Evertz down-converter (set to down-convert HD to NTSC)
1 × Miranda on-board down-converter (for Steadycam use only)
1 × Rane sound delay line

VTRs etc:
1 × HDW F500 HD VTR
2 × High Grade NTSC DV playback kits with integral monitors

Camera support:
1 × Dolly
2 × Tripod heads
2 × Tall tripod legs
2 × Short tripod legs
1 × Steadycam rig (to be supplied by Steadycam operator as and when required)

Figure 23.1 *The Children of Dune equipment list*

vary the camera settings from the Panavision recommended settings for a write out to film. This way I would discover what HD, when both shown as digital projection and as 35 mm film, would look like.

23.2.1   The studio shoot

The picture was scheduled to be shot in 3 days, 1 day to film the 'interlocutor' in a coved studio where the floor would be blue but the walls black, so there would be a colour for the artist to stand on but the background would be a complete void. Not an easy concept no matter what you are going to record it on. Further, the director's vision of this scene would be that it would be very severely top lit with the minimal amount of fill light. The other 2 days would be all over central London, including The Houses of Parliament, Millbank, the new London Council Offices, Tower Bridge, some back streets in West London, Panavision Europe's own offices and a North-East London flat. A lot of locations were in difficult parking circumstances with a large camera; it was a good job my young camera team liked a challenge!

The day in the studio was not scheduled to have much of a lighting budget and the 'dolly' consisted of a tripod on a rolling spider which could run on plastic piping as rails, not my normal scene, and I had offered to operate myself to help with the budget. I love operating when I can and that may have influenced my decision to take the job. The 'dolly' rarely went in exactly the same place twice. As most of the time I only had to keep a mid shot on the actor that was not too difficult, but when we went for close-ups my focus puller was in for something of a challenge.

The lighting scheme could not have been simpler; two par cans were rigged next to each other in the roof of the studio centred on the artist and very slightly in front of him. The only other lighting was an 800-watt redhead bounced off a polystyrene board. Simple, effective and when Chris saw the result on our 24-inch monitor he declared it exactly what he had envisaged. A good start to the shoot. Realizing that with a totally black background the sometimes excessive depth of field on HD was not an issue, for there was nothing there to be sharp, I could work without any ND (Neutral Density) filters and at least give my focus puller a decent chance; nevertheless, with only two par cans as a key light he still only got T3.2, which with that shifting track kept him on his toes. The 'panda effect' look of an actor very top lit with dark eye sockets is far from my normal style, but I have to give it to Chris, it was powerfully effective in this context. The 4-foot square polystyrene reflector put a nice dot in the eyes as well as brightening the eye sockets to a point where I could accept them. I may be old school, but it seems to me that the script, the writer, the director and particularly the actor might all be wasting their time if it is impossible for the audience to read the meaning on the actor's face. It does not matter how dark the face is so long as you can read what is going on behind it. To my mind most of that communication comes from the eyes, hence I hate it if I can't see an actor's eyes.

23.2.2   The location shoot

We were very lucky with the weather, particularly as we only had 2 days to shoot our exteriors. It was very bright with big majestic clouds with enough breaks in them to give us sun for the shots without waiting around too much. It also gave me a chance to show off what the camera was capable of. One of the silly rumours going the rounds about HD is that it won't handle a bright sky. I had bright skies in abundance, so this was my opportunity to show that they were not a problem. If you refer to Figure 23.2, you will see a still pulled directly from the HD tape. The scene concerns a chap who works for the police and whose job it is to stop people committing suicide, and the chap on the left is trying to throw himself off the top of a building site. Even in black and white and reproduced here, you can see the big sky holding up very well indeed. I assure you it looks even better on the big screen.

Because we were going to so many locations and, to ease the parking problems, we were travelling in private cars, I decided to work solely from a 9-inch monitor run off batteries. For really difficult shots I would dive under a cloth to check my exposure on the colour monitor, but found I rarely changed it from the setting I had made using the black and white viewfinder. When travelling a lot during the shooting day, you must be aware that control knobs on both the viewfinder and monitor can easily get knocked, so the first thing to do on arrival at a new location is to switch the camera on, leave it and the monitor for a few minutes – this can easily be the time it takes you to set the shot up – then switch the camera to bars output and line both the monitor and the viewfinder up. You can get a detailed description of how to line up your monitor quickly and efficiently in Chapter 15 of this book. The line-up procedure is exactly the same when lining up a black and white viewfinder as for a colour monitor, except you simply ignore the fact that there is no chroma control.

Figure 23.2 A still taken directly from the master HD tape of *Birthdays*

There were several important scenes in *Birthdays* where, because of the time pressure, we had shot a take before someone turned up with the monitor. With a carefully lined up viewfinder, I was very pleased with my exposure even when the scene contained one of our big skies. In retrospect, I think having finished product to look at, even be it only in black and white, made me braver with my exposure – it seemed I was not making that little cautious allowance I might when using a spotmeter and this was very much to the benefit of the pictures.

23.2.3   Exterior tracking shots

There were two major tracking sequences in *Birthdays*, one where the camera is static on a doorway through which our hero bursts and runs, in profile, down a street, and a second where he literally chases after the camera. This being a very low budget production, the only vehicle available that was not full of equipment was the director's Peugeot 306 hatchback. We did the burst through the door and into a profile run first. I simply got in the back seat, wound the window right down and rested the camera complete with the 6:27 mm zoom on the open window ledge.

There are some advantages to a heavy camera. I could have opted to take the HD SDI adapter and battery off one end of the camera and used a prime lens on the other end; it would have been just as nicely balanced, but I chose not to. A heavy camera clearly has a greater mass and therefore a greater inertia, so the camera simply does not want to change direction if it can help it. The result was that under the initial acceleration the camera wanted to tilt to the right; we were travelling right to left, but experience had taught me to expect this, so I had my right hand on the top handle to correct this yaw to the right. Once we were under way, the inertia of the camera smoothed out virtually all the bumps in the road and we had as smooth a tracking shot as I could have wished for with a much more sophisticated tracking vehicle.

The second tracking shot with the hero running after the camera I approached in a different way. Still a great believer in tracking with as heavy a camera as is practicable, I got the director to fold down the back seat of his Peugeot 306 and took a long hard stare at the available space. To everyone's amazement, including my own, we got the camera, again rigged with the 6:27 mm zoom lens, HD SDI adapter and battery into the back of the car mounted on our baby legs and metal spreader. Again, I was banking on the mass of the camera smoothing things out and it did, quite wonderfully. Having got the camera in, the biggest problem was getting myself and my focus puller in as well; it was a good job we had become friends by then as it was a very tight fit.

23.2.4 Interior lighting

There is one scene in *Birthdays* where our hero and his best friend have a drink in a bar. It is, supposedly, lit by tungsten light and has a soft, intimate atmosphere. Normally in these circumstances I would reach for my filter box and add a little diffusion, but you might remember I had forsworn such tricks on this shoot. I also wanted to warm up the scene a little. Basically, the two friends end up having an argument, so I wanted this to happen in a very attractive environment, thus heightening their conflict between place and dialogue.

The warmth I achieved with two crossed key lights from each end of the room; they were 2K blonds and I bounced them both off folding Lastolite reflectors. I am a great fan of Lastolites, particularly on a heavy schedule; they are quick to rig if you use their proprietary universal support brackets, are not expensive and give a wonderful light. They come in a variety of colours, but on this occasion I stuck to gold.

The cross keys worked to give an effect I use often; the key for one of the protagonists provided the backlight for the other, in both directions. The only fill I used was a Mizar bounced off 2-foot square of polystyrene board immediately in front of the two shot. The lighting plot can be seen in Figure 23.3 and a still from the master HD tape of this scene is shown in Figure 23.4.

23.2.5 Adding gain

Appropriate though this looked, I still missed some diffusion in front of the lens. I had been experimenting to try to grasp what effect on the image quality adding gain to the image might have. Expecting it to be detrimental, I had been quite surprised. On a low-key, particularly a warm low-key scene, it did not appear to reduce the apparent picture quality by any discernible amount, but added a certain texture. I know video engineers will tell me that what I have really added is picture noise. I accept this, but it does not look like any video noise I have ever experienced before. It looks remarkably similar to moving from a modern high quality film stock of around 200 ASA to an equally high quality one of around 500 ASA. These days you will not really notice added grain but there will be a change in texture.

Had I been shooting *Birthdays* on film I would have gone up to a higher film speed for the bar scene. I did not need the added exposure and would have added ND filters to counter this, just as I did with the HD camera. I would have done it solely to get a texture to the image more appropriate to the

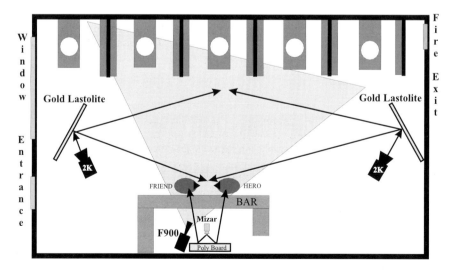

Figure 23.3 Banquets with practical hanging lamps over

Figure 23.4 The bar scene from *Birthdays*

scene. In adding 6 db (one stop of exposure) to the bar scene I put the effective ASA rating of the HD camera up to 640 ASA, very close to the 500 ASA film stock I would have chosen if shooting on 35 mm, and I got a surprisingly similar, apparent, effect. I have now seen this scene written out to 35 mm film and shown on a large screen, and am still very impressed with the result and will most certainly be using this trick again.

23.2.6   Editing

Chris's company, Stage 2 Screen, had recently purchased a Targa 3000 off-line editing suite which was capable of handling images in full HD format, so at the end of shooting Panavision supplied him with a Sony HDW F500 VTR for an afternoon and he played all the material directly into the editing server. Initially, there were some issues with producing EDLs (Edit Decision Lists) as we had shot at 24P and the Targa was working at 25 fps, but these were quickly overcome. As this was Chris's first film on HD, he was determined to go down the 24P route and make no compromises; it was a brave decision as it was still quite early days for HD, but we both learnt so much on *Birthdays* that has stood both of us in good stead on later projects.

23.2.7   Viewings

I have now seen *Birthdays* on a 24-inch monitor, projected digitally and projected from a 35 mm print. I have to say I am very happy with the look of the pictures in all three presentation mediums. It seems that the pictures adapt themselves in some subtle way to each type of screen. What we have learnt is that for a top of the range digital projector, a tape graded on a well set up 24-inch monitor looks perfect. If, on the other hand, the digital projector is less than top of the range and will therefore not have as full a tonal range, making a tape copy with deeper blacks will improve the screen image immeasurably. Peter Swarbrick was the first to demonstrate this to me when we went to show another HD movie at the National Film Theatre in London. We were disappointed in the blacks even after carefully setting up the projector, when Peter made the blacks deeper simply with a control in the VTR. I therefore recommend you make two copies of your product if it is to be shown digitally, each to give the best picture depending on the grade of the projector. Do label them very carefully though, for if you get the wrong one on the wrong projector you will be very disappointed at the result.

Part 6

Post-Production

24
Post-production

While this book is primarily dedicated to an explanation of the HD process with regard to capturing the image, it seems necessary to touch briefly on some of the post-production issues that might affect other decisions that may need to be made before you set up the cutting room. There are also some matters which should be considered before shooting starts in respect of how you intend finally to deliver the movie.

24.1 Generations

There is a level at which, although it might be technically possible, it may be unwise to make too many succeeding copies of the original tape. When you make another copy it is referred to as making another generation, where the camera original is thought of as the first generation. I have canvassed several of the major post-production houses in Soho, London, and the general feeling is that to be absolutely certain you will have no problems it is best not to go more than six generations within the HDCAM format. This is no criticism of HDCAM, it is simply a precaution that one might adopt with any electromechanical tape format.

Allowing only six generations may, at first sight, seem restrictive, but with just a little forethought it is very easy to keep well within this parameter.

24.2 How the choice of edit suite affects the generation game

An efficient, secure and probably most expensive editing format would be to cut in a non-linear editing suite that works entirely within the HD standard of 1080 lines by 1920 horizontal pixels. With this system you would play all your camera master tapes into the edit server and there they would stay until you had arrived at your final locked-off cut. It would then be a simple matter to play out the finished product to a single HDCAM tape and this would become your cut master. You would probably then perform a tape-to-tape grade and from the graded master you would copy however many customer copies you need. At this time you would be very wise to simultaneously make a backup copy, identical in every way to the master, from which you intend to make your customer copies. The flow chart for this route is shown in Figure 24.1. The generations are shown as large grey numbers and, as you can see, using this route to your customer copy only requires going down a very safe and secure four generations.

Better still, if you have cut in the HD format why not arrange to grade the final cut while the material is still in the edit server? In a high-end post house this should be possible and would remove one generation of copy, the cut but ungraded master, from the chain. If this is possible it offers an even

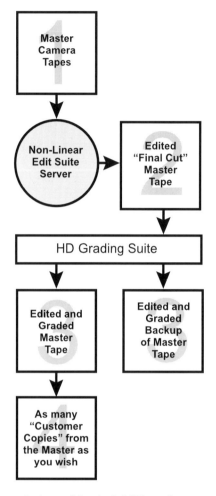

Figure 24.1 The generations created when editing in full HD quality

more secure route; its flow chart is shown in Figure 24.2 and again the generations are shown as large grey numbers. As you can see, the customer copy using this post-production route is now only a third generation copy.

Quite considerable cost savings can be made if a conventional non-linear edit suite, working with standard PAL or NTSC images, is used. The savings mount rapidly if you are likely to be editing for any appreciable length of time. There are basically two ways of approaching this: you can have an HD VTR in the edit suite all the time or you can have the HD camera master tapes transferred to Beta SP or Digi Beta and then play them into the edit server with a much cheaper VTR.

When you have arrived at a final locked-off cut, you ask the edit machine to produce an Edit Decision List (EDL), which is usually a record of all the time code positions of every cut or dissolve, or indeed any other effect the suite is capable of, and this is most often saved to a floppy disk. This floppy disk is then used to drive a conform suite consisting of two play-out HD VTRs and a record HD VTR, which work together to create a single tape with all the cuts etc. that you created in the cutting room. The play-out machines will hold the camera master tapes so the conformed master is still only a second generation copy. This conformed master will then go into a grading suite where it will be graded tape-to-tape to produce a conformed and graded master tape and this will be a third generation copy. At this point it is very wise to simultaneously make an identical backup copy.

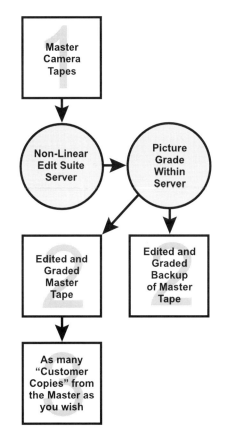

Figure 24.2 The generations created when editing in full HD quality and grading within the edit server

From the conformed and graded HD master you can make as many customer copies as you wish, safe in the knowledge that if there should be any disaster you still have an identical backup copy. Your customer copies will be fourth generation, still a very safe level of reproduction. Figure 24.3 shows the flow chart for an editing process that utilizes either down-converted broadcast standard tapes for the edit suite or HD tapes, and yet again the generation is shown as a large, grey, number.

24.3   The route to a film copy

Once you have a graded master copy of your final cut there is still a long way to go if you wish to end up with a film copy. It takes around a couple of seconds to write all the information from a single frame of picture onto conventional 35 mm film. It is impossible to pause an HD tape with sufficient stability of image to be writing for this amount of time. Most tape-to-film processes therefore transcribe the HD master tape into a large disk array having full random access facilities. It is now possible to pull down just the limited information the printer needs at any given moment in time.

There is a further problem; the information is stored on the tape in a very different way from the requirements of a disk array and the disk array may feed out information in a different way to the requirements of the photographic printing machine. It is in these conversion processes that the post house making your first photographic copy adds their signature to your work. Using a computer program often described as an algorithm, the post house makes these conversions and they can affect many of the parameters of the image, such as colour space, colour grading and overall density.

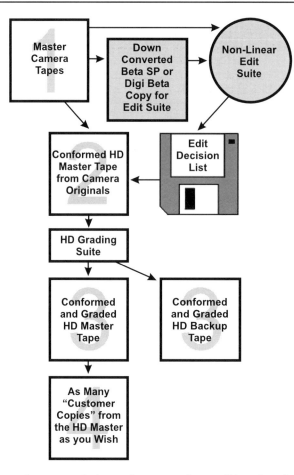

Figure 24.3 The generations created when going to non-linear editing via a down-converted tape

These conversions differ both in technical and artistic quality from post house to post house and will most likely produce differing results, again depending on the photochemical laboratory used to process the written out film and then make the release prints. This is the main reason I advocate so strongly making tests using both the camera and lenses you intend to use and sending this test right through your chosen post-production process some time before you commence principal photography.

What type of photographic master you make the first copy will depend, more than anything, on how many prints you envisage requiring. With some processes it is possible to go direct to a print, but as the transfer process from tape to film is very expensive it is more common to make an intermediary. If you are going to require a large number of prints you will need a greater number of negative copies to print from, as the mechanical life of a negative is limited. In this instance you would probably make your first copy an intermediate positive. From this you might make six intermediate negatives and each negative might print 50 times. You can now safely produce 300 prints.

If you only envisage needing less than 50 copies, you might go straight from your tape to an intermediate negative and make all your prints from this single negative.

It is possible to introduce conventional photochemical grading procedures at any point in the photographic process, though it is usually wiser to grade this way as early in the chain as possible.

Whatever route you choose, make a test right through the process and try and decide your route before you start shooting.

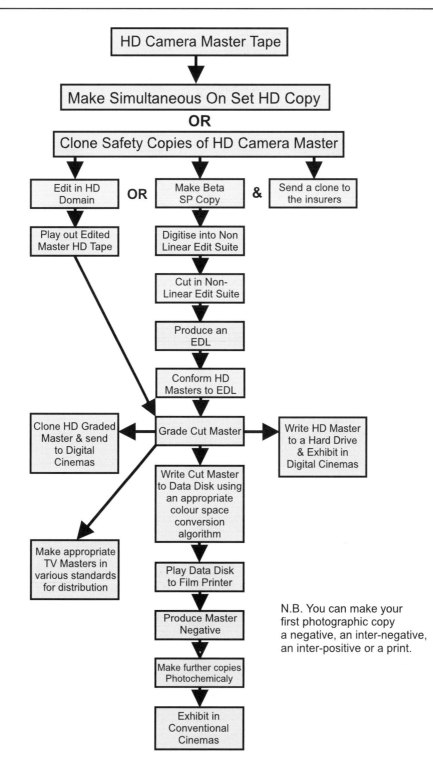

Figure 24.4 Post-production flow chart

24.4   Non-photographic distribution

24.4.1   An international standard

The introduction of the HDCAM format with its Common Image Format (CIF) system of recording has made it possible to lay down a standard for the international exchange of HD tapes. This has been decided as 24P HDCAM. Therefore, if you are intending to deliver your product on tape this is almost certainly your best option, for one of the main reasons it has been chosen is that a 24P signal can, more easily than any other available on HD, be converted into any local digital signal.

24.4.2   Where might it be shown?

You can take an HD tape and show it directly on an HD television station, down-convert it to standard definition television format, play it into a server in a cinema to show digitally, deliver it via satellite or fibre optic to a cinema, or even simply hook up an HD VTR to a digital projector in the cinema and show it from that. Once you have a 24P HDCAM master tape the possibilities are endless.

In order to try and display some of the options from camera master tape to final screen, look at Figure 24.4. The centre line of this flow chart shows the most common route from camera to cinema screen, which is to include a photographic print. Running alongside that route you can see some of the interesting digital-only routes, which are clearly shorter.

24.5   Time code considerations

Just as you should test in advance your film-out route, so you should test your non-linear edit suite with some tape shot with the camera set exactly as you intend to set it up for the shoot. You then need to make a few cuts and play out a tape and an EDL. The reason for this is that if your camera frame rate and the edit frame rate do not exactly match, it is possible that you can cut very successfully but the suite may make a nonsense of your EDL. This can happen, for instance, if you shoot at 24 fps but cut and try to play out at 25 fps. Some editing suites will do this happily and some may not. Make a test.

Part 7

The Sony HDW F900 Camera

25
The camera head

If you remove the lens from the camcorder you will find, just behind the lens mount, a fixed flat filter behind which are two discs which hold the four exposure control filters and the four colour control filters. Immediately behind those there is what appears to be another flat glass plate. It is not a plate but a very sophisticated beam splitter.

25.1   The infrared filter

The first piece of glass behind the lens is, in the Sony camera, a simple infrared filter. In the Panavision camera it is a little more sophisticated. The Panavision filter also absorbs infrared, but the wavelengths that are allowed to pass are extended.

One of the items that contributes to the 'video look' is the traditional red response of video cameras. If you look at Figure 25.1 you will see the three colours where the curves represent both the colour response of film and the human eye, for they are very similar. The dotted line to the right shows how a video camera is deficient in red response. Traditionally, camera manufacturers have corrected this by electronic amplification within the camera's circuits. It is this amplification that causes deep reds to appear as deep orange.

Panavision have taken a different approach. By modifying the infrared filter and by using sophisticated coatings within their lenses, they have extended the amount of red entering the splitter block in such a way as to compensate for the deficiency of the red receptor. They then turn the red amplifica-

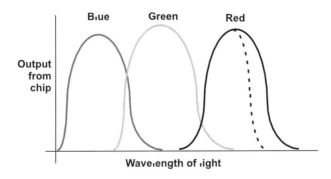

Figure 25.1 Three-chip video camera colorimetry

tion down considerably. This allows the Panavision 900F to create a colour image which is considerably more acceptable to eyes trained in the film world.

25.2   The filter wheels

Just behind the infrared filter there are two filter wheels, each containing four filters. One wheel contains a clear glass and three neutral density filters. These filters represent respectively no reduction in exposure, a reduction of two stops, a reduction of four stops and a reduction in exposure of six stops. On the Panavision camera, the label on the camera telling you the value of each setting on the wheel is marked both in stops and in the density value. The stops are as above and the density values are marked as CLEAR, 0.6, 1.2 and 1.8. The Sony camera marks them quite differently as CLEAR, 1/16, 1/32 and 1/64, thus showing the reduction in exposure as a fraction of the exposure using the clear glass.

The second filter wheel deals with colour correction and is the same on both the Panavision camera and the Sony camera. This I find strange, for coming from a film background I think Sony overcorrect the colour temperature and I would have expected Panavision to install conventional film correction. The four filters on the colour correction filter wheel are: CROSS, a four-point star filter, 3200K, 4300K and 6300K. The international nominal daylight that is used in film requires a correction to 5600K and I would prefer this sometimes, so in those cases I leave the setting to 3200K and put a conventional Wratten 85 filter in the matte box.

When rotating either the neutral density wheel or the colour compensation wheel, do make sure that when you stop rotating the wheel it is firmly in the indent and therefore correctly positioned.

25.3   The beam splitter

In order for a modern video camera to function, the image from the lens must be split up into its red, green and blue components, and each of the resultant images must then be delivered to a receptor dedicated to that colour. This is because the receptors representing each pixel are only brightness sensitive; they have little or no sensitivity to colour. It is therefore necessary to present each of the three sensors with only the colour they are to interpret.

While all this separation is happening, it is vital that each colour image travels through a light path which contains identical amounts of both air and glass. In order for this to be achieved three prisms are cemented together, as in Figure 25.2. Between the mating surfaces of the prisms are two dichroic mirrors, one reflecting blue light only and the other red only. Dichroic mirrors are used instead of filters because they enable a far brighter image to be separated.

A dichroic mirror works on the principle of coating a sheet of glass with interference layers which have both a low and a high refractive index. These layers have a thickness of approximately one-quarter of the wavelength of the light which is to be separated. For instance, a mirror which has a maximum output of 700 nanometres (nm) and a minimum output of 350 nm is therefore a red reflecting mirror. If the sheet of glass upon which the mirror is coated were to have a higher refractive index than the layer, then the maximum output will be 350 nm and it is therefore a blue reflecting mirror.

Looking at Figure 25.2 you will see that a full, three-colour image enters the block and arrives at the first interface which holds the blue dichroic mirror. All the blue portion of the image is then reflected away, and is then reflected a second time by the outer surface of this, the first prism, finally exiting this prism and arriving at the blue image receptor.

Both the red and green elements of the image pass cleanly through the blue dichroic mirror and the second prism in the block. At the back of the second prism is the red dichroic mirror, which separates off the red portion of the image, sending it to the far side of that prism, where it is reflected yet again and exits this prism to arrive at the red image sensor.

The green image, having passed cleanly through both the blue and the red mirrors, travels through the third prism to arrive at the green image sensor.

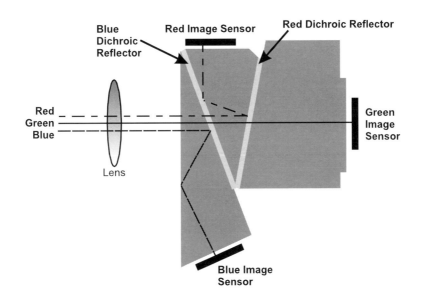

Figure 25.2 Light path through a video camera beam splitter

   The third prism may look unnecessarily thick; this is to add sufficient glass to the light path of the green image for it to match exactly the distance travelled by those of both the red and blue light paths. This is essential, for the taking lens will have formed an image in which all colours arrive at their point of focus precisely the same distance from the back of the lens.

25.4   The head amplifiers

Immediately behind, indeed virtually attached to them, each sensor chip has a dedicated amplifier. This is necessary because the output from each pixel sensor is very small and must be increased before the subsequent processing stages can successfully be accomplished.

   At this early stage the signal is not yet in its digital form; as light is an analogue phenomenon, the output from the chips is also analogue. Immediately after the head amplifiers, the signal is sent to a circuit which interprets the values into separate digital values. Every processing board in the camera from now on will be functioning in the digital domain. It is from this fact, the image being turned into a digital signal so early, that the camera attains its extraordinary reliability and repeatability.

26
Digital imaging

26.1 The history of digits

It is widely thought that one Claude Elwood Shannon, who died at the age of 84 in 2001, single-handedly laid the foundation for what became known as information theory, that branch of mathematics concerning the transmission of data in a digital form.

In what has been called the most important Masters Thesis of the twentieth century, *A Symbolic Analysis of Relay and Switching Circuits*, published in 1938, he first put forward the notion that it was possible to solve problems simply by manipulating two symbols – one and zero – in an automated electrical circuit.

Later, in his work *A Mathematical Theory of Communication*, he first coined the term 'bit' as the fundamental unit of information which encapsulates digital certainty as in true or false, on or off, yes or no. He was also the first to show how to design circuits to store and manipulate bits. It was Shannon who set in motion the route to the compact disc, cyberspace, digital television and the digital movie camera.

I think I should have rather liked Claude Shannon, for although preferring to work alone, he was friendly and liked to start his day at noon with a game of chess against the director of the Mathematics Centre at MIT, then working on late into the evening. He had a fascination for juggling and produced a paper on the underlying mathematics of juggling. While working at the Bell Labs, he could occasionally be seen juggling while riding a unicycle down the halls.

26.2 Colour depth

An often overlooked parameter of the feel of a camera's picture quality is colour depth. In a digital camera the whole tonal range is broken up into very small units and each unit is assigned a value. The number of units that constitute the complete tonal range of each individual pixel determines the colour depth; more units equals greater depth. Also, the more units that are used to record the complete tonal range of the picture, the smoother will be the transition from one tone to another and the subtler will be the final image.

Before we explore this function of the camera we need to understand how a digital camera records tonality and it is here the name digital is derived.

If, for instance, you decided to divide the complete tonal range of the image into 1000 parts from each pixel's output, and should you record them mathematically, you would have to read any number between 0 and 1000. This would be complicated as your recording and playback process would have to be capable of recognizing 1000 different units of measurement.

In order to overcome this the digital camera records using a binary code. A binary code uses a combination of zeros and ones to write any value. The number of zeros and ones you use in the code determines the number of different values you can record.

If you are only going to use two combinations of zeros and ones you can write four combinations, which are:

00, 01, 10 and 11.

Already you have two advantages. You only have to use two numbers in order to write, in code, any of four values. Secondly, and just as important, your recording and playback machines only have to recognize either a zero or a one, the equivalent of ON or OFF, and even a pretty stupid machine can tell if it is on or off. It also needs to understand the code in order to write or reconstitute the zeros and ones into a picture; fortunately, with modern electronics this is relatively easy.

In the example above, we have only used two digits in our code. Or, in digital speak, we have recorded using 2 bits of information to write our code, hence this would be known as a 2-bit format.

Very fortunately, as we start to use more bits to write our code the number of values we can encode goes up quite astonishingly. The F900 camera head is working in a 12-bit code, so let us see how many values that might be able to handle.

If we increase our code length to 4 bits, we can record 16 values as there are that many combinations available; these are:

0000, 0001, 0010, 0011, 0100, 0101, 0110, 0111, 1000, 1001, 1010, 1011, 1100, 1101, 1110 and 1111.

The mathematical function works like this. If you had a 1-bit code you could only record two values, the first represented by zero and a second represented by one. Increasing the code to 2 bits multiplies the number of values by 2. In fact, every time you add a digit to the code you will increase the number of values you can record by a multiplication of 2. Figure 26.1 shows the progression up to the remarkable 4096 values recorded by the F900's 12-bit encoding system.

If you were to be reading the specification of a camera, you might not think there was a huge difference between one where the camera head uses a 10-bit code and one using a 12-bit code, but as we have seen the difference is between the tonal scale being broken down into 1024 values and 4096 values. This might make a huge difference to the perceived picture quality.

1-bit	0											
	$2 = 2$ values											
2-bit	0	1										
	$2 \times 2 = 4$ values											
4-bit	0	1	0	1								
	$2 \times 2 \times 2 \times 2 = 16$ values											
6-bit	0	1	0	1	0	1						
	$2 \times 2 \times 2 \times 2 \times 2 \times 2 = 64$ values											
8-bit	0	1	0	1	0	1	0	1				
	$2 \times 2 \times 2 \times 2 \times 2 \times 2 \times 2 \times 2 = 256$ values											
10-bit	0	1	0	1	0	1	0	1	0	1		
	$2 \times 2 \times 2 \times 2 \times 2 \times 2 \times 2 \times 2 \times 2 \times 2 = 1024$ values											
12-bit	0	1	0	1	0	1	0	1	0	1	0	1
	$2 \times 2 \times 2 \times 2 \times 2 \times 2 \times 2 \times 2 \times 2 \times 2 \times 2 \times 2 = 4096$ values											

Figure 26.1 The effect of adding more bits to the binary code

26.3 Resolution

The finite resolution of the camera, as distinct from the lens, is determined by the number of pixels available in the taking area. In the F900 camera, each chip has a picture area containing 1080 pixels from top to bottom and 1920 pixels from side to side, giving a total of 2 073 600 pixels per chip. It should be remembered that there is one chip dedicated to each of the primary colours and therefore the whole colour picture is made up of the aggregate of the three chips – 6 220 800 pixels.

One often hears arguments as to the image resolution needed to satisfy the human eye on a large cinema screen. Many, predominantly from the post-production community, will claim that a '4K' resolution is required and that the F900 camera is inadequate for it only has a '2K' resolution, the 'K' in this instance referring to the number of horizontal pixels used. 'K' in this context represents 1000.

Yet the evidence on the screen clearly shows that pictures originated on the F900 are at least as sharp as any other from whatever source. One should not always be swayed by any other argument than the evidence of your own eyes in these matters. As I have said elsewhere, one of my favourite sayings is 'if it looks right it is right'.

26.4 Data quantity

It is interesting to note the quantity of data being processed just behind the three chips in the camera. First, let us look at the information we are trying to record. We have seen that there are 6 220 800 pixels being deployed to capture the whole image and that each pixel's digital output can have the choice of 4096 different values. Therefore, the total number of options is:

6 220 800 × 4096 = 25 480 396 800.

This, of course, is not necessarily the number of units being recorded, just the number of options. What the camera has to record is the 12-bit binary code from every pixel and this sum goes as follows:

1080 vertical pixels × 1920 horizontal pixels × 3 chips × 12 bits of binary code per pixel = 74 649 600 bits of information per picture.

That is all very well but we are recording a moving image and even at the camera's slowest frame rate of 24 fps a single second of moving image will require:

74 649 600 × 24 = 1 791 590 400 bits of information to be recorded each second.

Just for fun, a complete recording tape lasting 50 minutes at 24 fps will store:

1 791 590 400 bits × 60 seconds × 50 minutes = 5 374 771 200 000 bits of information per tape.

Quite astounding!

27
Frame rates and scanning

27.1 Frame rates

The F900 camera can be set to run at eight frame rates: five are progressive scan and three are interlace. The first three to consider are those that replicate conventional film shooting rates. They are:

- 24 fps progressive scan – exactly replicates the cinema projection rate.
- 25 fps progressive scan – exactly replicates the frame rate used when shooting film for European television using the PAL transmission system.
- 30 fps progressive scan – exactly replicates the frame rate used for shooting high quality commercials in the USA.

The next two progressive scan frame rates are exclusively for use when replicating film shot for television, and when it will only ever be shown on the US NTSC television transmission system. They are:

- 23.98 progressive scan – replicates film shot only for television transmission on NTSC where the 3:2 pull-down system is to be used.
- 29.97 progressive scan – replicates film shot only for television transmission on NTSC where frame-for-frame transfer is to be used.

In addition there are three interlace frame rates. These are:

- 50i – for use when shooting exclusively for the European PAL system where an interlace image is required, sport perhaps (see later).
- 60i – for use when shooting pure US NTSC standard.
- 59.94i – for use when greater compatibility with the US NTSC transmission format is required.

The choice of the best frame rate to shoot at can be complicated and confusing, as your post-production route can sometimes be a greater influence than anything else.

27.2 Interlace scanning

Traditional television systems scan the pixels on the odd-numbered lines first, as in lines 1, 3, 5, 7, 9, etc., and then return to the top of the picture to scan the even-numbered lines as in 2, 4, 6, 8, 10, etc. How the picture is segmented is shown in Figure 27.1. For the small screen, and for transmission, this has some advantages. Its disadvantages, however, show up dramatically when the picture is transferred to film and shown on a theatrical sized screen.

Original Scene   Lace Scans   Interlace Scans

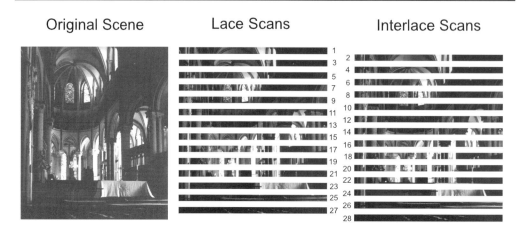

Figure 27.1 The effect of splitting up an image into lace and interlace scans

27.3   Interlace motion artefacts

In Figure 27.2 the picture will both scan and reproduce quite well, even on a theatrical screen, but let us analyse how the exposure was actually made. Motion picture film is projected at 24 frames per second (fps) and the nearest interlace frame rate the F900 camera can achieve in an interlace format to that rate is 50i. An interlace rate of 50i dictates that the lace lines will be scanned in one-fiftieth of a second, followed by the interlaced lines also being scanned in one-fiftieth of a second; thus, the whole

Figure 27.2 Original scene – no motion

image will have been recorded in one-twenty-fifth of a second, very close to 24 fps. But this is not the whole story.

If you think of the exposure time for the whole image, you might expect image blur to be the same as a still camera taking the same picture at one-twenty-fifth of a second – you would be quite wrong.

The edge definition of the image will actually be dictated by the exposure time of a single line of information. As we are shooting at an interlace rate of 50i a lace, or interlace, line will be scanned in one-fiftieth of a second divided by 540, the number of lines scanned in one-fiftieth of a second and half the total number of lines. Therefore the shutter speed, if you will, for a single line will be one-twenty-seven-thousandth of a second. That is:

$$\frac{1}{50 \times 540} = \frac{1}{27\,000}$$

Therefore the edge definition of any moving object will be very sharp indeed and this degree of edge definition is not natural to the human eye.

There are further complications. If you look at Figure 27.2 and imagine that the camera is still, the sky does not move but the balloon is floating from the left of the picture to the right, how would a picture created using an interlace scanning format record the image? As we have seen, the image will be cut up into lace and interlace lines; this will not affect the sky for it is still, but the balloon will be a little further to the right as each line is scanned. Further, after the lace scan is completed, the interlace scan will commence and by this time the balloon will be even further to the right.

If you look at Figure 27.3 you will see an exaggerated depiction of this. What has occurred is referred to as a temporal (time) artefact. There are two unnatural effects. Firstly, the balloon has become lozenged shaped. During the lace scan the bottom of the balloon has been dragged to the right with respect to the top of the balloon; this is shown as dark lines. Exactly the same thing happens to

Figure 27.3 Movement photographed using interlace scanning

the interlace scan, with the additional problem that the top of the balloon is now further to the right than the bottom of the balloon at the end of the lace scan; this is shown as lighter lines. This is because as one line follows another, the balloon will have moved a little further to the right of frame.

On a television screen these errors are so physically small that we hardly perceive them and we have all watched television so much by now that our eye/brain combination has come to accept that this is correct. We do not, however, accept it in the cinema, where it can look very odd indeed.

It is interesting to note that there is a prominent school of thought that for some subjects the interlace method of scanning is preferable, at least on television. Think, for instance, of a sports programme, particularly golf. When those shots where the camera operator follows a flying golf ball in quite a tight shot with an interlace picture are displayed as two sets of lines, the edges of the ball will be sharp. As we shall see, if this were photographed on film or in a progressive scan mode the ball would be a perfect circle but would also be quite out of focus due to movement blur.

27.4 Progressive scan motion artefacts

Unlike interlace scanning the F900 camera, when in progressive scan mode, does not scan the pixels during the exposure. The pixels are switched to expose for the time set in the menu and at the end of that time exposure mode is switched off and read mode is switched on. When the predetermined shutter closed time has elapsed the pixels will switch back to expose mode. This might be described as single image capture. This effect is perhaps more important to the cinematographer than the fact that the pixels, during the read period, are scanned progressively.

The nearest analogy I can think of is to ask you to imagine a pixel to be a bucket standing out in the rain, where rain represents light, with a lid on its top and a tap on its bottom. Starting with the lid on and the tap closed, the exposure sequence would go like this:

Lid on – tap closed.
Lid comes off – bucket begins to fill.
At end of exposure time – lid closes.
Tap opens and we measure the amount of water in the bucket.
When all the water has run out the tap closes.
Lid opens for next exposure.

So what we have is a discrete exposure time separated from the read time, exactly the same as a film camera, where a discrete exposure time is separated from the pull-down time by a mechanical shutter.

Just to be pedantic there is a very slight difference in the effect of a switched shutter in the F900 and the rotating shutter in a film camera. In the F900, both opening and closing the shutter is completely instantaneous. In a film camera, the mechanical shutter will spend just a fraction of the exposure time crossing the frame during both opening and closing. This will happen in either a vertical or horizontal manner depending on the design of the camera. This is a next to irrelevant matter in real terms. As no one I know can tell from an image projected on a screen whether the camera shutter was running horizontally or vertically, they are hardly likely to be able to tell if it was instantaneous. In theory an instantaneous shutter is an advantage: witness the fact that camera designers try and incorporate as large a diameter shutter as is practicable in order to reduce the opening and closing transition time.

If our balloon were to be photographed using either film or the F900 camera set to progressive scan, we would expect the image to be very different to that described for an interlace recording. There will be no distortion due to the passage of time, but there will be some motion blur just as there would be if you used a still camera at a similar, relatively slow, shutter speed. Figure 27.4 shows this effect. The balloon is now slightly out of focus due to motion blur, and on the trailing and leading edges there is a partial exposure due to the balloon moving during the exposure and therefore leaving less exposure over these areas. This is good.

Bear with me and carry out a little experiment. Hold your hand out at arm's length from you with your fingers apart and raised vertically. Now, watching your hand carefully, wave it reasonably rapidly from side to side. Your fingers should look blurred at the edges and darker in the middle

Figure 27.4 Film and 24P motion blur

of the finger than at their edges, exactly like our balloon. This motion artefact is therefore desirable as it replicates the way the eye/brain perceives movement.

One thing to note: you probably were only able to perceive the phenomenon acting upon your fingers because I asked you to concentrate on them and watch carefully. In normal life, your eye/brain combination would simply have accepted it as quite natural.

27.5 Three/two pull-down

This method of displaying a film or tape shot at 24 fps only applies in the US NTSC domain. The US television system is based on their 60 Hz mains supply and is so organized as to show a complete frame in one-thirtieth of a second, the lace part of the image lasting one-sixtieth of a second followed by the interlace portion shown in the following sixtieth of a second. Clearly there is a discrepancy between the conventional cinema frame rate and the American television frame rate.

This is overcome by what is known as the 3:2 pull-down method, so named for a film telecine machine is so organized as to pull the film through in this stuttering manner. The same basic solution is used for an HD tape shot at 24 fps when shown on American television.

The scanning sequence needs to increase the available frames by one-quarter, so the scan is organized to go as follows:

1st film frame	One lace scan + one interlace scan
2nd film frame	One lace scan + one interlace scan + one extra lace scan
3rd film frame	One interlace scan + one lace scan
4th film frame	One interlace scan + one lace scan + one extra interlace scan
5th film frame	One lace scan + one interlace scan
6th film frame	One lace scan + one interlace scan + one extra lace scan

7th film frame   One interlace scan + one lace scan
8th film frame   One interlace scan + one lace scan + one extra interlace scan
9th film frame   One lace scan + one interlace scan
And so on

Clearly this will give rise to a certain amount of motion stutter, particularly with horizontal motion. Most of the American public are so used to seeing their movies on television scanned this way that they are hardly aware of it, but a European asked to watch a film scanned in this way will almost certainly realize something is amiss, even if they cannot put their finger on what it might be.

The Sony HDW F500 desktop digital recorder/player can be fitted with an extra board to allow an HD tape shot at 24 fps to directly output in the 3:2 pull-down format, so that any device downstream of it will believe it is being fed from a telecine operating in this mode. It is possible, with the correct boards installed, to output this directly as an NTSC signal still in the 3:2 format.

27.6   An argument for 30 fps

If you were shooting exclusively for US television there is a strong argument for setting the camera to 30 or 29.97 fps. These are the frame rates used for very high quality commercials in this environment. Shooting film at 30 fps is usually considered to be too expensive and it is more usual to shoot narrative scripts at 24 fps and telecine them using the 3:2 pull-down system simply to save 20 per cent of the film stock and processing costs.

With the introduction of very high quality digital projectors into cinemas, you might find yourself in a position where you knew you were only ever going to have your product shown this way and decide to shoot HD at 30 fps. This would also apply if you added a US television transmission to the mix, but not if you know you need a theatrical print at 24 fps. Virtually all high quality digital projectors can show images at 30 fps simply at the throw of a switch. As increasing the frame rate from 24 to 30 fps measurably improves motion artefacts and dramatically reduces flicker, particularly in the highlights, there is a very strong argument for adopting this frame rate when appropriate.

Indeed, in 1988 the SMPTE (Society of Motion Picture and Television Engineers of America) published a report urging the cinema industry to convert to 30 fps as they were convinced the increased quality of motion rendition, reduction in flicker and increase in perceived definition were well worth the extra 20 per cent in film and processing costs. They were totally ignored by the industry.

My belief is we should keep a very careful watch on this decision when shooting HD. When shooting at 24 fps a camera tape lasts 50 minutes and costs something like £50 or $70. That's £1.00 or $1.40 per minute. When shooting at 30 fps, a camera tape lasts 40 minutes and therefore the cost will be £1.25 or $1.75 per minute. Surely now we have HD we can afford 25 pence or 35 cents a minute of screen time in order to gain such a considerable increase in picture quality?

28
The on-board VTR

28.1 The HDCAM format

The HDCAM format writes the information to the tape in exactly the same way whether it is recording a progressive scan or an interlace scan image. Every frame in either scanning format is recorded as a totally separate and individual part of the recording. Each picture frame is recorded in 12 diagonal stripes across the tape. This, and the phenomenal head to tape speed required to record such a huge amount of information, is achieved by using a helical scanning drum (see below).

Four playback and record heads are used, with newly introduced signal processing and error correction and concealment circuits so powerful that perfect pictures can be recorded and replayed even if one of the four heads completely ceases to function.

Each frame is laid down onto the tape as two separate segments; this must not be confused with the way an interlace picture has traditionally been recorded, it is a completely different process. When recording a 24 fps progressive scan image, each segment will be laid down in one-forty-eighth of a second. This is known as the segmented frame format and is approved by the ITU (International Television Union) in its recommendation 709-3.

28.2 Helical scan

If the tape were to travel straight past a static recording head, as in a conventional sound-only tape recorder, the tape would have to travel at a terrific speed to be able to record the quantity of information being delivered by the recording head. The use of a helical scanning drum maintains the required record head to tape speed while dramatically reducing the linear tape speed.

It does this by wrapping the tape, which is half an inch wide, around most of a drum, approximately 3 inches (75 cm) in diameter. As can be seen in Figure 28.1, the tape is not wrapped around the centre of the drum but makes first contact at one edge and leaves the drum adjacent to the opposite edge. The tape path has therefore described part of a helix, a shape just like one turn on a screw thread, and from this comes the term helical scan.

This helical wrapping of the tape would not, in itself, increase the record head to tape speed but, as the drum is made to rotate, the relative head-to-tape contact speed is dramatically increased. There are four record heads, each halfway between the outside edges of the drum and spaced at 90° angles around the drum. As the tape is wrapped around more than 180° of the drum, and there are four heads on the drum, there will always be at least two heads in contact with the tape. Because the tape is wrapped in a helix around the drum, the recording head will, relative to the tape, travel not only along the tape but from one edge of the tape to the other. By switching the record heads on and off sequentially, strips of recording can be laid down at a shallow angle across the tape, as shown in

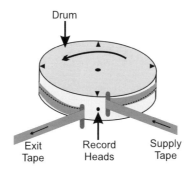

Figure 28.1 The helical scan recording drum

Figure 28.2. In addition, there are a series of linear, static, recording heads to lay down several control tracks and the time code track.

28.3   Mechanical considerations

While the VTR might not be quite as robust as we might wish it to be, this is mainly a result of weight requirements. If treated with respect, the VTR will give years of unfaltering service. It does, after all, come from a fine and very reliable lineage – the Digi Beta camera and before that the Beta SP camera. In both these cameras it proved to be very reliable indeed.

28.4   The scanning drum

The scanning drum is made to the highest accuracy, while being very light. The use of high quality materials and the manufacturers' considerable experience in designing portable video recorders ensures that there will be little or no difficulty in obtaining reliability, providing the operator understands how to treat the device. The drum is so light not just as a contribution to the portability of the camera as a whole, but to reduce the inertia associated with spinning the drum at a high speed. This reduction in the inertia of the drum brings two benefits: it can be brought up to operational speed very quickly and will consume very little power to keep it spinning. This second factor reduces the drain on the battery and therefore indirectly contributes to a reduction in the weight of the on-board battery.

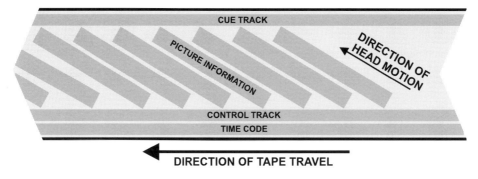

Figure 28.2 Layout of information on HDCAM tape

28.4.1 The drum lacing mechanism

In order to remove a loop of tape from the cassette and wrap it around three-quarters of the drum, the mechanism has, first, to open the door of the cassette as it enters the door of the VTR. Two rollers then come behind the short, straight, length of tape that is free at the mouth of the cassette. These rollers then travel round the drum in a circle larger than the diameter of the drum but allowing the tape to wrap around the drum. Again, due to weight considerations, this mechanism is made of high quality but very light materials.

28.5 Operational considerations

There is little chance of the VTR failing to operate, though there are precautions that should be taken. While the cassette door opens by itself it must be closed manually; please do this gently but firmly. Experience with old and tired SP and Digi Beta cameras leads some operators to bang it shut; banging it shut will eventually lead to its having always to be banged shut and this is doing no good at all to the mechanisms contained within the VTR.

28.6 A jammed mechanism

Perhaps this is a good moment to mention an invasive operation that one, occasionally, has to carry out on the camera. On the opposite side of the camera to the operator, at the bottom of the camera casing, roughly halfway along the camera body, is a rubber plug about a centimetre in diameter. If you remove this plug it reveals a red plastic button with a Philips type cross-head slot in it.

Should you have an electrical breakdown such that the camera will not unlace the tape and let you remove the cassette you can, with the camera switched off, insert a cross-head screwdriver into this button and, turning it *anticlockwise*, very, very gently hand crank the lace/unlace mechanism, thus allowing you to retrieve the cassette. A warning – if you turn this button clockwise you will very likely damage the lacing mechanism. Strangely, there is no easily visible indication on the camera as to which way one should turn the button, though if you look very closely at the button you will see the tiniest arrow, but it is almost invisible. The gear ratio is very low, so this will take some time. I have had to do this a couple of times and would counsel you to carry out this procedure only as a last resort. It is much safer for your tape and your camera if you can get the camera back to the supplier, where a more thorough and safer method can be deployed. You should only consider this mechanical unlacing of the camera if your rushes on the tape are very important and retrieving them is a matter of the greatest urgency.

Part 8

A Selection of Other Cameras and Equipment

29

The Panavision HDW 900F and its system

Panavision have taken the production of their version of the camera very seriously. At first glance it might seem to be the basic Sony camera with a clever lens and a few film style bits and pieces, but this is very far from the case. Figure 29.1 shows a Panavision camera built up with a 4:1 zoom, follow focus, etc. The original camera is shown as a pale image and all the Panavision parts are shown in their full density; from this you can see just how extensive are the modifications and the additional equipment that is available. The rig shown is far from the limit of the number of accessories that you might choose to add to the camera, such as on-board monitors, electronic zoom controls, scale illumination light and many other helpful parts which may be fitted.

29.1 External modifications

29.1.1 The top handle

As can be seen in Figure 29.2, the original handle on top of the camera has been completely removed and replaced with a handle of an entirely different configuration. Near the front of the new handle there is a wedge which is fitted to the camera with a quick release catch; at the rear of the handle there is a female dovetail on the camera into which the male dovetail on the handle fits; on the top of the handle there is a locking wheel. The front portion of the handle has a drilled plate, which is there to enable the camera to be underslung on a Steadycam rig. Milled into this plate is a slot into which the camera control unit can be fixed.

There is also another version of the top plate available which has a reduced handle size and a considerably increased mounting plate with many drilled holes. This might be useful if you are planning to mount the camera from the top plate in some unconventional manner.

29.1.2 The viewfinder support

Just ahead of the handle, and below it, is a carrier and lock for a pair of rails that at the front carry a long dovetail plate on which the viewfinder can be mounted. The rails are quite long so that, with the viewfinder extension removed, the shortened viewfinder can be positioned well ahead of the handle so that the eyepiece can be positioned in exactly the right relationship to the shoulder pad under the camera for comfortable hand holding.

In Figure 29.3 the camera is shown in a hand-held configuration. I have used the camera rigged in this way very successfully. A prime lens is fitted to reduce weight and size, the HD SDI box and the battery are removed and Panavision 'Bull's Horns' hand-held hand grips are fitted. When using the

Figure 29.1 Panavision additions and modifications to the Sony camera

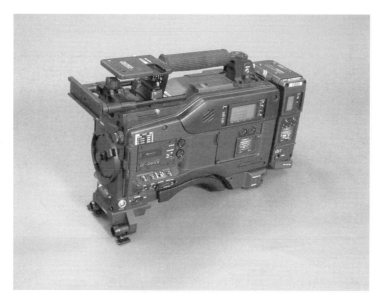

Figure 29.2 The Panavision camera body

camera in this configuration I expect the camera grip to be following me, probably wearing a 12-volt battery belt to power the camera, and I will have persuaded the director to accept a black and white monitor picture so that there will only be a single BNC lead coming out of the side of the camera from the Y socket.

This is a very manageable and operator-friendly way to use the Panavision camera.

29.1.3 The viewfinder

The Panavision viewfinder comes in three parts, as can be seen in Figure 29.4. There is an attachment bracket which fits onto the camera viewfinder support rails, into which can be locked either the

Figure 29.3 The Panavision camera in hand-held mode

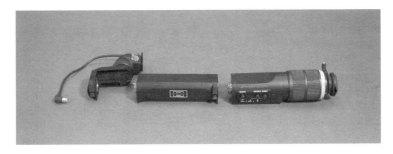

Figure 29.4 Exploded view of the Panavision viewfinder

viewfinder itself or the viewfinder extension unit. If the viewfinder extension unit is to be used then the viewfinder itself locks into the end of the extension unit. The locks are very positive, so there is no physical rattle in this unit. There is no degradation in the image in the viewfinder when using the extension unit, as it is only a box containing 12 wires.

29.1.4 The camera front plate and lens mount

Panavision removed all the external parts of the original Sony B4 lens mount and replaced it with one of its own, which has the same configuration as its motion picture mount but is, in fact, slightly larger. This is facilitated by completely replacing the front plate of the camera. The new lens mount is so large and robust that there is now insufficient space for the camera control plate and this is why Panavision fit this plate into its own casing and fit it with a flying lead, enabling it to be mounted in a number of positions around the camera.

When Panavision first decided to join forces with Sony to produce a camera and lens combination for George Lucas to use on *Star Wars II*, Panavision chose to develop a version of the existing 11:1

zoom lens; this lens was originally designed for their 35 mm film cameras. Due to the imaging chip in the digital camera being two and a half times smaller than a 35 mm frame, the new lens had to produce the smaller image but, in addition, become two and a half times sharper to allow for the greater magnification when shown in the cinema. All subsequent Panavision lenses have been specifically computed for HD and have at least the same resolving power.

The only problem with this 11:1 zoom lens was its weight – 8.5 kg ($18\frac{3}{4}$ pounds); there was no way a Sony B4 lens mount was going to support a lens of this weight, so a new front plate to the camera and a reconfigured lens mount became essential.

Just below the lens mount there is a socket to enable a conventional video lens to be driven from the camera. At the bottom of this plate, and on the operator side of the camera, is a new socket into which the flying lead going to the camera control unit plugs in.

29.1.5　The camera base plate

Panavision completely removed the original camera base plate. It has to be said that most camera technicians from the film world find Sony's method of attaching the camera to a tripod most unsatisfactory; put bluntly it simply is not rigid enough. There are two distinct advantages to the new method of mounting the camera; by fitting a standard Panavision dovetail great rigidity is achieved. This dovetail has an extension bar going right to the back of the camera, where there is a very strong locking block tensioned by a knurled screw. As the camera is longer, front to back, than most film cameras, the considerable length of this extension bar gives the camera/tripod junction great rigidity in all three dimensions.

The new front base plate of the camera has two wings left and right and, slightly below the dovetail, these wings carry the mounting and locking units for the rails that can extend forward of the camera to carry all the lens accessories you would expect to be able to attach to any Panavision film camera. The positioning of the rail mounts has been arranged to have exactly the same relationship to the optical centre of the lens mount, again allowing total compatibility with the company's film cameras.

29.1.6　The voltage distribution box

On the opposite side of the camera to the operator, and at the front of the camera body, there is a plate with three dovetails. Several accessories can be fitted on these dovetails but the rear of the three is usually used to hold the voltage distribution box, as shown in Figure 29.5. There are two sockets at the rear of the box, the top of which takes a lead from the back of the camera carrying the 12-volt supply. The lower socket is a dedicated supply for the eyepiece heater known as Panaclear. The front of the box has four outlets, two giving 12 volts and two supplying 24 volts.

This box is very useful, for most professional video cameras work on 12 volts and although some film cameras work off 12 volts, many now run off 24 volts. By giving both outputs it is possible to power any camera accessory from either world, no matter which voltage it requires.

29.2　Internal modifications: the internal filter

Panavision have only carried out one physical modification within the camera and have made two significant modifications to the electronic specifications.

The physical modification has been simple but significant. If you look into the camera lens port there is a fixed filter immediately visible; this is in front of the two in-camera filter wheels. This filter has been changed from the Sony specification so that, in combination with the Panavision lenses, the way red is processed and recorded is much more like the spectral analysis of the human eye, and film, than any previous video camera. Hence, as we have seen in other chapters of this book, one of the video 'signatures', that of dark reds being recorded as dark orange, no longer happens.

Figure 29.5 The Panavision voltage distribution box

29.3 Electronic modifications

29.3.1 Red amplification

The first electronic modification relates to the above. In most video cameras the inability of the camera to be sensitive to enough red frequencies of light is compensated for by electronically amplifying the red signal. As Panavision have cured this problem optical in their cameras they dramatically turn down this red amplifier.

29.3.2 Electronic definition enhancement

Traditionally, video cameras have had circuits within them to improve the apparent sharpness of the image. It is relatively simple, electronically, to make a hard edge in a scene look harder or, therefore, sharper. This is done primarily for two reasons: either the recording format is not up to the required level of data information storage or the lens in use is simply not up to the job. Both reasons usually pertain. In the video world recording formats have to be cheap and lightweight, and therefore are not going to be capable of recording the amount of data required for a first class image. The HDCAM format overcomes the recording problem.

The price video professionals have been used to paying for their lenses is much less than film crews have been used to. Despite this, video cinematographers expect a huge zoom range, a wide maximum aperture and light weight, as they might often have to put the camera on their shoulder.

There is another way of enhancing the apparent sharpness of a video image, which is more subtle than simple edge enhancement. It requires the electronic circuits to analyse the central fine detail of an image and decide which parts of this information are essential and which are not. The essential parts will then be recorded.

Everything described above has worked exceptionally well for television. When Digi Beta was introduced many years ago its introduction was derided by some traditionalists for having something like a two times compression ratio in its recording format and having at least three electronic levels of image enhancement. Digi Beta is now the standard by which all subsequent formats are judged – how things have moved on.

But with the introduction of a truly high definition tape format, which has ambitions to be seen on a large cinema screen, things have changed again.

The Panavision camera, with its associated lenses, has taken the whole format another step forward. They were determined to throw off the 'video look' and the modifications to the camera, and the Primo Digital lenses enabled them to turn down to a minimum the red amplifier and turn off, completely, all the image enhancement circuits – their lenses are quite sharp enough without this assistance.

29.4   Why Panavision HD?

There is no doubt that at least some of the product going from set to cinema screen will move from a photochemical recording medium to a digital tape medium. The important thing for me, as a DoP, is that the pictures are still just as exciting. Panavision seem to have given me the tape storage medium that allows me to make just as exciting pictures as I could ever manage with film. I am driven by exciting pictures, not a storage medium, so whatever the director or the producer want to record a good script on, I no longer think of as a major reason for agreeing to shoot a picture.

And as a final note – a good script is a good script and nothing is more important than that to the success of a movie.

30
The Sony HDW F750/F730 HD camera

In 1999, Sony transformed the professional camcorder market with the introduction of the HDW F900, described in the previous chapters, which utilized three 1920 × 1080 pixel chips and recorded on a half-inch tape in what was another step up for portable videotape recording, and which used a recording format they named HDCAM. This pixel array and recording format quickly became the international norm. This camera was firmly aimed at being able to replace 35 mm film.

In 2002 Sony brought out three additional cameras, the HDW F750, F750P and the F730; these still used the international HD pixel standard of 1920 × 1080 and the HDCAM recording format. Whereas the F900 utilized a 12-bit analogue to digital processor, the F750/F730 cameras use a 10-bit processor, and despite this the images from these cameras look every bit as good as those from the F900 when shown on television, which is the intended market for these cameras. I think most viewers seeing the images from an F750 on television would think they had been recorded on 35 mm film. These remarkable cameras are easily capable of a camera/recording stock cost combination below, sometimes significantly below, that of Super 16 mm film and yet deliver a superb picture quality comparable to 35 mm film.

30.1 Frame rates

There are two models designed for the NTSC environment, both of which record in the 60i (interlace) format, or more accurately 59.94 interlace. These are the HDW F730 and the HDW F750. The F750 uses exactly the same picture head block and imaging chips as the earlier F900: three $\frac{2}{3}$-inch FIT chips. The F730 uses three $\frac{2}{3}$-inch IT chips. Though there is only a small reduction in overall picture quality when changing from an FIT chip to an IT chip, there is a significant reduction in cost, so the F730 is aimed at the more cost-conscious end of the market and the F750 at the quality-conscious customer.

There is a second model of the F750, intended for the PAL environment and known as the F750P, which is switchable between 25 fps progressive scan and a 50 interlace format.

All three cameras record onto HDCAM tape exactly as with the HDW F900.

30.2 The camera body

All the HDW 700 series cameras share the same camera body and their switches and controls are identical. The body is a few inches shorter front to back than the F900 and around 7 pounds lighter; in fact, it is smaller and lighter than a conventional Digi Beta camera. There are none of the multiple frame rates available as with the F900, only those discussed above. Figure 30.1 shows an F750P fitted with a 20 mm Zeiss DigiPrime lens and a Crosziel matte box. At the rear of the camera can be seen two

Figure 30.1 The Sony HDW 750P HD camera

aerials that are attached to the slot-in radio receiver, thus allowing the sound recordist to feed back a mixed output to the tracks on the videotape without the use of a cable. This unit can be more clearly seen in Figure 30.2, which shows the back of the camera.

The switch block that controls most of the camera functions and the menus has been somewhat redesigned from the ones on the F900 and the Digi Beta cameras, which are similar to each other. In Figure 30.3 you can see the new layout; the most significant change is the moving of the rotary encoder wheel from the front plate of the camera to the end of the camera control switch block, where it is more easily accessed. Also in Figure 30.3 you can see that just below the filter code plate there are now two assignable switches whose functions can be selected from within the menus.

The lens centre to base plate height has been significantly reduced, thus lowering the centre of gravity, which makes the camera even more suitable for hand holding.

30.3   Add-in boards etc.

There are a couple of potentially very useful add-in boards for the camera; one operates as a built-in down-converter which can output SD SDI or an analogue composite signal, the choice being select-able within the menu system. This board will be a great attraction to users in the television industry, for without any additional kit they can now view the camera's output on conventional broadcast monitors. As can be seen in Figure 30.2, there is no external change when the down-converter board is fitted, both HD SDI and the SD SDI or composite BNC sockets are conveniently placed at the back of the camera on the operator side. The cannon plug in this illustration is providing an external DC supply.

The second add-in board is a picture cache that allows several minutes of recording to be con-tinually recorded without the VTR being switched on. Once the VTR is activated, the cache starts to dump down its contents while still taking in new images; when the VTR run/stop control is hit the tape runs on for the chosen cache time to complete the recording.

In the 60i versions of the camera, cache times of 0, 1, 2, 3, 4, 5, 6 or 7 seconds may be selected and in the 25P/50i version 0, 1, 2, 3, 4, 5, 6 or 8 seconds may be chosen. There are no moving parts to this board as it utilizes solid-state memory and therefore should prove very reliable.

Figure 30.2 The rear of the HDW 750

Figure 30.3 The HDW 750 switch block

As we have seen, a radio receiver can be slotted into the back of the camera. Also, a GPS unit can be fitted on the top of the viewfinder and the position of the camera recorded either on the tape itself or onto the set-up memory card which, as in the F900, is a Sony memory stick.

30.4   Image control via the menus

There are most of the image controls accessible via the menus that one would expect on an F900 or, indeed, a Digi Beta camera; some have changed and there are a few new ones. The most interesting, and possibly unfamiliar, F750/F730 menus are outlined below.

30.4.1   Multi matrix

Multi matrix allows for selective colour enhancement or alteration. Any particular colour can be selected or 'grabbed' and have its hue changed over a range of approximately 22.5 degrees. This allows for secondary colour correction normally only possible in post-production and is performed at full bit depth.

30.4.2   Auto tracing white balance

If the auto tracing white balance function is deployed the camera will continuously monitor the ambient light colour temperature and adjust the camera's settings accordingly. Therefore, if you have this function switched on and take a shot where, with the camera running, you go from an outdoor environment lit by daylight and move to an interior scene lit with tungsten light, the camera will automatically adjust the colorimetry to make both environments look colour correct. A lot of the time this function works surprisingly well.

30.4.3   Colour temperature control

There is a page in the menu called preset white where you can simply add overall blue or overall red to the scene, thus giving either a cooler or warmer look. This works simply and well.

30.4.4   Selectable gamma curves

The camera allows for multiple points in the gamma curve where it can be adjusted or modified, thus achieving a contrast range appropriate to the scene. Within the menu system there are also a number of preset gamma curves, which are:

Gamma calculating pattern A

- No. 1: SMPTE 240M standard which sets an initial gain of 4.0.
- No. 2: ITU-R.BT709 standard which sets an initial gain of 4.5.
- No. 3: BBC gamma setting which gives an initial gain of 5.0.

Gamma calculating pattern B

- No. 1: Sensitivity is equivalent to 50 ISO.
- No. 2: Sensitivity is equivalent to 100 ISO.
- No. 3: Sensitivity is equivalent to 200 ISO.

I would not necessarily advise deploying any of these settings if there is any chance of your material going out to film, but for a purely television presentation they can be very useful. This holds true for all the gamma settings, as well as black stretch.

30.4.5   RGB gamma balance

This adjustment alters the colour balance of the mid tones without affecting black or white.

30.4.6 Variable black gamma range

This function makes possible fine adjustment of the tonal reproduction on the darker parts of the scene without affecting the mid tones; while doing this it maintains the absolute black level. The variable range is LOW, MID and HIGH.

30.4.7 Black stretch

When variable black gamma range is performed, it can be limited to picture luminance without affecting any other factors of the video signal. This can be very helpful in a dark scene when you wish to bring out more detail in the darker parts of the scene but wish the absolute black to stay black.

30.4.8 Adaptive highlight control (auto knee mode)

With this function switched to ON the camera's ADPS system will monitor the whole of the picture and adapt the knee point/slope settings for optimum reproduction of the scene. For instance, if you are shooting an interior with a bright window in shot, switching this function on should bring down the exposure just within the image contained by the window.

30.4.9 Knee saturation function

Sony refer to their TrueEye processor, which basically controls the highlights in a high contrast scene. For instance, if knee correction is applied only via the RGB channels, skin tone when very brightly lit will occasionally look yellow and Sony claim applying this function should bring it back to a clear colour. It does seem to work.

30.4.10 The triple skin tone detail control

In addition to the usual single skin tone detail and colour control found on most current Sony cameras, there are now three separate settings and the range of adjustment allows for modification to far more colours than just skin tone. Within each setting it is possible to grab a single colour and substantially modify it, and this can be done to three individual colours. It works well and allows you to do far more than you might with a red enhancement filter; for a start, it works on all colours.

30.4.11 Level depend detail

This function provides detail enhancement in extreme highlights; it automatically limits the amplitude of edge signals in high contrast areas. Detail aliasing in these areas can be dramatically reduced.

30.5 Meta-data handling

The camera can record a UMID (unique material identifier) signal which is standardized as SMPTE 330M. The purpose of this is to record information on the tape at every shot change. This data can include a universal label, an instance number, a material number, the time and date, spatial co-ordinates, the country, the origin and a user identifier code.

30.6 The Sony Tele-File system

The Sony Tele-File storage system allows information such as shot data, shot marks etc. to be recorded onto an optional cassette label with a built-in memory IC so that all this information can travel with the cassette for the rest of its working life. This can significantly speed up the post-production process if used carefully.

30.7   The optional HD SDI adapter

Although a single HD SDI source comes out of the back of the camera, there are occasions when more sources might be required and also access to all four of the on-tape sound tracks may be needed. The optional HD SDI adapter allows for all of this.

30.8   An overview

The HDW F700 range of cameras are a very significant step forward in the move to a worldwide common standard of HD acquisition in the television industry. Even the most expensive model has a lower price tag than a Digi Beta camera did on its introduction 10 years previously and we all know how popular that camera became.

The HDW F730 is such an economical camera to purchase that it is hard to conceive how the take-up will not be at least as successful as was Digi Beta – this time the cost is less and the leap in quality of much greater significance.

The HDW F750P, with its 25 fps progressive scan capability, is tailor made for the European, and particularly UK, single camera television drama market, where it offers all the convenience of Digi Beta, a significant reduction in costs compared with the traditional acquisition medium, Super 16, and brings picture quality up to that usually expected of 35 mm origination.

31
The Thomson Viper HD camera

Thomson has taken a very different approach to other manufacturers in that a primary design parameter was that there should not be any data compression within the camera. Technically, this would be described as a 4.4.4 signal. This means that the data stream coming out of the back of the camera is so large that it takes two BNC cables to transfer it to some form of recording format. Thomson has named the form in which the data leaves the camera FilmStream. With the current state of data recording technology there is no tape format that can cope with this much information and, if no compression is to be used, it must be fed to a server or some form of hard disk recording format. At its introduction the camera could not be used as a camcorder, so the purity of the data coming from it was both its main advantage and its greatest drawback, for recordings could only be made on rather unwieldy equipment.

31.1 The camera body

Figure 31.1 shows the operator side of the camera, which is fitted with its extension eyepiece and an Angenieux zoom lens. Figure 31.2 shows the other side of the camera. Some film technicians who have seen the camera have taken to its appearance, for it is not dissimilar in shape to the camera body of several current 35 mm film cameras, particularly so if you look at the front of the camera body in Figure 31.2, where you can see the housing for the mechanical shutter that is needed with the Thomson system.

31.2 Outputs from the camera

At the rear of the camera in Figure 31.2 you can see three BNC plugs, the left hand of which is sending HD SDI to a straightforward monitor and the right-hand two are, together, taking the FilmStream signal away for storage.

It is also possible to fit an alternative back to the camera which will add an additional output, giving a down-converted PAL signal using a single BNC cable.

31.3 Recording a FilmStream signal

Figure 31.3 shows the hard disk recording unit used by the rental house Arri Media, which was the first company to acquire Thomson Viper cameras in the UK. This unit contains eight disks, giving a total of approximately 40 minutes of recording time if FilmStream is used and around 1 hour if the HD SDI signal is recorded. The storage unit is reasonably transportable, weighing roughly the same

Figure 31.1 The Thomson Viper camera fitted with an Angenieux zoom lens

Figure 31.2 The adapter back giving both an HD SDI output and a FilmStream output

as a flight case containing two loaded 1000-feet 35 mm magazines. A half size unit is available. The disk recorder will work from a mains electricity supply or a 24-volt DC supply.

31.4 The director's friend

Unfortunately it is not possible to send data directly from the camera to the hard disk recorder, as the information must first be processed into a form the recorder can handle. Arri Media initially chose to

Figure 31.3 The eight-disk hard disk recorder

use a device known as 'the director's friend' for this purpose and this can be seen together with the Thomson camera in Figure 31.4. As well as processing the data before sending it to the hard disks, the director's friend can also display a certain amount of image adjustment on one of its screens or send it to a conventional monitor. It will be possible to record these adjustments and recall them at some later post-production stage. Any adjustments that are made are not recorded on the hard disks, for that is always a pure signal from the camera. The adjustments will be recorded on a separate data track.

The director's friend is a large clamshell, the lower half of which contains the processors and has a keyboard on its uppermost surface, while the lid has two 14-inch TFT LCD screens, the left-hand screen showing the information relating to the image capture software and the right-hand screen showing the image after manipulation, as can be seen in Figure 31.5.

The director's friend will work from a mains electricity supply or a 24-volt DC supply.

31.5 The beam splitter

The Thomson camera uses a beam splitter in the same way as the Sony camera. If you refer to Chapter 25, Section 25.3, you will find a full explanation of how this works.

31.6 The Viper's CCD array

The Viper is primarily designed to produce the standard HD format image using 1920 pixels horizontally with 1080 pixels vertically, giving a total of 2 073 600 pixels for the complete image, this being the current international HD standard. The Thomson HD-DPM chip is a little cleverer than this, for while it has 1920 pixels horizontally it has four times as many sub-pixels vertically, which can be grouped in various ways to give some interesting imagery. If every four vertical sub-pixels are grouped

Figure 31.4 The Thomson Viper camera with the director's friend

Figure 31.5 The director's friend

together then the standard 1080-line HD image is recorded. If every three pixels are grouped together then very nearly the equivalent of a cinemascope aspect ratio can be recorded, still with a full 1080-line vertical resolution. The actual aspect ratio formed using three-pixel grouping will be 2.37:1. Alternatively, if every five pixels are grouped together then an HD 16 × 9 image will be outputted in the 720-line format. This ability to switch between formats using sub-pixels to make up various vertical pixel groupings gives the camera a distinct advantage over cameras with a fixed 1080 vertical pixel array, especially when shooting in the equivalent of an anamorphic format, for then a conventional chip will only have a vertical resolution of a little over 800 lines.

31.7 The mechanical shutter

All CCD imaging devices are sensitive to light at all times, though they can be electronically switched to convert photons into electrons or dump the electrons, which effectively switches the pixels off and is commonly known as an electronic shutter. If the Thomson chips are left on all the time there will be some image blur or streaking of moving highlights evident in the image. The Viper therefore uses a mechanical shutter to provide a brief period in every frame cycle during which the imaging chip will not have light reaching it, and in this period the information is dumped to a play-out-only chip, which is kept continually in the dark, and this releases the imaging chip for the next frame.

The Viper can be set with the mechanical shutter permanently open, but the streaking and blur described above will be evident; there may be some occasions where for artistic reasons this may be preferred.

The mechanical shutter has an opening of 312°. The exposure time can be further reduced electronically down to one-thousandth of a second.

31.8 Frame rates

The Viper can be set to record in a large number of format combinations. It will work in a 1080-line progressive scan mode, both in a 16 × 9 format and a 2.37:1 format; it will also work in a 1080 interlace format and a 720-line progressive scan format. Figure 31.6 shows which frame rates are available at the different vertical resolutions in both the available progressive scan and interlace settings.

31.9 Resolution

Although the Thomson camera has 4320 vertical sub-pixels, it always groups them into a configuration of 1080 vertical master pixels. It would be wrong to think that the sub-pixels contribute

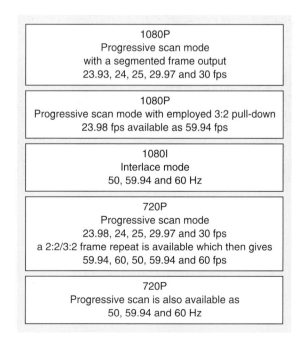

Figure 31.6 Frame rates available on the Thomson Viper camera

to a greater resolution, for it is the combined sub-pixels that are outputted as a single unit of pixel information and therefore this is the resolution of the data that leaves the camera.

31.10   The camera's processor configuration

Figure 31.7 shows a block diagram of the processor stages within the camera. The analogue signals from the three colour dedicated CCDs are converted to a 12-bit digital signal immediately behind the chips. If the camera is being used in the higher information FilmStream mode, the signal is then converted from the line 12-bit signal to a logarithmic 10-bit signal and is then sent to some recording device that can handle this information. Additionally, the add-on camera back can convert the RGB digital signal to an HD SDI or PAL viewing signal. If no viewing facility is required, the add-on converter can be dispensed with and the camera can be set to output a pure FilmStream signal, an RGB signal or a YUV signal.

31.11   The camera back

If any viewing facilities are required from the camera, a relatively small back can be attached to the camera to convert the signals to more convenient formats. The block diagram of the basic back is shown in Figure 31.8, where the raw output from the camera is converted from a parallel FilmStream mode to a serial FilmStream mode and four other processors are used to output a conventional HD SDI output. The back and its BNC connectors are clearly shown in Figure 31.2.

31.12   The arguments for a logarithmic recording format

Thomson put forward a strong argument for firstly converting the output from the imaging chips to a binary digital signal and then translating this signal to a logarithmic digital signal. The argument is mainly based on two suppositions. Firstly, that the human eye, and film, both respond to light in a

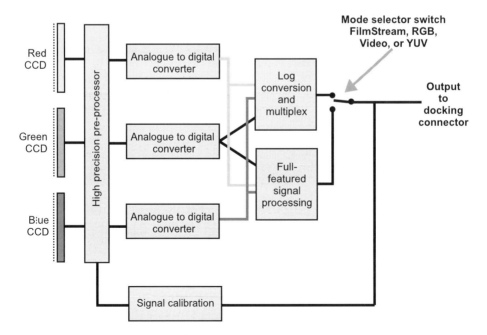

Figure 31.7 Simplified block diagram of the Viper camera's processors

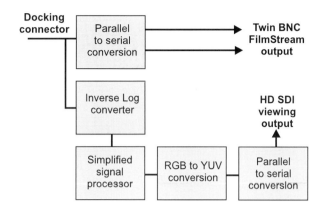

Figure 31.8 Simplified block diagram of the processors in the camera back

logarithmic way and that storing the data in a logarithmic form makes it much more compatible to the image a human being would expect to see in a film image. Secondly, the human eye sees much more colour and the brain is much more aware of the densities in the darker parts of an image. A logarithmic interpretation of a picture will provide much smaller steps between values in the darker parts of an image than it will for the lighter parts so, again, it is conforming itself to a more human response.

They further claim that a linear 12-bit information stream will contain no more information than a 10-bit logarithmic data stream, as the greater information in the shadows is so much better catered for in the logarithmic version that the gross data contained within it is higher than the same picture stored in a linear format.

31.13   Lenses for the Viper

There is no question that the Viper camera is capable of full HD resolution and that outputting a full 4.4.4 signal, at least theoretically, provides a fuller digital interpretation of that image. The 4.4.4 signal is also arguably more robust, particularly if considerable post-production work is envisaged. Given the above, it would be a terrible waste if the optical image provided to the imaging chips were not able to resolve a circle of confusion much better than one covering two pixels. In my opinion, very near a one-pixel resolution must be achieved before the advantages of the Thomson approach will be seen on the screen, especially on a cinema screen.

Judging lens resolution can be a tricky matter; all manufacturers claim their products to be exceptional and, as we have seen elsewhere in this book, judging the resolution of an image is not always that easy, as both resolution and contrast play their part in the way we humans make our conclusions.

It would be wonderful to see an image from the Viper that has been formed by a Panavision lens, but as both companies are head to head looking for similar business and the two cameras use entirely different lens mounts, the Viper using the Sony B4 mount, this seems very unlikely at the moment. Thomson must, therefore, look elsewhere for their lenses.

Arri Media in London are keen to send the Viper out with Zeiss prime lenses and I think they are absolutely right. As I haven't had the opportunity yet either to bench test or photographically test most of the non-Panavision lenses, what follows can only be my opinion. I am of the opinion, just as I am when recommending lenses for the Sony camera, that, at present, only Zeiss and Panavision manufacture lenses that can bring the absolute best out of the currently available HD cameras that work in the 1080 × 1920 pixel format.

31.14   Monitors for the Viper

As the Viper can easily deliver a standard HD SDI signal, exactly the same monitors are available as with the Sony HDW F900. Unless you can afford the newer progressive scan monitors, when you pan the camera you will see horizontal stuttering, again exactly as with the F900 and again just as with the F900 this is not recorded but is simply a monitor problem. Upgrading to a progressive scan monitor cures the problem completely.

31.15   Camera accessories

The Viper is totally compatible with Arriflex camera accessories; the base plate can be supplied to conform with the normal positioning of Arriflex lens support bars and therefore all lens control and matte boxes you would expect to order with a film camera are available with the Viper.

Tripods and tripod legs are probably best sourced from the same kind you would use with a 35 mm camera, though the more robust ones that you might choose to use with 16 mm equipment should work more than adequately.

31.16   Shipping the Viper

The Viper is a robust camera, but as with all sophisticated equipment it must be treated with respect. Standard motion picture precautions will more than suffice.

32
The Sony HDW F500 VTR

32.1 An overview

I asked a colleague how he would describe the F500 and his reply was 'big, heavy, clever and complicated'; that about sums it up. The clever bit is the most interesting, for it can be fitted with a number of converter boards that effectively make it, in the right circumstances, into a standards converter.

Those of you who are familiar with Digi Beta VTRs will find that, in the main, the F500 is familiar to you, though the menu is considerably more sophisticated, as it has to be able to control many more functions.

As this book is primarily about cinematography, i.e. picture acquisition, I will not go into the VTR in any great detail, although I think it useful to know its main features. I have also added the instructions for changing the frame rate, as it is sometimes necessary to carry out this procedure in the field.

32.2 Editing and playback

The F500 is fitted with a playback head to enable pre-read editing, which allows basic editing to be carried out with a single VTR.

32.3 Simultaneous playback

Separate playback heads are fitted to the record drum immediately behind the record heads, allowing the recording to be checked at the same time the recording is made.

32.4 Slow motion replay

Using what Sony describe as dynamic tracking, the F500 can provide a noiseless continuously variable picture replay at speeds from −1 up to +2 times normal playback speed. This allows for a certain amount of slow motion and reverse action effects to be achieved.

32.5 High speed picture search

If you are starting with a 24P recording, the F500 can search forwards or backward at up to 60 times normal playback speed and still provide a recognizable picture.

32.6   Digital jog sound

The F500 will replay sound on all four channels of digital audio within a speed range of −1 up to +1 times the correct playback speed.

32.7   Vertical interval time code (VITC) read/write

The F500 can read and write time code at any speed. The VITC facilitates play, still and slow motion, all with precise time code information.

32.8   The control panel

The control panel, in the main, will be familiar to anyone who has used a Digi Beta VTR. It has direct access keys to configure the machine, and machine set-ups can be stored on a removable PCMCIA SRAM memory card.

32.9   Remote control

A remote controller is available which replicates all the most important image control functions.

32.10   In/out capacity

The F500 can take in and give out a number of different types of signal:

- HD SDI input and outputs for digital, uncompressed, 10-bit component signals conforming to SMPTE 292M with a bit rate of 1.5 Gb/s. These signals carry HD video, four channels of digital audio and some additional data.
- HD SDTI input and outputs for digital HDCAM signals containing the compressed HD video and four channels of audio within the familiar 270 Mb/s standard SDI wrapper. This allows the HDCAM signals to be, for example, routed through existing SDI infrastructures on conventional SDI-based disc recorders. Using HD SDTI inputs and outputs, perfect copies, or clones as they are referred to, can be made with no loss of quality.
- Analogue composite outputs are available if an optional down-converter board is fitted (Sony reference code HKDV-501A).
- Digital audio inputs and outputs are available; there are two pairs of AES/EBU digital audio, both in and out.
- Analogue inputs and outputs are available on all four channels, together with the cue track on analogue in and out. Two additional analogue monitor outputs are also included.
- Using reference signals, the F500 can be synchronized to either 525, 625, 1125/59.94 or 1125/60 signals.

32.11   Optional plug-in boards

There are a number of optional plug-in boards that can extend the facilities within the F500. They include:

- A high definition to standard definition down-converter board – Sony code HKDV-501A.
- An HD line converter board – Sony code HKDV-502.
- An SDTI interface board – Sony code HKDV-506A.
- An HD 3:2 pull-down board to allow compatibility between 24P recordings and an NTSC requirement that has the same signal as one would get from a telecine machine. The Sony code for this board is HKDV-507.

32.12 Cassettes

In addition to the smaller cassette used in the Sony HDW F900 camera, the HDW F900 VTR will accept a larger cassette. When running at 24P the smaller cassette runs for 50 minutes, whereas the larger cassette will last for 155 minutes, making it possible to record most feature films on a single cassette.

32.13 Changing the frame rate

To change the frame rate on the F500, carry out the following procedure:

1 Close to the bottom left-hand corner of the LCD information screen on the front of the VTR there is a small hole, behind which there is a rubber membrane; it is marked Maintenance. Using something hard with a blunt tip – an unfolded paper clip is ideal – press the membrane. The Maintenance information display will now be shown on the LCD screen.
2 While pressing the SFT (Shift) key, also press the F8 (Maintenance execute) key. This will cause you to enter the Maintenance mode menu.
3 Press the F9 (Others Check) key to set the OTHERS CHECK screen.
4 Press the F9 key again (System Menu) to set the SYSTEM MENU screen.
5 Press the F2 (System Frequency) key as many times as necessary to select the system frequency mode you require (system frequency is Sony speak for frame rate) and then press the F9 (Execute) key. The message to confirm the selection will be displayed. If it is OK, press the F9 (Execute) key again. System initialization will be executed and a new setting will be performed. Please see below for the frame rates that are available.
6 Turn OFF the power once and then turn it ON again. The VTR will now run in your chosen frame rate.

32.14 Available frame rates

Sony refer to the film world's phrase of frame rate either as the system frequency or as a number plus PsF, as in 24PsF. PsF stands for Progressive Segmented Frame, which is not just the frames per second but the actual recording format, the information actually being written to the tape in a format known as segmented frame.

If you are going through the procedure above and have reached part 5, as you continue to press the F2 key again and again you will sequence through the following frame rates. They are written as they will appear on the LCD screen:

23.98PsF
24PsF
25PsF
29.97PsF
30PsF
50i
59.94i
60i

An 'i' indicates the fields per second when using an interlaced scanning format.

32.15 Power supplies

The HDW F500 will run on any mains supply from 100 volts through to 240 volts, either at 50 or 60 Hz (hertz – cycles per second). In itself it is not equipped to run from a battery supply.

33
The Sony HDW F900 menus

33.1 Using the menus

How you access the Top Menu depends on the setting 'Resume', which is found on page 11 of the Maintenance Menu. Depending on this setting, access is gained either by holding the rotary encoder in and moving the switch at the front of the camera to MENU (these switches can be seen in Figure 33.1), or you will find TOP displayed in the top right-hand corner of the screen whenever the menu is brought up on the screen, and the Top Menu can be accessed by rotating the encoder until the cursor points at the word Top and then clicking the encoder. The rotary encoder lives on the right of the camera control panel, which on the Sony camera is sited below the lens mount. On the Panavision version, the panel is on a flying lead, as shown in Figure 33.2. The Top Menu will appear in the viewfinder, as in Figure 33.3.

Figure 33.1 The camera front switches

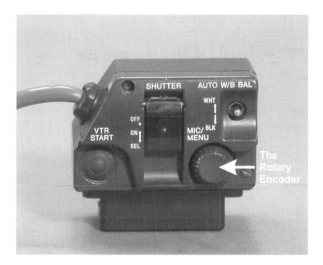

Figure 33.2 The rotary encoder

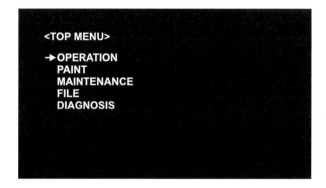

Figure 33.3 Top Menu

To change pages in the menu, set the cursor to the page number by rotating the encoder wheel, and then click the encoder wheel. This will change the cursor into a '?'; if you now rotate the wheel the pages will change. You can go both forwards and backwards.

To change a settings value, scroll the cursor till it points to the line you wish to change and click the wheel; again the cursor will change into a '?'. Now rotate the wheel and the value of the setting will change. To save a change, click the wheel a second time. If you wish to cancel a change, press the menu switch on the side of the camera to the cancel position.

Each successive press of the switch to cancel will sequence the screen from item selection, then back to the page selection and finally back to the Top Menu.

When you have finished your settings, return the display switch to OFF and the menus will disappear from the viewfinder.

33.1.1 The layout of the menus

If you think of the Top Menu as a library within which are usually five books and within each book are pages containing various settings, you will understand the structure of the menus. There is a sixth book, Service, but this is usually disabled when the camera reaches a crew.

The books in the library you will most often meet are entitled Operations, Paint, Maintenance, File and Diagnosis, as in Figure 33.4. Contained in each book are a number of pages, each with its own name, as shown in Figures 33.5–33.9.

Be warned: some of the pages should never be modified by the camera crew. In Figures 33.5–33.9, pages that the crew might, with some caution, modify are shown as white boxes containing black lettering. Pages that do not need to be modified are shown as black boxes with white lettering. In the following section, which describes the function of the pages and settings, only those pages it is safe to modify are described.

33.1.2   Using the menus – some warnings

If you have read my book *Digital Cinematography*, you will know that when shooting Digi Beta I advocate careful use of the menus to create a 'look' for each film and sometimes each scene. This is because I believe with the limited, but adequate, tonal range of the Digi Beta camera, images can be improved by careful manipulation and selection of the tonal range to be recorded.

For the HD cameras, with their considerably greater tonal range, I recommend very limited use of menu manipulation when using either the Sony or the Panavision versions of the HDW F900. Indeed, with the Panavision lenses and modifications to the optical colorimetry, it is a very rare occurrence for me to change any of the standard Panavision settings. This is especially true if the final product is going to be transferred to film.

There is a very real danger of altering settings in the menu in such a way that one is pandering to the characteristics of the monitor, particularly if you are shooting a low-key scene. This is especially true if you are tempted to adjust gamma and even more so should you adjust black gamma. This is because compressing the blacks may look better on the limited tonal range of a cathode ray tube but will not be appealing when displayed on a cinema screen, with its ability to deliver many more tones.

As an example, should you be tempted to set black gamma RGB to its maximum of 50 per cent and Y to 50 per cent, you will have done something which, in film terms, would be the equivalent of force processing only the darker one-third of the tonal range by nearly two stops. Were you able to do this in the photochemical world, you would expect to see that the shadows have gone milky and become very grainy. This is very like an image recorded with these settings will look like when printed out to film. Unfortunately, as a large proportion of this effect happens to tones that respond differently on a cathode ray tube, you might not discover your error until late in post-production.

For these reasons I recommend you make only the slightest or, better still, no changes to any of the gamma settings.

You should not infer from these warnings that what you see on the monitor is not an accurate guide to what you will see on a cinema screen, it is providing you have the camera set to recommended

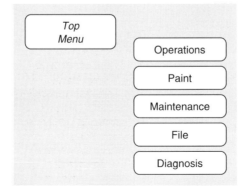

Figure 33.4 Top Menu libraries

Figure 33.5 Operations Menu

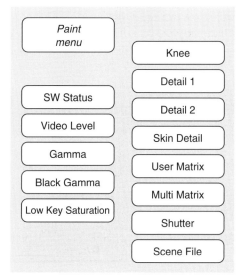

Figure 33.6 Paint Menu

Figure 33.7 Maintenance Menu

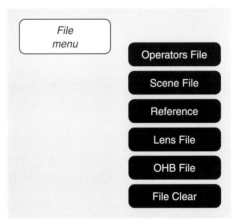

Figure 33.8 File Menu

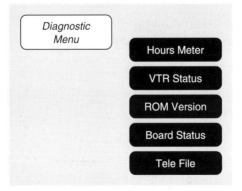

Figure 33.9 Diagnostic Menu

film characteristics. It is only when some settings, particularly within the gamma area, are altered or set unusually that there might be a significant difference in the final look of the images as seen on the cathode ray tube and as seen from a print projected on the cinema screen.

33.2   The Operations Menu

There are nine pages in the operation menu, as shown in Figure 33.5 in the previous section (33.1.2). Each page contains several operator selectable options. For each page there is an illustration showing how the viewfinder screen will look with the page up and the settings shown on this figure will be the Sony recommended settings unless otherwise stated. There is also a further figure showing the Sony settings, or my own preferred settings for the Panavision camera, and a brief description of the effect of the setting.

33.2.1   VF DISPLAY page

The first page deals with the messages that can be displayed on the viewfinder screen. All the options can be set to one of three values: ON, OFF and 3S. If 3S is selected then the warning will only be displayed for 3 seconds on the viewfinder screen when a status is actually changed.

Figure 33.10 shows how the viewfinder screen will look with the Sony settings. Figure 33.11 shows both the Sony recommended settings and the settings I prefer when using the Panavision camera. The extender, zoom and iris warnings are switched off as the Panavision lenses do not have these facilities.

33.2.2   '!' IND page

At the bottom of the viewfinder, just outside the screen, there is a small orange LED on which can be seen, when it is alight, an exclamation mark. This page controls which occurrences cause the LED to light up. It should be noted that there can be many of the lines causing it to light or simply one.

On every line, if the selected setting agrees with the normal setting the light will not come on, i.e. the '!' LED only illuminates when you deviate from the normal settings.

Operators vary enormously as to liking or disliking this function. If they are from a video background they often like it, but those from a film background invariably find it annoying. If I am operating the camera I tend to turn everything OFF except GAIN and SHUTTER. Figure 33.12 shows how the page will look and Figure 33.13 both the Sony On/Off recommendations and their selection of what they recommend as the 'Normal' setting, and this is followed by the settings of On/ Off and 'Normal' settings that I prefer.

```
<VF DISPLAY>                      → 1      TOP

    EX      :    ON        BATT   :   ON
    ZOOM    :    OFF       TAPE   :   ON
    ND      :    ON        TC     :   OFF
    CC      :    ON        AUDIO  :   OFF
    IRIS    :    ON
    WHITE   :    ON
    D5600K  :    ON        MESSAG :   ALL
    GAIN    :    ON
    SHUTT   :    ON
```

Figure 33.10 VF DISPLAY page

<VF DISPLAY>			
	Sony	**PV/PW**	
Ex	ON	OFF	Sets the lens extender display
ZOOM	OFF	OFF	Sets the zoom position display
ND	ON	ON	Sets the ND filter display
CC	ON	ON	Sets the Colour Correction filter display
IRIS	ON	OFF	Sets the iris aperture display
WHITE	ON	ON	Sets the white balance memory display
D5600K	ON	OFF	Sets the D5600K mode display
GAIN	ON	ON	Sets the gain value display
SHUTT	ON	ON	Sets the shutter speed/mode/reading display
BATT	ON	ON	Sets the power supply voltage/battery life display
TAPE	ON	ON	Sets the tape run out display
TC	OFF	OFF	Sets the time code display
AUDIO	OFF	OFF	Sets the audio level display
MESSAG	ALL	ALL	Sets a message to be displayed at the centre of the viewfinder when each setting is changed

Figure 33.11 VF DISPLAY functions

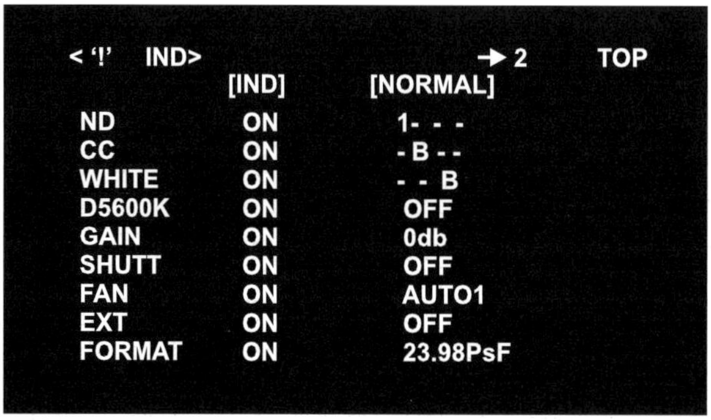

```
< '!'  IND>                        → 2    TOP
                 [IND]      [NORMAL]
      ND          ON        1- - -
      CC          ON        - B - -
      WHITE       ON        - - B
      D5600K      ON        OFF
      GAIN        ON        0db
      SHUTT       ON        OFF
      FAN         ON        AUTO1
      EXT         ON        OFF
      FORMAT      ON        23.98PsF
```

Figure 33.12 '!' IND page

33.2.3 MARKER page

Figure 33.14 shows how the screen will look when you bring this page up. Figure 33.15 shows the choices you have on each line.

This page deals solely with the lines and boxes you can display in the viewfinder in order to frame for different aspect ratios. Remember the camera always records 16:9, so having the right aspect ratio that you are finally going to deliver the picture in, or the primary aspect ratio of the major producer, displayed can be vital. There are a number of preset aspect boxes already programmed into the camera, plus the ability to programme a box of your own. By setting the number of pixels you wish the box to represent in separate vertical and horizontal settings, any ratio you desire can be brought up. For instance, with a horizontal setting of 1920, the full number of pixels available horizontally, and a vertical setting of 800, you will have a full frame box of an aspect ratio of 2.4:1.

<'!' IND>					
	SONY	**Sony**	**PV/PW**	**PV/PW**	
	IND	**NORMAL**	**IND**	**NORMAL**	**Options**
ND	ON	1 - - -	OFF	- 1 - -	1,2,3,4 and combinations of these options
CC	ON	- B - -	OFF	- B - -	A,B,C,D and combinations of these options
WHITE	ON	- - B	OFF	P - -	P,A,B and combinations of these options
D5600K	ON	OFF	OFF	OFF	ON, OFF
GAIN	ON	0 db	ON	- - L	L,M,H
SHUTT	ON	OFF	ON	ON	ON, OFF
FAN	ON	AUTO1	OFF	AUTO1	AUTO1, AUTO2 MIN, MAX
EXT	ON	OFF	OFF	OFF	ON, OFF
FORMAT	ON	23.98PsF	OFF	24PsF	23.98PsF 60i, 59.941, 50i 30PsF, 29.97PsF 25PsF 24PsF, 23.98PsF

Figure 33.13 '!' IND recommendations

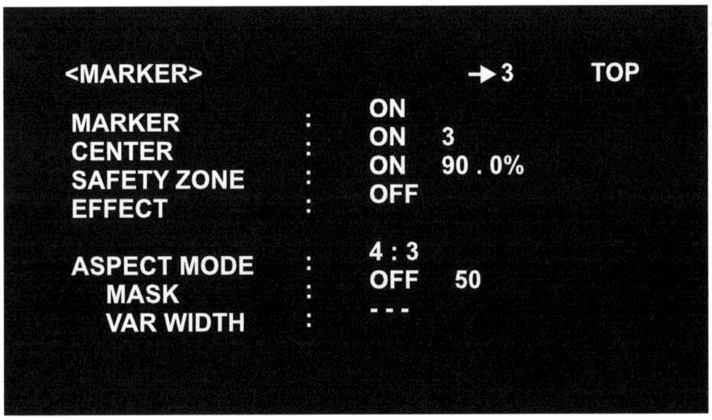

Figure 33.14 MARKER page

33.2.3.1 MARKER

MARKER simply switches the whole effect ON or OFF, so in OFF mode you will see absolutely nothing but the full area of the viewfinder. ON switches on the settings you select in the following lines. There is also a switch on the viewfinder body that carries out the same function.

33.2.3.2 CENTER

CENTER chooses the markings you prefer in the centre of the screen and will come up correctly in whatever aspect ratio you choose unless the line file offset is on. Figure 33.16 shows the four available choices here in 16:9 format.

<MARKER>				
	Available	**Sony**	**PV/PW**	
MARKER	ON or OFF	ON	OFF	Sets ALL the viewfinder markings ON or OFF
CENTER	ON or OFF 1,2,3 and 4	ON	ON and 3	Sets the centre cross ON or OFF
SAFETY ZONE	ON or OFF 80,90,92.5 and 95	ON @ 90%	ON @ 90%	Can be set to OFF or 80%, 90%, 92.5% or 95%
EFFECT	ON or OFF	OFF	ON	Sets the effective pixel area display ON or OFF
ASPECT MODE	16:9, 15:9, 14:9, 13:9, 4:3, VAR H, VAR V, 1035, VISTA 1 and VISTA 2	4:3	VISTA 1	Sets the aspect mode grey area display
MASK	ON or OFF 0–100%	OFF and 50	OFF and 50	Switches the grey area ON and OFF
VAR WIDTH	0–1920 VAR H 0–1080 VAR V	- - -	- - -	You can manually set an aspect ratio in numbers of pixels and lines

Figure 33.15 MARKER functions

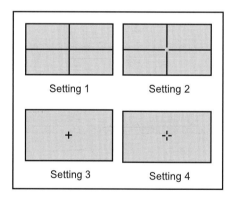

Setting 1   Setting 2

Setting 3   Setting 4

Figure 33.16 CENTER settings

33.2.3.3 SAFETY ZONE
SAFETY ZONE selects the percentage of the whole chosen. Again, the percentage both horizontally and vertically will automatically be correct for the chosen aspect ratio.

33.2.3.4 EFFECT
EFFECT, which stands for Effective Area, simply puts a bright line around the whole 16:9 picture area. This can be very useful when photographing very low-key scenes, where it might be hard to tell the difference between the edge of the image and the surrounding viewfinder housing.

33.2.3.5 ASPECT MODE

ASPECT MODE selects any of seven preset formats or allows you to set your own using the number of pixels you wish to shoot to in separate horizontal and vertical modes. The options are shown in Figure 33.15.

33.2.3.6 MASK

MASK switches ON or OFF the ability to have the unused area shaded. Figure 33.17 shows how the viewfinder screen will look if MASK is switched on in all the seven pre-selectable formats. A second line in the MASK section allows you to choose the density of the greyed out area. You might like to start at around 50 per cent, which is my preference.

Figure 33.18 shows how the viewfinder image might look if the EFFECT were On, the CENTER set to setting 3 and the ASPECT MODE set to Vista 2, which is set up to show a 2.4:1 aspect ratio, the equivalent to shooting in 35 mm film with anamorphic lenses.

33.2.4 GAIN SW page

This page sets the amount of gain, or image amplification, that will be applied when the external gain switch is set at any of its three positions: L, M or H. All three positions can be assigned either −3, 0, 3, 6, 12 or 18 db. It should be noted that in this application 6 db increases the exposure by a factor of 2, the equivalent of one stop.

Sony ship the camera with L set to 0 db, M set to 6 db and H set to 12 db. I prefer to set the positions to L at 0 db, M at 3 db and H at 6 db, as shown in Figure 33.19. My reasoning for this is twofold, for unlike the Digi Beta camera I don't believe there is any improvement in the image using

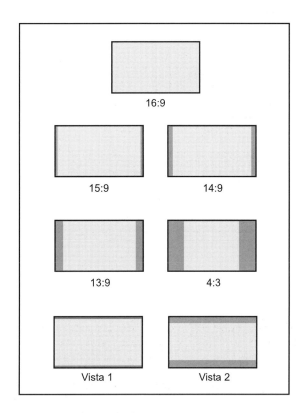

Figure 33.17 The seven pre-selectable MASK formats

Figure 33.18 Viewfinder image with particular MARKER page settings

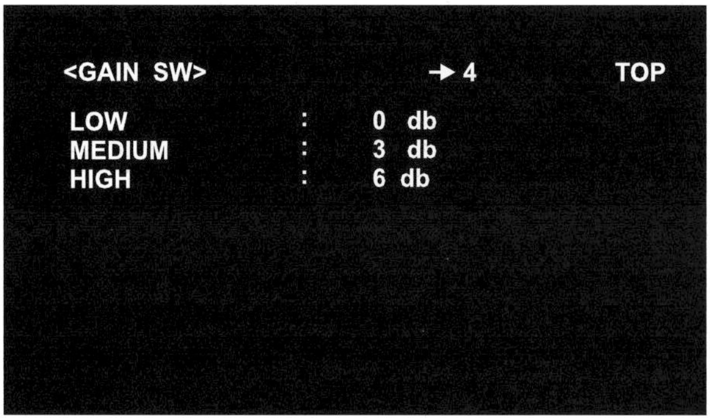

```
<GAIN SW>                    ➜ 4            TOP

LOW              :    0  db
MEDIUM           :    3  db
HIGH             :    6  db
```

Figure 33.19 GAIN SW page

−3 db. Indeed, as the HD camera's tonal range is so long, I think the highlights suffer a little with negative gain and with so much longer tonal range the advantages disappear. My second reason to use different settings from Sony is that as I am trying to obtain such a high quality image it seems foolish to use more than 6 db of gain, as higher settings will noticeably reduce the image quality.

33.2.5 ZEBRA/VF DTL page

This page deals with the brightness level at which the zebra indicators will switch in. The zebra is a diagonal banding that can be arranged to overlay the image areas of a predetermined brightness. This effect is only seen in the viewfinder. It is used to show when a specific set brightness is reached and stays on over all the tones in the scene that are of this brightness or brighter. There are two available settings and it is common to set one at just above correct skin tone to show when facial tones are overexposing and the other to 100 per cent, or a little lower, to warn when peak white is reached. I find the zebra effect disturbing in the viewfinder and not terribly useful, so most of the time I keep it switched off. On rare occasions, say when shooting outdoors without a monitor, I might use zebra 2 set at 100 per cent in order to keep a watch on the exposure of a bright sky. Figure 33.20 shows the Sony recommended settings and Figure 33.21 my preferred settings, where all the effects are off but zebra 2 is chosen and set at 100 per cent so that it can be switched in as easily as possible. There is also a spring-loaded switch on the viewfinder body that allows the zebra effect to be switched on momentarily.

Viewfinder detail is an artificial sharpening program, which only affects the image in the viewfinder. I don't like this effect, so keep it switched off.

33.2.6 AUTO IRIS page

Figure 33.22 shows the layout of the AUTO IRIS page, where it is possible to select one of six areas over which the exposure will be assessed. On the right of the screen is a graphic illustration, where the grey area in the box is the area that will be used to determine the exposure. Figure 33.23 shows the six areas that can be chosen.

The second line of selection allows you to cause the exposure to be set on the lens to be either greater or less than the factory setting. The figures can be set from −99 (this will cause the iris to become nearly fully closed) to 99 (which will cause the iris to become nearly fully open). I find the most successful way of making this adjustment is to set the camera up with an 18 per cent grey card filling the frame and then take a reading with the override set at zero. You can then adjust the figures and take more readings, noting how far the iris ring on the lens has moved.

For exterior photography with the Sony camera, I sometimes find it useful to set the override, using the 18 per cent grey card, to whatever figure gives me one-third of a stop less exposure than the factory setting.

```
<ZEBRA / VF  DTL>              ➔ 5           TOP

ZEBRA              :       on
                   :       1
ZEBRA1             :       70%
ZEBRA2             :       100%
VF  DTL            :       On
```

Figure 33.20 ZEBRA/VF DTL page – Sony settings

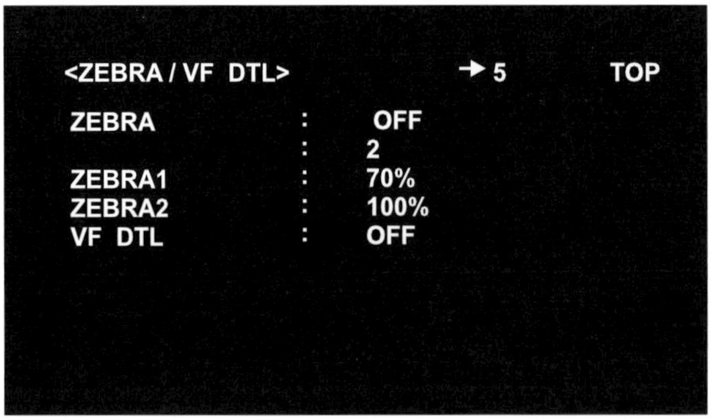

```
<ZEBRA / VF  DTL>              →5        TOP
ZEBRA            :    OFF
                 :    2
ZEBRA1           :    70%
ZEBRA2           :    100%
VF  DTL          :    OFF
```

Figure 33.21 ZEBRA/VF DTL page – my preferred settings

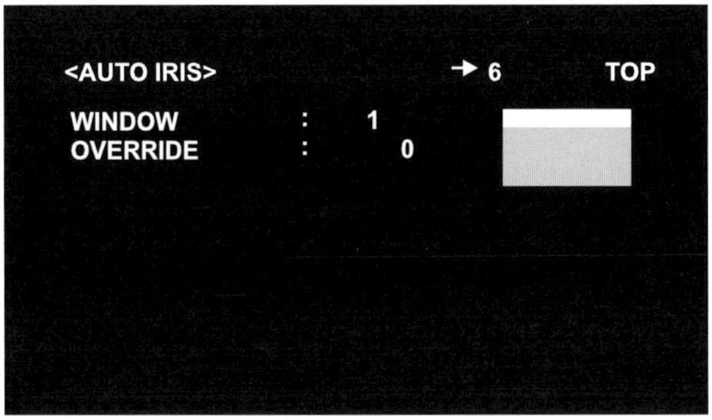

```
<AUTO IRIS>                    →6        TOP
WINDOW           :    1
OVERRIDE         :    0
```

Figure 33.22 AUTO IRIS page – Sony settings

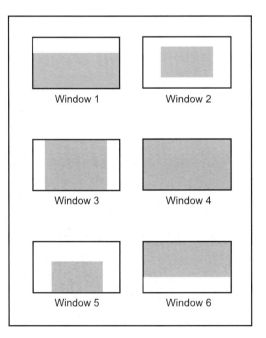

Window 1   Window 2

Window 3   Window 4

Window 5   Window 6

Figure 33.23 The six areas that can be chosen on the AUTO IRIS page

Although the Panavision lenses have the capacity to have their iris set by the camera, the company, to date, has not incorporated this facility and therefore this page is inoperative on their version of the camera.

33.2.7 BATT ALARM page

There are two levels of battery alarm, one which tells you the battery is getting low and a further one which tells you the battery is about to have so little power it will fail to run the camera. On this page you also have to set the type of battery you wish to power the camera, both via the on-board battery adapter and via the cannon DC in the socket on the back of the camera.

For any type of battery other than lithium, an Anton Bauer or when using the AC power adapter, you must select Others 1 and Others 2.

Figure 33.24 shows how the screen will look when this page is selected and Figure 33.25 the various options that are available, with a brief description of what each means.

It should be noted that this page is also in the Maintenance Menu and it is only here that the voltage settings can be changed.

33.2.8 OTHERS page

This page is basically a collection of three settings that are simply not covered anywhere else. The top line allows you to change the camera from having the correct response when the scene is illuminated with tungsten light having a nominal colour temperature of 3200°K to one having the correct response to nominal daylight with a colour temperature of 5600°K. This effect is not nearly as successful as using a filter to make the correction.

The other two lines in the menu refer to the assignable switch located at the bottom of the camera near the front on the operator's side. This switch is spring loaded in both an upward and downward direction. As can be seen in Figure 33.26, there are a number of possible options available for each of the two directions. Panavision set this switch to operate a sequential run/stop when pushed upwards and to replace the lens VTR return switch when pushed downwards. I agree with this choice, as it gives both the operator and the focus puller a convenient way of switching the camera on and off and being able to replay the last few seconds of a take. The page will therefore appear in the viewfinder as in Figure 33.27.

33.2.9 OPERATOR FILE page

Using this page you can store all the settings you have made in the pages of the operation menu. Unlike the Digi Beta camera, you have to store each of the main menus separately; there is no global storage page available. It is also possible to store the Operation pages separately.

```
<BATT ALARM>              ➜ 7        TOP

BATT
 TYPE: LITHIUM
   BEFORE END:  11.5V
   END        :  11.0V

DC IN
  TYPE : AC  ADP
   BEFORE END:  - - -
   END        :  - - -
```

Figure 33.24 BATT ALARM page

<BATT ALARM>		
	Setting	**Description**
BATT TYPE	**LITHIUM, ANTON OTHERS 1 OTHERS 2 AC ADP**	Select the type of battery you wish to use on the battery adapter on the back of the camera here.
BEFORE END		As the battery voltage drops, the battery warning showing the battery is wearing out will come on at the voltage set here.
END		As the battery voltage drops, the battery warning showing the battery is about to die will come on at the voltage set here.
DC TYPE IN	**LITHIUM, ANTON OTHERS 1 OTHERS 2 AC ADP**	Select the type of battery supply you wish to send to the camera via the DC socket on the back of the camera here.
BEFORE END		As the battery voltage coming to the camera via the DC socket drops, the battery warning showing the battery is wearing out will come on at the voltage set here.
END		As the battery voltage coming to the camera via the DC socket drops, the battery warning showing the battery is about to die will come on at the voltage set here.

Figure 33.25 BATT ALARM options

The FILE ID, CAM CODE and DATE lines allow you to write camera identification notes so that you can identify the settings you store. This is valuable as the memory stick can hold up to five separate scene files and if you store more than one you will need to be able to tell them apart. FILE ID allows memory stick identification rather than scene file ID and it is necessary to write the ID before you write data or it does not store the ID.

Figure 33.28 shows how this page will look in the viewfinder. Figure 33.29 shows the available options.

33.2.10   LENS FILE page

In Figure 33.30, the first line allows you to choose from the 16 available files the appropriate one for the lens you currently have on the camera. The second line shows the name of the lens and the last line shows the maximum aperture the chosen lens is capable of. Figure 33.30 shows how the page will appear in the viewfinder.

This page is not used on the Panavision version of the camera.

<OTHERS>		
	Setting	**Description**
D5600K	**ON or OFF**	Resets the camera from being a tungsten device where the correct colour temperature is 3200°K to a daylight device where the correct colour temperature would be 5600°K when in preset white
ASSIGNABLE 1	**OFF, D12db, D24db, VTR S/S REC REVIEW**	Any of the settings opposite may be selected
ASSIGNABLE 2	**OFF, D12db, D24db, VTR S/S REC REVIEW**	Any of the settings opposite may be selected

Figure 33.26 Options on the OTHERS page

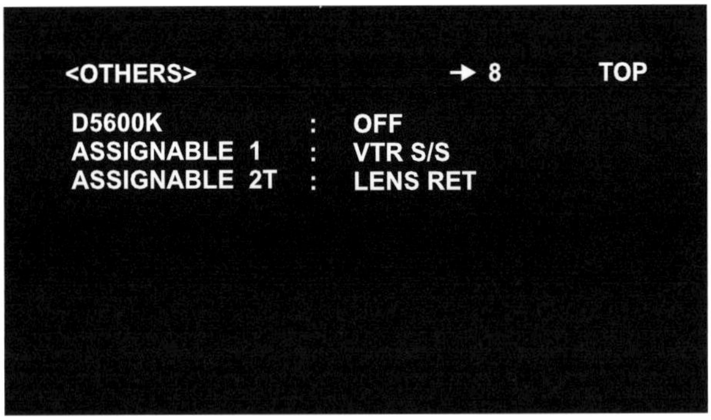

```
<OTHERS>                    ➜ 8        TOP
D5600K            :   OFF
ASSIGNABLE  1     :   VTR S/S
ASSIGNABLE  2T    :   LENS RET
```

Figure 33.27 OTHERS page

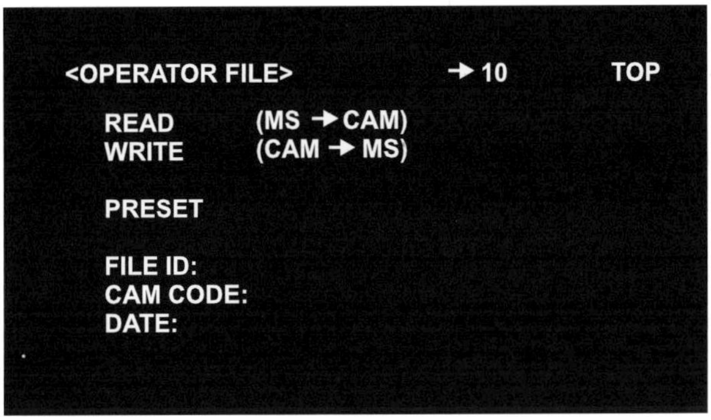

```
<OPERATOR FILE>             ➜ 10       TOP
     READ      (MS ➜ CAM)
     WRITE     (CAM ➜ MS)

     PRESET

     FILE ID:
     CAM CODE:
     DATE:
```

Figure 33.28 OPERATOR FILE page

<OPERATOR>		
	Setting	**Description**
READ **(MS → CAM)**	By pressing the rotary wheel you will carry out this operation	Executing this command causes the operator file on the memory stick to be read and loaded into the camera
WRITE **(CAM → MS)**	By pressing the rotary wheel you will carry out this operation	Executing this command causes the operator file in the camera stick to be written to the memory stick
PRESET	By pressing the rotary wheel you will carry out this operation	Executing this command causes the operator file in the camera to return to the factory settings
FILE ID		Writes comments to the file such as camera identification
CAM CODE		Displays the camera name of the file you have created
DATE		Shows the date on which the file was created

Figure 33.29 OPERATOR options

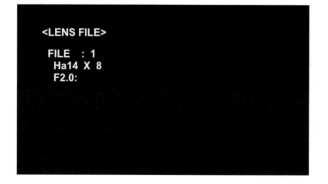

Figure 33.30 LENS FILE page

33.3 The Paint Menu

The Paint Menu is used to adjust the way in which the camera manipulates the image and is, in the main, where one modifies the look of the image. Great caution should be taken before embarking on any radical changes, for some of the adjustments do not look the same on the monitor as they will when the image is finally written to film. Even more importantly, it is just these settings which are hard, if not impossible, to undo in post-production.

As I have stated elsewhere, the camera has an extraordinary long tonal range and is therefore recording so much information that virtually anything you can do in the camera can also be done in post-production. I think it wisest to leave image modifications to that stage of production, where they can easily be redone if not liked in the final cut. If you are tempted to make changes, then I strongly advise that you shoot a test and have it printed *exactly* as you intend to post-produce the final film. If you like the result, only then is it safe to proceed with the main production.

If you leave the settings as recommended by your supplier, then it should be perfectly safe to trust what you see on the monitor, as no self-respecting supplier would let you leave with a camera that was showing pictures on the monitor that did not closely represent the final result you will get on the final film print, but do make sure you have lined up the monitor correctly using the procedure described elsewhere in this book. It is still a good idea to send a small test to your chosen laboratory, if only for your own peace of mind. This may be insisted upon in any case by your completion bond insurers.

If, on the other hand, your work is only ever going to be shown on television, then you can make any changes you like the result of on the monitor, for the image is only ever going to stay within this, or a similar, television medium. In the main, it is the swapping of medium that changes the look of the picture in unexpected ways if you use unusual or not recommended settings.

Gamma and black gamma should only ever be changed with extreme caution, for it is this parameter where there is the greatest difference between an image as seen on a cathode ray tube and the same image when written out to film and projected on a cinema screen. Unless asked to do otherwise, Panavision send their cameras out with settings that are most favourable to a film-out image.

It is also in this area of image control that the computer program used in the laboratory to convert an HDCAM image to the kind of data needed by the laser printer will be having most effect. So please, if you change any of the gamma settings, have your chosen laboratory make a test print before you proceed.

33.3.1 SW STATUS page

This, the first page of the Paint Menu, is simply a series of On/Off switches for some of the more important functions in this menu. Figure 33.31 shows the Sony recommended settings that are, in my

```
<SW STATUS>              →P1      TOP

FLARE          :    ON
GAMMA          :    ON
BLK GAMMA      :    OFF
KNEE           :    ON
WHT CLIP       :    ON
DETAIL         :    ON
LVL DEP        :    ON
SKIN DTL       :    OFF
MATRIX         :    OFF
```

Figure 33.31 SW STATUS page – Sony recommended settings

opinion, more suited when shooting for a television end-product. Figure 33.32 shows the settings preferred by Panavision, which are more appropriate when the final image is to be on film.

Figure 33.33 describes the effect of setting lines on this page to either ON or OFF.

Some of the functions on this page have pages of setting of their own and on these pages may also be an On/Off selection. If the On/Off is changed on the individual page, then the setting will automatically change on the SW STATUS page. SW STATUS is therefore an indicator of successive pages.

33.3.2 VIDEO LEVEL page

The VIDEO LEVEL page is where the white balance and black level can be manually set. Figure 33.34 shows the settings suggested by both Sony and Panavision, and will come up when the white balance switch is moved to Preset. If you have taken a white balance on Preset A or B, then the adjustment that the camera has automatically made will show on this page, as changes to white level red and blue settings, when the white balance switch is moved to A or B.

Flare correction, on the third line from the bottom, is a useful tool which will not affect very much of the image, but that which it does affect it can improve considerably. The most graphic example I have seen was on a low-key scene with candles in shot. Somehow, the candle flames were not as believable when panned across as I had expected. Turning the flare corrector circuits ON sorted the problem out immediately.

Figure 33.35 shows the available settings and gives a brief description of the function of each line on this page.

33.3.3 GAMMA page

Adjusting the settings in the GAMMA page away from the manufacturer's settings can be a very dangerous thing to attempt. This is particularly true if you are judging the effect of changes on a monitor and are ever going to write out the image to film. If you are absolutely certain that your images are only ever going to be shown on a television screen then it is a safer procedure. This is because the overall gamma of the television system and the film to cinema screen image routes are very different.

Changes made within this page can be very difficult, if not impossible, to reverse in post-production.

Sony and Panavision set up this page identically with one exception. Sony use table number 2 and Panavision prefer table number 5, as shown in Figure 33.36.

Figure 33.37 shows the available settings on each line of the GAMMA page, together with brief descriptions of the function of the changes available on each line within the page.

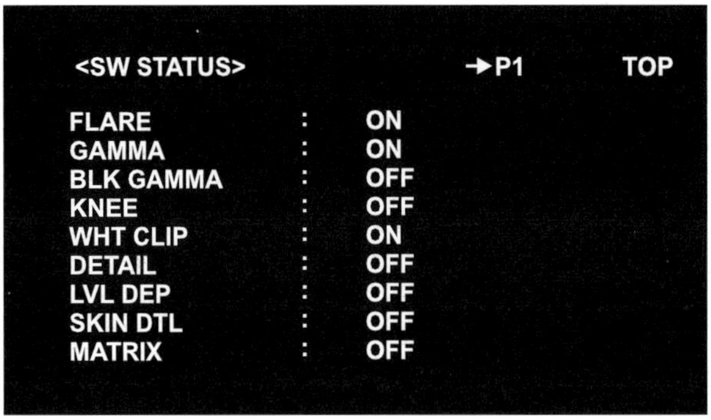

Figure 33.32 SW STATUS page – Panavision recommended settings

<SW STATUS>		
	Available setting	**Description**
FLARE	ON or OFF	Sets the flare correction circuit to ON or OFF
GAMMA	ON or OFF	Sets the gamma correction function to ON or OFF
BLK GAM	ON or OFF	Sets the black gamma correction to ON or OFF
KNEE	ON or OFF	Sets the knee correction circuit to ON or OFF
WHT CLIP	ON or OFF	Sets the white clip function ON or OFF
DETAIL	ON or OFF	Sets the function for attaching the detail signal, which some feel improves the resolution, to ON or OFF
LVL DEP	ON or OFF	Sets the level dependence function to ON or OFF
SKIN DTL	ON or OFF	Sets the skin tone detail function to ON or OFF
MATRIX	ON or OFF	Sets the linear matrix correction to ON or OFF

Figure 33.33 Effect of SW STATUS settings

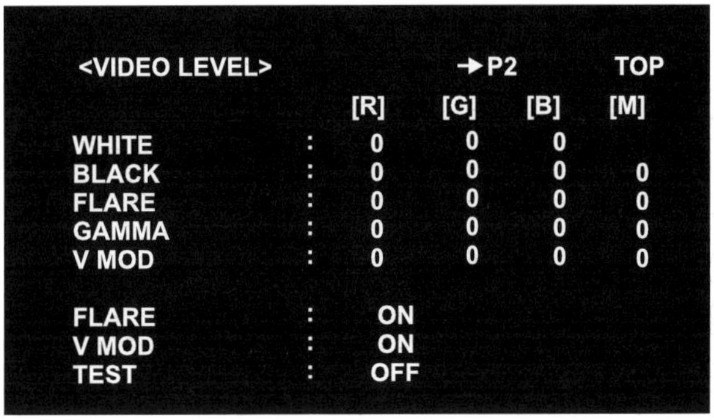

Figure 33.34 VIDEO LEVEL page

<VIDEO LEVEL>		
	Available setting	**Description**
WHITE	−99 to 99	Adjusts the white level of the Red, Green and Blue channels
BLACK	−99 to 99	Adjusts the black level of the Red, Green, Blue and Master channels
FLARE	−99 to 99	Adjusts the flare level of the Red, Green, Blue and Master channels
GAMMA	−99 to 99	Adjusts the gamma correction curve of the Red, Green, Blue and Master channels
V MOD	−99 to 99	Adjusts the V modulation shading of the Red, Green, Blue and Master channels
FLARE	ON or OFF	Switches the flare correction circuit ON or OFF
V MOD	ON or OFF	Sets the V modulation shading ON or OFF
TEST	OFF, 1 or 2	Selects the test signal OFF: No test signal 1: Provides an analogue waveform test signal 2: Provides a digital waveform test signal

Figure 33.35 VIDEO LEVEL settings

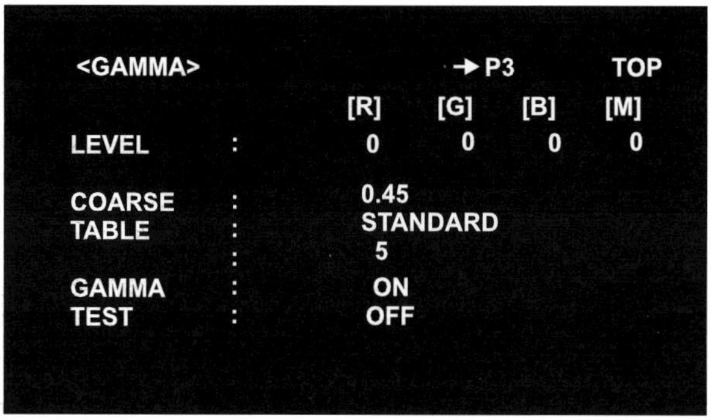

Figure 33.36 GAMMA page

<GAMMA>		
	Available setting	**Description**
LEVEL	−99 to 99	Adjusts the gamma correction curve of the Red, Green, Blue and Master channels
COARSE	0.40, 0.45 and 0.50	Sets the correction curve of the master gamma in three distinct steps
TABLE	STANDARD, FILM 1, 2, 3 and - - -	Selects the gamma table category Selects the table number in the gamma table category
GAMMA	ON or OFF	Switches the gamma function ON or OFF
TEST	OFF, 1 or 2	Selects the test signal OFF: No test signal 1: Provides an analogue waveform test signal 2: Provides a digital waveform test signal

Figure 33.37 GAMMA page settings

33.3.4 BLK GAMMA page

If adjusting the overall gamma is dangerous, adjusting black gamma can be suicidal. For instance, if the Y range were brought up to the maximum setting, 50 per cent, then in film terms you would have done the equivalent of force processing the lower half of the tonal range by some two stops. Though force processing only a portion of the tonal range is impossible, the effect would be to dramatically bring up the grain in the shadows and lighten the blacks. This is exactly what happens in this camera, though the grain is replaced by electronic noise, much the same thing.

This effect is just about impossible to correct in post-production and any attempt to do so may well be very expensive.

Both Sony and Panavision agree as to the settings for this page, which include all the functions set to OFF, as shown in Figure 33.38. A brief description of the function of each line within this page is shown in Figure 33.39.

33.3.5 LOW KEY SAT page

This is another page of controls which both Sony and Panavision normally leave both at zero and switched off. While very occasionally one might use this alteration to the image if it was only ever going to be shown on television, I would strongly advise leaving this control set to OFF if there is any possibility of the image being transferred to film, as it produces an image which cannot be created using the conventional photochemical process and therefore appears to be very false when seen in the cinema.

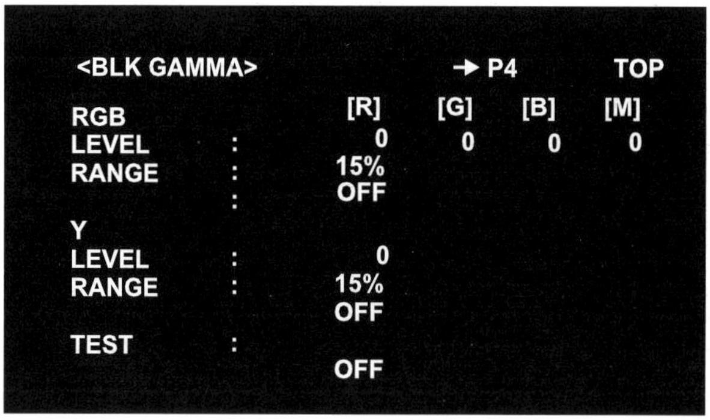

Figure 33.38 BLK GAMMA page

<BLK GAMMA>		
	Available setting	**Description**
RGB LEVEL	−99 to 99	Adjusts the black gamma of the Red, Green, Blue and Master
RGB RANGE	15, 25, 35 and 50%	Sets the upper limit of the video level which the RGB black gamma affects
	ON or OFF	Switches the RGB black gamma correction function ON or OFF
Y LEVEL	−99 to 99	Adjusts the Y black gamma in order to modify the contrast of the image without changing the chroma phase of the dark part of the image
Y RANGE	15, 25, 35 and 50%	Sets the upper limit of the video level which the Y black gamma affects
	ON or OFF	Switches the Y black gamma correction function ON or OFF
TEST	OFF, 1 and 2	Selects the test signal OFF: No test signal 1: Provides an analogue waveform test signal 2: Provides a digital waveform test signal

Figure 33.39 BLK GAMMA settings

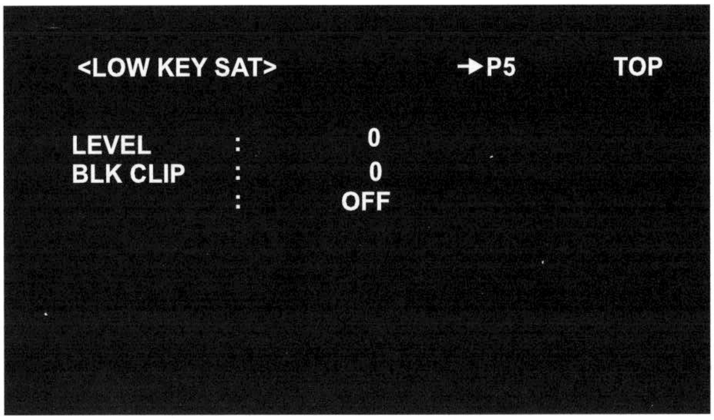

```
<LOW KEY SAT>                →P5        TOP

LEVEL        :        0
BLK CLIP     :        0
             :       OFF
```

Figure 33.40 LOW KEY SAT page

<LOW KEY SAT>		
	Available setting	Description
LEVEL	−99 to 99	Sets the saturation level for the dark part of the image
BLACK CLIP	−99 to 99	Sets the lower limit of the video level which the low key saturation affects
	ON or OFF	Turns the low key saturation effect ON or OFF

Figure 33.41 LOW KEY SAT settings

Figure 33.40 shows how the viewfinder will appear and Figure 33.41 the function and range of effect of each line on the page.

33.3.6 KNEE page

The word knee is used in a video context to describe a modification to the highlight portion of the tonal range, much as shoulder is used in photochemical photography. The point setting determines the point on the response curve that the slope value will start to come into effect. The slope setting determines the angle to which the response curve changes from a straight line to one moving more rapidly upwards or downwards. In photochemical photography this effect is known as rolling off into the highlights. Figure 33.42 shows the effect of adding a little roll-off to the knee response curve.

Sony ship the camera with all the relative values set at zero, while Panavision prefer to alter only the settings to the white clip, giving red, green and blue a value of 11 and leaving master at zero. Figure 33.43 illustrates how the page will appear in the viewfinder when set to the Panavision recommended settings. Figure 33.44 describes the functions of each line on the page.

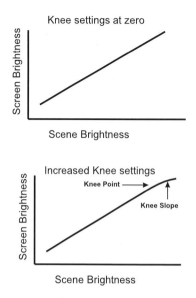

Figure 33.42 Effect of adding roll-off to the knee response curve

<KNEE>		→ P6		TOP
	[R]	[G]	[B]	[M]
POINT :	0	0	0	0
SLOPE :	0	0	0	0
WHT CLP :	11	11	11	0
:				
:				
KNEE	OFF			
KNEE SAT :	OFF			
WHITE CLIP :	ON			
TEST :	OFF			

Figure 33.43 KNEE page

33.3.7 DETAIL 1 page

On this page you can choose whether you wish to electronically enhance the edge definition within the picture. The decision to use this function and at what setting depends both on personal preference and, more likely, the quality of the lens you intend to use. If you are in the unfortunate position of having to use a standard definition lens on your high definition camera, it might be possible to give the appearance of greater sharpness using this function. Beware though, for increasing the electronic enhancement of the edge definition will cause the overall appearance of the picture to start to look like it is coming from a rather cheap video camera. It is a function much disliked by cinematographers with a film background.

Sony ship the camera with all the relative settings at zero, but with the detail and level depend switched on. At the factory settings there will still be a small amount of enhancement present. The Panavision Primo Digital lenses have such superior definition that Panavision switch both detail and level depend off. This is, perhaps, one of the reasons many cinematographers with a film background believe the Panavision version of the camera, with the associated Primo Digital lenses, to be far superior to any other.

<KNEE>	Available setting	Description
POINT R, G, B & M	−99 to 99	Sets the knee point level when the setting of the auto knee function is set to OFF
SLOPE R, G, B & M	−99 to 99	Sets the knee slope level when the setting of the auto knee function is set to OFF
WHITE CLIP R, G , B & M	−99 to 99	Sets the white clip level of the Red, Green, Blue and Master
KNEE SATURATION LEVEL	−99 to 99	Sets the knee saturation level
KNEE	ON or OFF	Sets the knee correction circuit to ON or OFF
KNEE SATURATION	ON or OFF	Sets the knee saturation to ON or OFF
WHITE CLIP	ON or OFF	Sets the white clip function to ON or OFF
TEST	OFF, 1 or 2	Selects the test signal OFF: No test signal 1: Provides an analogue waveform test signal 2: Provides a digital waveform test signal

Figure 33.44 KNEE page functions

Figure 33.45 illustrates how the screen will appear in the viewfinder of a Panavision camera. The only difference looking down a Sony camera will be that the bottom two rows will have the legend ON. Figure 33.46 describes the effect of changes on each line on the page.

33.3.8 DETAIL 2 page

The fine detail function on this page changes the width of the edge definition without changing the detail's edge level in the horizontal direction.

The knee aperture function compensates for decreases made by the knee aperture in the detail level at the high luminance level part of the scene. Some versions of the camera do not have the knee aperture function on this page.

Both Panavision and Sony ship the camera with these functions switched off, as shown in Figure 33.47. The available settings are shown in Figure 33.48.

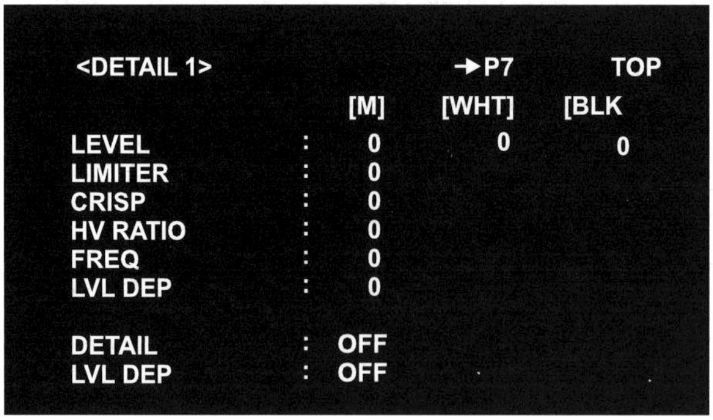

```
<DETAIL 1>                          →P7         TOP
                        [M]      [WHT]      [BLK
          LEVEL        :   0         0          0
          LIMITER      :   0
          CRISP        :   0
          HV RATIO     :   0
          FREQ         :   0
          LVL DEP      :   0

          DETAIL       : OFF
          LVL DEP      : OFF
```

Figure 33.45 DETAIL 1 page

<DETAIL 1>		
	Available setting	**Description**
LEVEL	−99 to 99	Sets the general level of the detail signal
LIMITER – MASTER, WHITE & BLACK	−99 to 99	Sets the level for clipping the excessive detail signal
CRISPENING	−99 to 99	Sets the level for suppressing the noise components contained in the detail signal
HV RATIO	−99 to 99	Sets the ratio between the horizontal detail signal and the vertical detail signal
FREQUENCY	−99 to 99	Sets the frequency of the horizontal signal
LEVEL DEPEND	−99 to 99	Sets the level at which the scene will start to be affected by the detail function
DETAIL	**ON or OFF**	Sets the function for attaching the detail signal designed to improve the resolution of the image to ON or OFF
LEVEL DEPEND	**ON or OFF**	Sets the level depend function to ON or OFF

Figure 33.46 DETAIL 1 settings

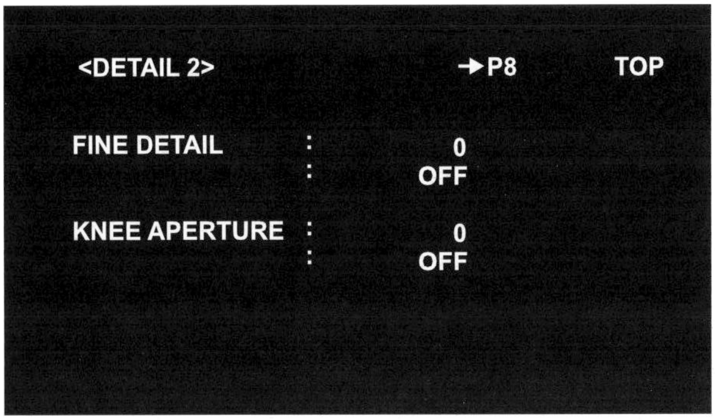

Figure 33.47 DETAIL 2 page

<DETAIL 2>		
	Available setting	**Description**
FINE DETAIL	−99 to 99	Sets the general level of the fine detail signal
	ON or OFF	Sets the fine detail function to ON or OFF
KNEE APERTURE	−99 to 99	Sets the knee aperture level
	ON or OFF	Sets the knee aperture function to ON or OFF

Figure 33.48 DETAIL 2 settings

33.3.9 SKIN DETAIL page

Imagine you are photographing an actress who is immensely talented but physically a little older than the age of the part she is playing. If you put an overall diffusion to help her with her close-ups, the audience might notice the change on the cuts to and from that shot. On the other hand, if you could reduce the detail only within the portion of the image that is skin tone (as with Skin Tone Detail) the audience is less likely to notice the effect at the cuts, but you will still have taken away some of the finer lines on your actress's face. Surely flattering photography of one's leading ladies is a prime objective of most cinematographers? I use this function when shooting with the Sony version of the camera.

Unfortunately, detail is a relative thing and as Panavision switch off the electronic detail enhancement completely, arguing that their lenses are more than sharp enough anyway, there is no enhancement to remove from the skin tones. You could add some back in order to be able to use Skin Tone Detail, but this would detract from the value of the Panavision Digital Primo lenses.

Only once have I used this function to age a male actor, by adding detail, but lighting is usually more successful as a route to this conclusion.

It should be noted that, even with the level set to maximum reduction of detail, the result is still fairly subtle.

A useful addition to this menu compared with that in, say, a Sony DVW 790 camera is the provision of three channels so that one may set up three programmes each to suit a different actor, as shown in Figure 33.49. It is possible using this page to grab a skin colour when, perhaps, you wish to affect one actor in shot without affecting another. This will only work if there is a discernible difference between their skin tones.

The simplest way to set the affected skin tone is to move the cursor down to the AUTO position of one of the three available columns you wish to set and click the rotary encoder. Should you have chosen column 1, this will bring up an extra line which will read 'AUTO HUE 1: STANDBY'. You will also notice a small hatched rectangle has appeared in the centre of the viewfinder; this is this area you are about to use.

Zoom in so that the hatched area covers the section of skin tone in the scene you wish to affect. Click the wheel again and the new line should change to 'AUTO HUE: EXECUTING' and the hatched area will expand to cover all the areas within the scene that are about to be affected. After a few seconds the message will change to 'AUTO HUE: OK'. After a few more seconds the message will disappear, leaving the affected area hatch warning on.

You will notice that the SKIN GATE has changed to ON. To lose the function, move the cursor to SKIN GATE ON and click the wheel. The note will change to OFF and the hatching will disappear.

Figure 33.49 shows how the viewfinder will look with this page selected. Figure 33.50 describes the changes each individual line can make.

33.3.10   USER MATRIX page

What happens on this page is both useful and very foreign to a film-trained cinematographer. To a person with a television studio background, and who understands a vectorscope, it is simplicity itself. As the television technician will understand this page I will try to give the film technician a working knowledge of how to take advantage of it.

In the Sony HDW 900 camera the image from the three chips is encoded into three channels. One is luminance, the overall brightness of the image with no regard to colour. Then two more channels are recorded. One records the difference between the luminance channel and the output from the blue chip. The third records the difference between the luminance and the red channel. This is done because there is more than enough information in this method of recording to bring back perfectly the original image, but far less data has to be recorded than if the red, green and blue channels were recorded in full. Hence the adjustments on this page always refer to the effect of one colour upon another.

It is perfectly possible to rearrange the colour relationships on this page, but I strongly advise against this. However, there is a wonderfully useful function available here that the film cinematographer will understand and might possibly find very useful indeed. If all the six values shown in

<SKIN DETAIL>			➔ P9	TOP
SKIN DTL	:	OFF		
SKIN GATE	:	OFF		
		[1]	[2]	[3]
CH SW	:	(ON)	OFF	OFF
GATE	:	OFF	OFF	OFF
PHASE	:	AUTO	AUTO	AUTO
	:	0	0	0
WIDTH	:	0	0	0
SAT	:	0	0	0
LEVEL	:	0	0	0

Figure 33.49 SKIN DETAIL page

<SKIN DETAIL>		
	Available setting	**Description**
SKIN DETAIL	ON or OFF	When this setting is ON, the setting (1) of the channel 1 is always set ON. Sets the skin detail function to ON or OFF
SKIN GATE	ON or OFF	Sets the zebra indicator of the skin tone detail function to ON or OFF
CHANNEL SWITCH	ON or OFF	Sets each individual channel of the skin detail function to ON or OFF
GATE	ON or OFF	Sets each channel of the skin gate function to ON or OFF
PHASE	AUTO	Sets automatically the region of each channel the skin detail function affects
	0 to 359	Sets the centre phase of the chroma phase the skin tone detail function affects to each channel
WIDTH	⁻99 to 99	Adjusts the chroma phase width of the skin tone detail function to each channel
SATURATION	⁻99 to 99	Adjusts the saturation level of the skin tone detail function to each channel
LEVEL	⁻99 to 99	Sets the skin tone detail amount to each channel

Figure 33.50 SKIN DETAIL settings

Figures 33.51–33.53 are set at the same values then you can adjust the overall colour saturation of the image. I find that adjusting all the values to −7 or −10 will very subtly reduce the saturation, something film-trained eyes sometimes appreciate.

Panavision prefer the preset line to be switched off when shooting for a film output and I firmly agree with this. They also suggest that if you are going to sell the project to television only then the preset should be set to ITU-709; again I agree. Nevertheless, it might be prudent to check with the main investor's delivery department to find out if they have sufficient knowledge to give you advice. If in doubt, stay with the Panavision recommendations.

If your project is destined for delivery both as a film output and a television showing, then I am very firm in my recommendation. Shoot with the preset off. It is quite simple to transfer the camera

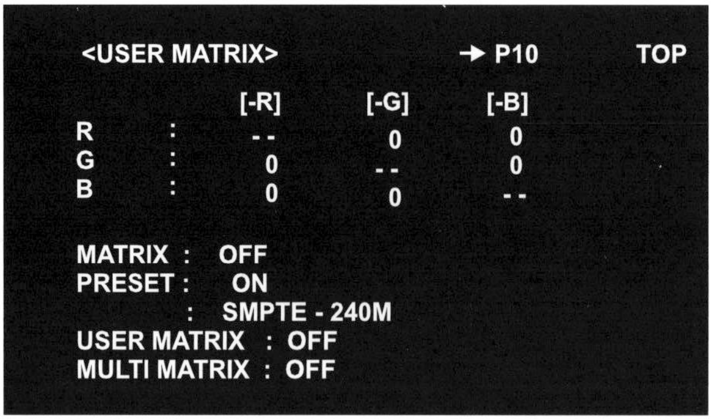

Figure 33.51 USER MATRIX page – Sony factory settings

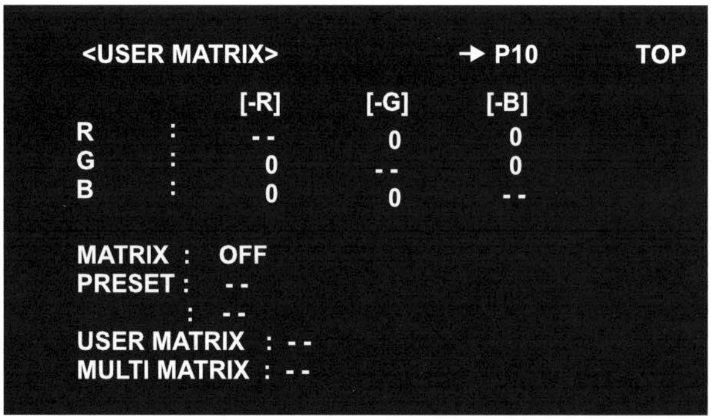

Figure 33.52 USER MATRIX page – Panavision settings for printing to film

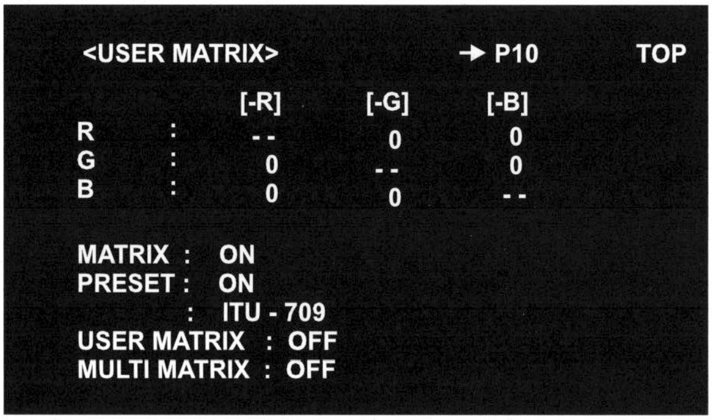

Figure 33.53 USER MATRIX page – Panavision settings for a TV-only shoot

original image shot with preset off to a version for television that will perfectly replicate the ITU-709, or any other preset, in post-production.

It should be noted that the purpose of the preset user matrices is to adapt the image from the camera so that it will look better on a cathode ray tube. Cathode ray tubes have a very different response, particularly with respect to gamma, than a projection screen. The phosphors on a cathode ray tube in the USA and the phosphors of a cathode ray tube in Europe are quite different. It is therefore essential that the cinematographer determines where the finished product will be shown. Again, if in doubt use a film setting, as it is very easy to add a television response curve to the image in post-production. It is quite difficult to remove that response curve later if you wish to make a film version.

There is a great danger in shooting with one of the presets on and then attempting a film output. It is very difficult, if not impossible, to undo the effect of a television preset in post-production. Please be warned.

Figure 33.51 shows the Sony recommended settings on this page. Figure 33.52 shows the Panavision recommended settings when shooting for a film output and Figure 33.53 the Panavision settings when the project will only be shown on television. Figure 33.54 describes the function of each of the lines on this page.

<USER MATRIX>		
	Available setting	**Description**
RED to GREEN & RED to BLUE	−99 to 99	Sets the linear matrix coefficient for Red to Green and Red to Blue
GREEN to RED & GREEN to BLUE	−99 to 99	Sets the linear matrix coefficient for Green to Red and Green to Blue
BLUE to RED & BLUE to GREEN	−99 to 99	Sets the linear matrix coefficient for Blue to Red and Blue to Green
MATRIX	**ON or OFF**	Sets the linear matrix function to ON or OFF
PRESET	**ON or OFF**	Sets the linear matrix correction coefficients to ON or OFF
	SMPTE-240M ITU-709 SMPTE-WIDE NTSC, EBU ITU-609	Selects a preset linear matrix from one of the preset linear matrices available in the camera's memory
USER MATRIX	**ON or OFF**	Sets the linear matrix correction function set by the user to ON or OFF
MULTI MATRIX	**ON or OFF**	Sets the multi matrix correction function to ON or OFF

Figure 33.54 USER MATRIX settings

There are six presets available on this page. This is because if you are going to one television system only, it is possible to choose here what may probably be the ideal setting. To determine which setting is best you must check with your post-production people.

If in any doubt at all shoot with the user matrix OFF. As with so many of the choices in the Paint Menu, all six of the presets can be replicated in post-production.

33.3.11   MULTI MATRIX page

Again, we see a page that the cinematographer with a television background will have no problem understanding and the cinematographer from a film background might be somewhat confused. The purpose of this page is to give the cinematographer control over separate, individual, colours. It is a complex page but it is possible to take just one colour in the original scene and change that colour to another completely independently from the rest of the scene. I am told that one can capture the colour of green grass and change it to purple; I confess I have never tried this. More usefully it should be possible to create the effect of a colour enhancement filter in any colour.

There is a great value in this page if, only occasionally, it might be useful. Suppose you are shooting a car commercial and the client would like the car to stand out. Using the USER MATRIX page you can reduce the overall saturation of the scene and then moving to the MULTI MATRIX page you can make the colour of the car stronger than it might be in real life. The client might be very pleased.

Figure 33.55 shows the Sony factory settings and Figure 33.56 the Panavision recommended settings. Figure 33.57 describes the effect of each line on the page.

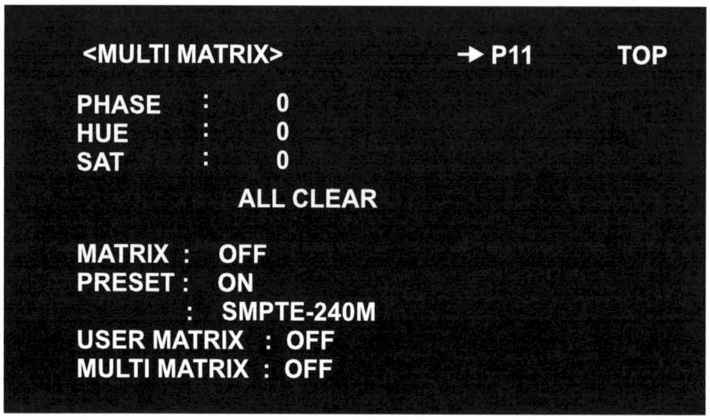

Figure 33.55 MULTI MATRIX page – Sony settings

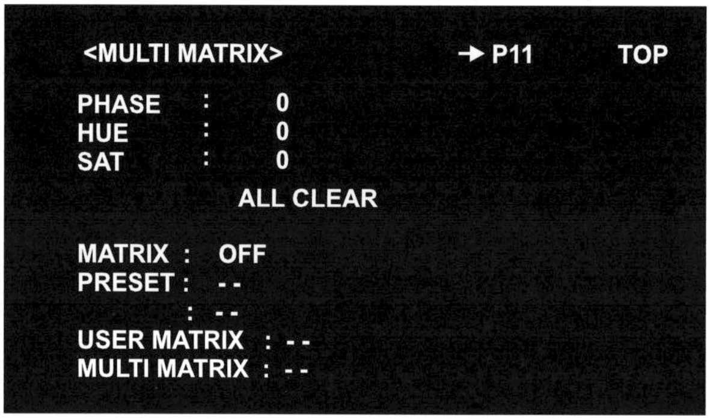

Figure 33.56 MULTI MATRIX page – Panavision recommended settings

<MULTI MATRIX>		
	Available setting	**Description**
PHASE	**0, 23, 45, 68, 90, 113, 135, 158, 180, 203, 225, 248, 270, 293, 315, and 338**	Sets the region in which the multi matrix correction function can be changed
HUE	**−99 to 99**	Adjusts the colour phase the multi matrix correction function affects in each of the 16-axis modes
SATURATION	**−99 to 99**	Adjusts the saturation level the multi matrix correction function affects in each of the 16-axis modes
ALL CLEAR	**Press the rotary encoder to execute this operation**	Clears the HUE and SATURATION values in each phase to zero. Note that the values in the reference file are not cleared
MATRIX	**ON or OFF**	Sets the linear matrix correction coefficient to ON or OFF
PRESET	**ON or OFF** **SMPTE-240M ITU-709 SMPTE-WIDE NTSC, EBU ITU-609**	Sets the linear matrix correction function to ON or OFF Selects a preset linear matrix from one of the preset linear matrices available in the camera's menu memory
USER MATRIX	**ON or OFF**	Sets the linear matrix correction function set by the user to ON or OFF
MULTI MATRIX	**ON or OFF**	Sets the multi matrix correction function to ON or OFF

Figure 33.57 MULTI MATRIX options

33.3.12   SHUTTER page

Within the DVW F900 camera the shutter opening time is set quite independently of the frame rate, much as the open angle of a mechanical shutter on a film camera can be set independently of the frame rate. A further difference is that the time of opening is expressed as a fraction of a second, more akin to the markings on a still camera.

Figure 33.58 shows the Sony factory settings and Figure 33.59 the Panavision standard settings. Figure 33.60 describes the function of each individual line. The available shutter speeds at the various frame rates are shown in Figure 33.61.

The second line on the page, ECS, allows you to widely vary by very small amounts the scan frequency, so that you can try and set the camera to match that of a television or computer screen you may be trying to photograph. The available range is shown in Figure 33.62.

S-EVS (Super-Enhanced Vertical Definition), the last function on the page, supposedly improves the vertical definition and reduces flicker when on, but at the expense of fast-moving objects becoming more blurred. I confess to having never found a use for this function.

The majority of the time you will have the shutter speed set to one over a number that is twice the frame rate. Therefore, if shooting at 24 fps, the shutter speed will be set at 1/48, thus exactly emulating a film camera shooting at 24 fps having a 180° shutter. Likewise, at 25 fps the shutter will normally be set at 1/50.

33.3.13   SCENE FILE page

It is possible to store up to five independent sets of paint parameters. It should be noted that it does not store every parameter within the Paint Menu. To store a Paint file you have set in the camera, rotate the rotary encoder until the arrow points at STORE and click the encoder in. The message 'STORE NO' will blink. Rotate the encoder until the arrow points to the file number you wish to file the camera settings under and click the encoder in. Now rotate the encoder until the arrow points to WRITE and click the encoder in. If you already had data filed in that number, the old data will be erased and replaced with the paint settings currently set in the camera menu.

To recall a file, choose the file number you wish to read just as in the above and rotate the encoder until the arrow points to READ; click the encoder in and the camera paint settings will revert to those stored on the file number you have chosen.

Figure 33.63 shows how the viewfinder will look with this page called up, while Figure 33.64 shows the available settings.

33.4   The Maintenance, File and Diagnostic Menus

There is just one page within the Maintenance Menu that concerns the camera crew. All the other pages do not concern the crew as they are there for the camera engineers to maintain the camera on return from a client or before issuing the camera to a client.

33.4.1   Page M7

Page M7 in the Maintenance Menu is, however, of interest to the camera crew, as it is here that one can change the camera's frame rate. Figure 33.65 shows the MULTI FORMAT page, M7, which allows camera frame speed to be changed.

The current frame rate can be checked without having to go into the menus by simply holding the MENU switch on the side of the camera to the STATUS position; the frame rate will be shown at the top of the viewfinder along with other information.

The camera is capable of eight frame rates – five progressive scan rates (23.98PsF, 24PsF, 25PsF, 29.97PsF, 30PsF) and three interlace frame rates (50i, 59.94i and 60i). The rates containing decimal points are provided to give compatibility with the American NTSC broadcast system.

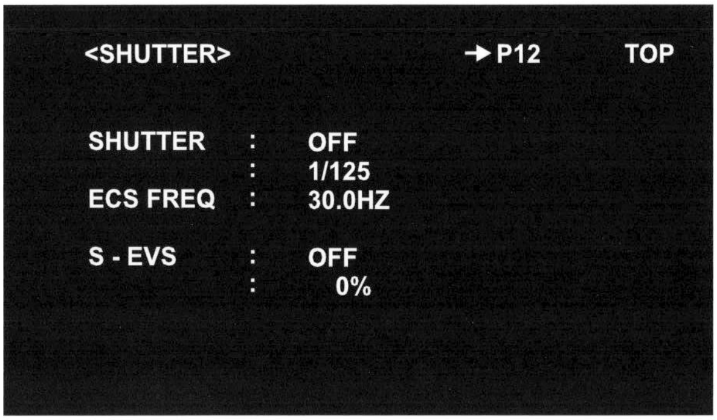

```
<SHUTTER>                          ➜ P12      TOP


SHUTTER      :    OFF
             :    1/125
ECS FREQ     :    30.0HZ

S - EVS      :    OFF
             :     0%
```

Figure 33.58 SHUTTER page – Sony factory settings

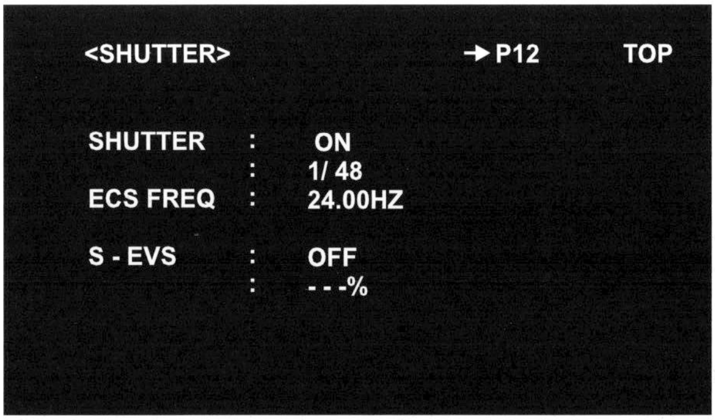

```
<SHUTTER>                          ➜ P12      TOP


SHUTTER      :    ON
             :    1/ 48
ECS FREQ     :    24.00HZ

S - EVS      :    OFF
             :    - - -%
```

Figure 33.59 SHUTTER page – Panavision standard settings

<SHUTTER>		
	Available setting	**Description**
SHUTTER	**ON or OFF** **See Figure 33.28**	Sets the shutter and the ECS mode to ON or OFF
ECS (Extended Clear Scan) FREQUENCY	**See Figure 33.29**	Sets the ECS frequency. This is adjustable manually in fractions of Hz
S-EVS (Super-Extended Clear Scan)	**ON or OFF**	Sets the EVS mode to ON or OFF
	0 to 100	Sets the S-EVS

Figure 33.60 SHUTTER options

Format	Shutter speed
60i, 59.94i	1/100, 1/125, 1/250, 1/500, 1/1000, 1/2000
50i	1/60, 1/125, 1/250, 1/500, 1/1000, 1/2000
30PsF, 29.97PsF	1/40, 1/60, 1/120, 1/125, 1/250, 1/500, 1/1000
25PsF	1/33, 1/50, 1/100, 1/125, 1/250, 1/500, 1/1000
24PsF, 23.98PsF	1/32, 1/48, 1/96, 1/125, 1/250, 1/500, 1/1000

Figure 33.61 Shutter speeds at various frame rates

Format	Extended Clear Scan frequency settings (Hz)
60i, 59.94i	30.0 to 5600
50i	25.0 to 5600
30PsF, 29.97PsF	30.4 to 2800
25PsF	25.3 to 2300
24PsF, 23.98PsF	24.3 to 2300

Figure 33.62 ECS frequency settings

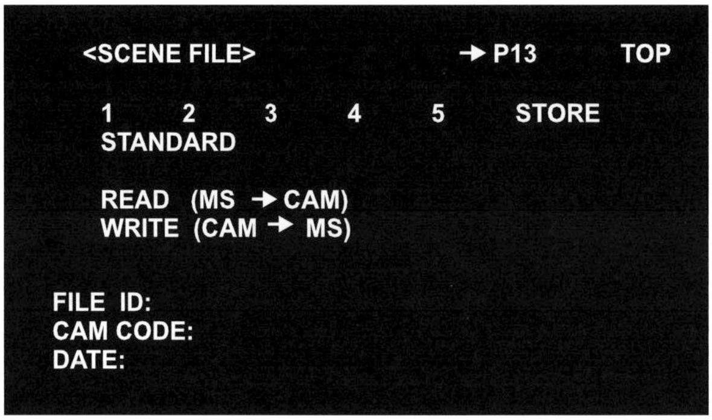

Figure 33.63 SCENE FILE page

<SCENE FILE>	
Item	**Description**
1, 2, 3, 4, 5, STORE	Saves and stores up to five different groups of settings as 'scene files'
STANDARD	Clicking on 'Standard' will return all the settings in the Paint Menu to the supplier's standard settings
FILE ID	Here you can name the file or write any other comments up to 14 characters
CAMERA CODE	Here you can give each camera a signature, e.g. scene number etc.
DATE	Here it is suggested you might like to write the date you filed the settings

Figure 33.64 SCENE FILE settings

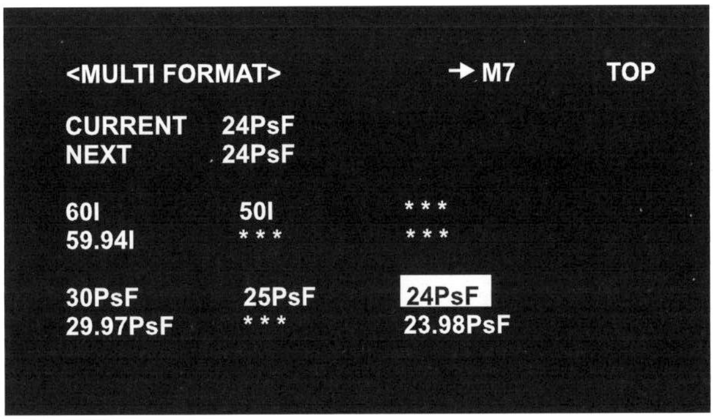

Figure 33.65 MULTI FORMAT page, M7

To change the frame rate carry out the following:

1 Turn on the MENU by moving the DISPLAY switch to the MENU position.
2 Go to page M7 of the MAINTENANCE MENU.
3 Move the cursor opposite the 'NEXT' frame rate number and push the rotary wheel in to change the cursor to a question mark.
4 Scroll through the list until you have highlighted the frame rate you wish to change to and then push in the rotary wheel again to enter the frame rate into the field. The frame rate you have chosen will now be displayed alongside the second line 'NEXT'.
5 Turn the camera power switch off.
6 Turn the camera back on.

7 Verify the new frame rate by holding the MENU switch to the STATUS position. Your new frame rate will be shown in the viewfinder.

In general, the File and Diagnostic Menus should never be touched by the camera crew. The File Menu duplicates some of the filing available in both the Paint and Operation Menus plus further facilities. The Diagnosis Menu is for the camera engineers to assess what maintenance may or may not be needed before the camera is issued to the client.

Index

Also available from Focal Press ...

Cinematography
Image Making for Cinematographers, Directors and Videographers
Blaine Brown

- The definitive guide to cinematography
- Up-to-date coverage of technical topics, including High Definition and digital imaging
- Full colour throughout brings issues of colour and light to life

Lavishly produced and illustrated, Cinematography covers the entire range of the profession. The book is not just a comprehensive guide to current professional practice; it goes beyond to explain the theory behind the practice, so you understand how the rules came about and when it's appropriate to break them. In addition, directors will benefit from the book's focus on the body of knowledge they should share with their Director of Photography.

Blain Brown is a Director of Photography based in the Los Angeles area.

'A gorgeous piece of work that bids to become a classic text on cinematography... Few books on cinematography meld aesthetics and pragmatics as deftly as this one'.
American Cinematographer

'The gorgeous illustrations bring movies to life and the modern approach that incorporates digital as well as film means that this book can be used for years to come'.
Judy Irola, ASC, Head of Cinematography, USC School of Cinema-Television

---

CONTENTS: Filmspace; Visual Language; Lens Language; Camera Dynamics; Cinematic Continuity; Exposure; Color Theory; The Tools of Lighting; Lighting as Storytelling; Controlling Color; Optics; Filters; Video and High Definition; Image; Set Operations; Professional Formats

---

2002 • 304pp • 254 x 180mm • paperback
ISBN 0 240 80500 3

To order your copy call +44 (0)1865 888180 (UK) or +1 800 545 2522 (USA)
or visit the Focal Press website: www.focalpress.com

Also available from Focal Press ...

Digital Cinematography
Paul Wheeler

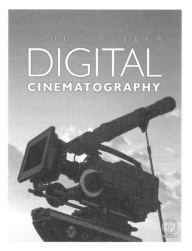

- The first step-by-step guide to high end digital camerawork
- Keep up to date with the very latest technology
- A practical 'on-the-set' guide that helps you get your job done

High end digital cinematography can truly challenge the film camera in many of the technical, artistic and emotional aspects of what we think of as 'cinematography'. This book is a guide for practising and aspiring cinematographers and DOPs to digital cinematography essentials - from how to use the cameras to the rapidly emerging world of High Definition cinematography and 24p technology.

Paul Wheeler trained at the BBC rising to become a Senior Drama Film Cameraman. A renowned cinematographer/director of photography and trainer, and previous Head of Cinematography at National Film & Television School where he still runs courses on Digital Cinematography. Previous Head of Cinematography on the Royal College of Arts MA course. Twice nominated by BAFTA for a Best Cinematography award and twice winner of the INDIE award for Best Digital Cinematography.

CONTENTS: Digital Cinematography; The Director of Photograph's Craft; Lighting; Lighting Ratios; Colour Temperature; Filters; The Shoot; Crewing; The Director of Photography's Preparation; Technical Preparation For A Shoot; The Technology; The Camera; The VCR; White and Black Balance; Time code and user bits; Delivery Systems; High Definition Television; The Sony DVW In-Camera Menus; The Sony DVW 700 Quick Reference List; The Sony DVW 700 Menus; The Sony DVW 90 Quick Reference List; The Sony DVW 790 Menus

---

2001 • 208pp • 106 illustrations • 246 x 189mm • paperback
ISBN 0 240 51614 1

To order your copy call +44 (0)1865 888180 (UK) or +1 800 545 2522 (USA)
or visit the Focal Press website: www.focalpress.com

Also available from Focal Press ...

Practical Cinematography
Paul Wheeler

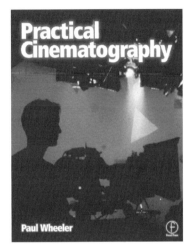

- Comprehensive coverage of all essential theory and techniques
- Many clear diagrams to supplement theories
- Written by a respected cinematographer/trainer

Practical Cinematography discusses the principles of cinematography and the expertise which is unique to the Director of Photography (DoP). It deals with all the basic theory such as colour temperature and sensitometry, and all the practical things a DoP needs to know, from the make-up of the crew to how to prepare an equipment list.

Paul Wheeler trained at the BBC rising to become a Senior Drama Film Cameraman. A renowned cinematographer/director of photography and trainer, and previous Head of Cinematography at National Film & Television School where he still runs courses on Digital Cinematography. Previous Head of Cinematography on the Royal College of Arts MA course. Twice nominated by BAFTA for a Best Cinematography award and twice winner of the INDIE award for Best Digital Cinematography.

CONTENTS: The camera crew; The motion picture camera; Lenses; Film stock; Basic sensitometry; The laboratory; Exposure meters; Lighting ratios; Three point image control; Using the 18 per cent grey card; Colour temperature; Camera filters; Depth of field; Testing; Composition and the rule of thirds; Lenses and perspective; Aspect ratios; Research; Preparing for a shoot; Future proofing film for television using Super 16mm

---

2000 • 178pp • 246 x 189mm • paperback
ISBN 0 240 51555 2

To order your copy call +44 (0)1865 888180 (UK) or +1 800 545 2522 (USA)
or visit the Focal Press website: www.focalpress.com

Focal Press

www.focalpress.com
Join Focal Press on-line
As a member you will enjoy the following benefits:

- an email bulletin with **information on new books**

- a regular **Focal Press Newsletter**:

    - featuring a selection of new titles

    - keeps you informed of **special offers, discounts and freebies**

    - alerts you to **Focal Press news and events** such as author signings and seminars

- complete access to **free content** and reference material on the focalpress site, such as the focalXtra articles and commentary from our authors

- a **Sneak Preview** of selected titles (sample chapters) *before* they publish

- a chance to have your say on our **discussion boards** and **review books** for other Focal readers

Focal Club Members are invited to give us feedback on our products and services.
Email: worldmarketing@focalpress.com – we want to hear your views!

Membership is **FREE**. To join, visit our website and register. If you require any further information regarding the on-line club please contact:

> Lucy Lomas-Walker
> Email: l.lomas@elsevier.com
> Tel: +44 (0) 1865 314438
> Fax: +44 (0)1865 314572
> Address: Focal Press, Linacre House,
> Jordan Hill, Oxford, UK, OX2 8DP

Catalogue
For information on all Focal Press titles, our full catalogue is available online at www.focalpress.com and all titles can be purchased here via secure online ordering, or contact us for a free printed version:

USA
Email: christine.degon@bhusa.com
Tel: +1 781 904 2607 T

Europe and rest of world
Email: j.blackford@elsevier.com
el: +44 (0)1865 314220

Potential authors
If you have an idea for a book, please get in touch:

USA
editors@focalpress.com

Europe and rest of world
focal.press@elsevier.com